The Messiah

Behold a white horse!

And
its rider
had a bow,

And a crown
was given to him,

And
he
went out conquering
to conquer.

And
the armies of heaven,
followed him
on white horses,

They
arrayed in fine linen
white and pure.

Rev 6:2, 19:11,14

White Horse = Heavenly Power
Rider = Second Coming of the Messiah
Armies = Those on the Messiah's Way

The Messiah's Unrealized Revolution

Discovered in the Gospel of Thomas

His Soul-Way Out of Religious Conflicts
And Into Personal & Global Peace

By

Robert W. North, PhD

Way of the Soul
www.7771.org

The Messiah's Unrealized Revolution

Discovered in the Gospel of Thomas

His Soul-Way Out of Religious Conflicts
And Into Personal & Global Peace

To Contact the Author

www.7771.Org

Because of the dynamic nature of the Internet, any Web addresses or links contained in this book may have changed since publication and may no longer be valid.

Cover and Book Design

Front Margin
www.frontmargin.com

ISBN-13: 978-0-9907795-0-6

Way of the Soul Publications

San Diego, California
www.7771.org

TABLE OF CONTENTS

PREFACE

In 1945, some Egyptian farmers discovered a huge, buried vase near Nag Hammadi, Egypt. Historians believe it was hidden by Christian monks in the 4th century, and that it probably contained portions of their library that they wanted to protect and preserve. Among the books was one entitled the "Gospel of Thomas." This Book begins with the remarkable statement that Jesus was the Book's author, speaking its words to a scribe by the name of "Thomas." Within 10 years of its discovery, scholars were able to divide the book into 114 "sayings," about half of which we read in some form in the New Testament. These and later scholars could not find any organization to the book; therefore, they concluded that it was largely a "collection" of sayings put together in the 1st or 2nd century.

About 18 years ago, living in a cabin in the desert outside of Santa Fe, New Mexico, facing a late life "meaning crisis," I sensed that I should fully immerse myself in the study of the Gospel of Thomas. Prior to that, I had studied for the priesthood as a Jesuit to seek and proclaim the real Jesus. However, after many years of deep study, I could not find him or his practical answers to my inner turmoil in Catholic theology.

After I left the Jesuits and after I earned a Ph.D. in Counseling at the University of Florida, I continued with my study of scripture hoping to find "the real Jesus." My Biblical scholarship specialty became the unearthing of the "signals" that ancient Semitic authors imbedded in their writings to tell us how to organize and interpret their works. Our present chapter, verse, paragraph, sentence, and stanza organization was imposed by translators and printers 400 to 500 years ago. When we use the artificial schemes they imposed, we do **not** read the text as the original authors intended.

Sitting in my cabin and reading Thomas using the learned ancient "Semitic signals, I could see that it was not a "collection" of sayings as scholars claimed, but a highly organized book. After I read it a second time, I was thrilled to exclaim, "This is the real Jesus. What a revolutionary message! The world needs to hear this now. If everyone lived this Gospel, all religious conflicts would end; and furthermore, I see a way out of my existential crisis!"

And so, with the help of colleagues I have spent years unearthing Jesus' core message in Thomas while cross checking the discoveries with his New Testament parables and main sayings. This is one of a series of books that present the results of our exploratory expedition. Our conclusions:

- The Gospel of Thomas is a coherent, intricately organized book of 131 wisdom poems, not 114 "collected" sayings as scholars have thought. About half of them are more ancient versions of Jesus' parables and sayings in the New Testament.

- Jesus probably *composed* the Gospel of Thomas. It is unlikely that anyone other than Jesus could have understood his sayings and parables so well that he could intricately organize them into a coherent Book.

- The Gospel of Thomas chapters are in the form of a Semitic literary style called a "chiasm" or "arch." You read the first chapter, then the last parallel chapter, then the second, and then the second from the last, and so on. The main concept is in the keystone (center) Chapter Eleven.

- When this new knowledge of Semitic signals is applied to the books of the Bible, it discloses the true organization of these books. They contain major and minor divisions, and within them, a type of Semitic poetry, not the columns of prose we read today.

- The newly discovered Semitic signals tell us how to read the text to understand the meaning of metaphors and passages. Most of the words and phrases such as "ark," "wilderness," and "walking on the sea" are primarily metaphors and not physical objects and actions. Further, many of the books should be read as pure allegories, or allegories that rely loosely on some historical information. They are not pure histories.

- The organization of most Biblical books and passages tell us how to understand the author's *embedded* dictionary and commentary. Thus, we have less need for external dictionaries and commentaries, and we can check the basis of current theology and interpretations.

- The organization of most Biblical books and passages is so tight that it betrays when a later copyist deleted or added text. Thus, we can correct ancient manuscripts.

- The Gospel of Thomas *combined* with Jesus' sayings in the New Testament fully explains his revolutionary, hitherto seemingly unknown, shocking "gospel" (Mk 1:14), "way" (Acts 9:2), and method for knowing the "will of God" (Mk 3:35). I call Jesus' approach, his "Way of the Soul." Its three major principles that he discovered through direct observation of his experience of people and nature:

1. We were born saved, innocent, pure, perfect, one with ourselves, others, plants, and animals; and *full* of the life of God.

2. We became "divided" from our real selves and from our brothers and sisters when we allowed adults to convince us that we were "good" when we blindly believed their religious and social dogma and "bad" when we did not. Jesus calls this way of thinking, psychological "death."

3. We become "one" again with ourselves, everyone and everything by making the ideas of authorities (clerics, parents, politicians, peers, professors, authors of scriptures, therapists, etc.) *secondary* to listening to our common soul-Voice which will guide us unerringly to peace and fulfillment. When we do that, we become more

fully "alive" by returning to being an all-loving child, but with the wisdom to guard ourselves from people who want us to be what we are not.

- Jesus' Way of the Soul is an expansion of Abraham's Covenant. Jesus criticized the Way of Moses, and by extension, all dogma-indoctrinating religions and institutions, which are what I call, the "Way of the Mind." Neither Jesus nor Abraham established a dogma-indoctrinating religion. Instead, they taught people to listen to and live from their soul-Voice. Their goal was to empower people to make their own decisions, not to control how they thought and acted.

- Jesus' revolutionary message is one that people attached to dogma-indoctrinating religion, to tradition, and to religious and secular authoritarian control would find not only hard to live but to be a deep personal and social threat. That would explain what motivated religious and secular authorities to murder him, why his followers hid Thomas, why they established many conflicting communities each with their own convenient interpretation of his message, why Paul the Apostle never quoted him, and why the Nicene Creed contains no statements from Jesus' parables and core sayings. As a result, most people today do not understand that dogma-indoctrinating Christianity is not the true gospel of Jesus.

- There are two forms of most religions: one part that is dogma-based, and the other, that makes soul-knowing primary. We often call the first "organized religion" and the second, "mystical religion." Jesus expanded upon and concretely systematized the latter. He was critical of the former.

SUMMARY

Jesus was a therapist, not a theologian, cleric, or nationalistic zealot. In Thomas, he lays out a theory of personal development that is a universal "Way" for everyone—including Atheists. Therefore, he was the Messiah who proclaimed the paradigm-shift solution for personal and world peace that we need today.

THE MESSIAH'S UNREALIZED REVOLUTION

In this book you will find:

1. 53 of Jesus' wisdom poems, explained from the full Gospel of 129 poems. I selected those poems and organized them so that they explain the main elements of his theory of personal development,

2. A comparison of Jesus' message with that of the Apostle Paul, which forms the basis of Christian theology,

3. An Overview of Jesus' Unknown Revolutionary gospel,

4. A Primer for living Jesus' Gospel, and

5. A Self-Examination that enables the reorder to measure his progress on Jesus' "Way,"

6. Evidence that Jesus was the Messiah with a message that, if lived, will bring unity to the world fractured by religious conflict, and

7. Evidence that Jesus composed the Gospel of Thomas.

COMPANION BOOKS:

Two companion books are available that present the entire Gospel of Thomas in its 21-chapter poetic organization. One is a Professional Edition and the other a Standard Edition.

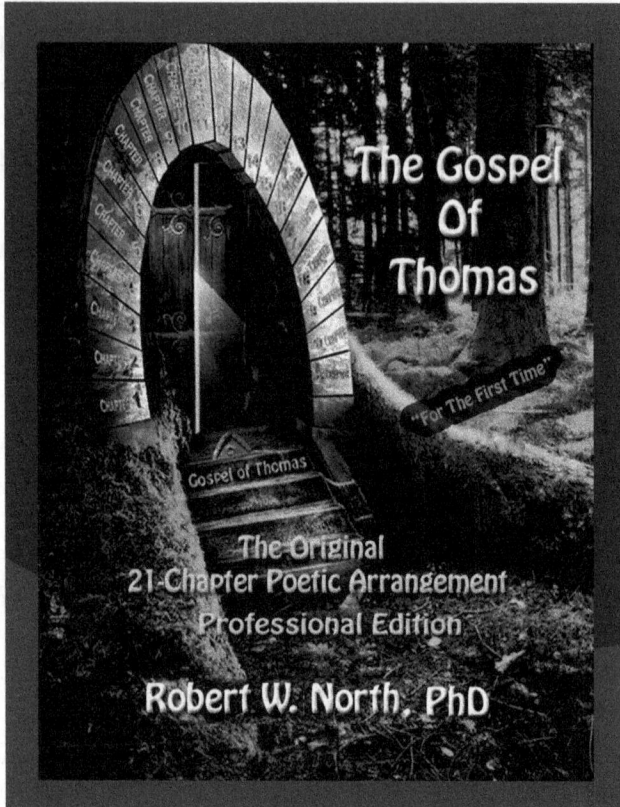

In both books you will find 131 of Jesus' Poems presented side by side in parallel with a full explanation of the poem's metaphors. The Professional Edition contains over 200 pages of Appendices for the serious Bible Student who wishes to understand Semitic Parallelism—the method I used to determine the organization of this Gospel. In the course of explaining Semitic Parallelism, I show that the organization of sections of Genesis and the Gospel of Mark can be determined using the same principles. When employed, the true meaning of those Bible sections emerge. As a result, the Professional Edition Appendices teach one to read the Bible in an entirely different, highly organized, and vastly more accurate way.

ADDITIONAL MATERIALS

- The digital version for electronic reading devices, tablets, phones and computers can be purchased *only* at www.7771. com. Software provided by book sellers, such as Amazon, cannot display the complicated layouts of these books.

- The companion books and forthcoming training materials can also be examined at www.7771.org.

- You may also register your interests at that site. We will be establishing forums for people to connect with others on Jesus' Way, offering free video and other guides and providing a bookstore for other authors who teach his Way.

- I and my colleagues welcome any feedback. If you wish, please contact us at www.7771.org.

ABOUT ROBERT NORTH

Robert North was a former member of the Society of Jesus (Jesuits). There he was educated in the classics, history, the humanities, and philosophy. After he left that order of priests and brothers, he earned a Ph.D. in Counseling at the University of Florida. While working in several colleges and universities, he continued the scripture scholarship that he began as a Jesuit. His focus has been on discovering the Semitic Principles used by the authors of the *Bible* and the *Gospel of Thomas* to organize their works.

OVERVIEW

INTRODUCTION

You are about to read a book of Jesus' wisdom poems. Because each could be considered a tree in a forest of meaning, and because it is easy to get lost in those trees and never see the forest, I am providing a brief Overview of Jesus' gospel or core message.

As you will see, Jesus' gospel is largely unknown. It has been misinterpreted since before he died. Theologians, clerics and others throughout the last 2000 years have misconstrued his intentions so much that people love the man without understanding his radical "way" (Acts 9:2). They think they are following him when, in fact, they are actually and unknowingly following what he criticized. Therefore, I will outline the key differences between what Christianity in general presents as Jesus' gospel with what you will understand it to be once you have read his wisdom poems.

THE WORLD VERSUS THE KINGDOM

Jesus observed that we can live in one of two "ways." Each has its own logic and core principles. One is the *normal* "way" that you perceive around you every day and that you probably live. The other is *hidden* behind our unwillingness to know it. In the *Gospel of Thomas* and in the New Testament (NT) Gospels, Jesus calls the hidden "way," the "world" as we see in Chapter 21, Poem 4 (Saying 110):

*Jesus
said this:*

Whoever
has discovered the world[1]

[1] *Whoever has discovered the world*: Whoever has seen the difference between the normal "way" lived by most people and the "hidden way"...

And
he
comes to be
rich[2]

Let him
abdicate
from the world.

[2] *And he comes to be rich*: And he comes to be wise on the hidden "way"...

[3] *Let him abdicate from the world*: Let him no longer live and rule himself on the normal "way." Let him instead, live on the hidden "way."

Jesus composed his parables, sayings and poems to disclose the hidden "way" and to teach people how to live it. That is his true gospel. He says that in Chapter 21, Poem 1 (Saying 108):

*Jesus
said this:*

Whoever
drinks out
of my mouth[1]

Will come to be
in my way[2]

And
those things[3]

Which
are
hidden[4]

Will appear
to him.[5]

[1] *Whoever drinks out of my mouth*: Whoever listens to me and nourishes himself with my wisdom.

[2] *Will come to be in my way*: Will follow the hidden "way"

[3] *Those things*: Those words, insights, concepts, logic about the hidden "way"

[4] *Which are hidden*: Which one hides from himself when he thinks that the normal "way" of the "world" is the only "way" to live.

[5] *Will appear to him*: Jesus promises that if one ponders his wisdom poems while both opening himself to living an entirely different "way" and with a willingness to abandon the "world," the hidden "way" logic, values, and insights "will appear to him."

In this poem, Jesus communicates a law of the universe: He who seeks the hidden way will find it. He implies that we are soul-connected to a universal intelligence that responds to us when we truly abandon our former normal "world" beliefs, become open, and ask for the wisdom to live differently.

Jesus calls the hidden "way," the "Kingdom" in Chapter 21, Poem 7 (Saying 113).

*His disciples
asked him:*

"The kingdom[1]

It
is coming
on which day?"[2]

*Jesus
responded:*

"The kingdom[3]

It
comes
not in watching.[4]

They
will say
not this:

'Behold here

Or
Behold there.'[5]

Rather
the Kingdom
of the Father[6]

It
is spreading
upon the earth [7][8]

And
men
peer
not upon it.[9]

[1] *Kingdom*: For the disciples: The "kingdom" is a Jewish country that will exist after the Messiah drives out the Romans. It will be a restored, evolved "kingdom," patterned after the one ruled by King David (Daniel 8:17-19).

[2] *Day*: In the Bible, a "day" is a moment or period of enlightenment. A "night" is the opposite. The disciples want to know when the enlightened Messiah would fulfill the prophesies that he would cleanse the temple of false teachings and bring everyone on earth into one government and into the worship the one true God (Isaiah 2:4; 9:5-10; Mal. 3:2; 4 Ezra 7:113; Zech 6:13; Ezek. 37: 21-24).

[3] *Kingdom*: For Jesus, a "kingdom" is the "hidden" "way" to live. In it, one rules over himself and his interactions in a manner entirely different from the normal "way." The "Kingdom" is not physical territory. It is a way of being with oneself and with things, plants, animals and other people. It is the extraordinary fulfilled life that we all unconsciously seek.

[4] *It comes not in watching*: The kingdom will not come because you disciples stand around watching for what you could not recognize from your normal "world."

[5] *They will not say "Behold here..."* Those who are satisfied with the normal "world" will not be able to see the alternative Kingdom way of living.

[6] *Kingdom of the Father*: The hidden Kingdom is the way God lives. Those in the "world" project false notions on God. They do not understand how the Father lives. (In other poems, Jesus calls God his "Mother." He experiences two persons in God.)

[7] *Earth*: Metaphorically, in Thomas and in the Bible, "earth" is our reflective consciousness.

[8] *It is spreading upon the earth*: Hidden people are living the hidden Kingdom all over the planet because of their enlightened consciousness.

[9] *Men peer not upon it*: Unenlightened people of the "world" do not see the alternative Kingdom way to live.

Jesus was not trying to heal the normal "world." That would be like healing cancer so it can continue to live in the body. Rather, He wants us to abdicate from the "world," and all of its rewards, drama, conflicts, values, principles, logic and relationships, to live in the Kingdom.

Now, I am going to ask you to consider something that I will not prove in this short Overview, but will prove in the rest of this book. The alternative hidden "way" of living that Jesus calls the "Kingdom" has been discovered by wise people before him. Also, it is being discovered today by people who are sick of the normal "world."

For example, the author of the Garden of Eden allegory discovered the hidden "way" and called it the Garden of Eden. He called the normal "world," "Nod," which means, the "way of Wandering." In the Abraham allegories in the Bible, the author calls the normal "world" the "land of your Father," "a foreign land" and "wilderness." He calls the alternative "hidden" "way" the "land that I (God) will show you," which has come to be called, the "Promised Land." The word "land" means "consciousness." So Abraham left one kind of consciousness to live another.

Buddha in his *Dhammapada* calls the normal "world," the "world of confusion." The alternative is the "world of clarity" which is on the other "side of the river" of "passions." The latter has become known as "Nirvana."

The words "Kingdom," "Garden of Eden," "Promised Land" and "Nirvana" are metaphors for the same hidden "way" of living. It is how we will find personal fulfillment in any situation. In contemporary terminology, it is the way to mental health and abundant life. These authors recognized that we will be emotionally sick forever if we live in the "world," "Nod," the "wilderness," and on this "side of the river." In other words, the conflicts that we see today in ourselves, our families, between groups, between religions, and between nations will never end unless most live on the hidden "way."

I am presenting in this book and in those accompanying it that Jesus composed the *Gospel of Thomas* to present his understanding of the hidden "way" and how to live it. He expanded upon the insights of the ancient authors. I also show that Christian theologians, beginning with Paul the Apostle and the Evangelists, either did not understand Jesus' gospel or deliberately hid it because it upset their normal religious, traditional "world." I also explain that Jesus followed Abraham, and that most Jews, Christians and Muslims do not.

Now, I will compare the normal "world" and the hidden "Kingdom" using Jesus' poems from the *Gospel of Thomas*.

ORIGINAL SIN VERSES THE LIGHT

Most Christians believe that people inherit original sin from Adam and Eve who long ago disobeyed God in the Garden of Eden. To remove that sin, they go through a baptism ritual. To maintain their purity, they believe in a creed.

When Jesus observed a new born child, he saw divine light, not original sin. He says that in the following poem from Chapter 3, Poem 3 (Saying 24):

*Jesus
said this:*

"The light
exists inward
of a man
of light [1]

[1] *The light exists inward of a man of light*: A person is born with a soul filled with light. It is his essence. He shares the divine life of God.

And
he
comes to be
light
to the world [2]

[2] *He comes to be light to the world*: A tiny child is the light in the world. The "world" is people living in darkness.

All of it. [3]

[3] *All of it*: A little child lives the divine in very way. He possesses the ability to know as God knows and to live as God lives.

If

he

does

not come to be

light [4]

The darkness

is

he" [5]

[4] *If he does not come to be light:* If a person does not live out what he is, and instead, lives the darkness of society...

[5] *The darkness is he:* When anyone chooses to not be his light self, he chooses to be a false self, that is, darkness in the world.

That is a shocking poem. Few look at another person and see God. However, Jesus observed a child and child-like adults and saw divinity, not original sin. He never distinguishes between divine and human life. For him, plants, animals and human beings live the life of God. Humans may fully live that life, as does a little child, by being himself. Or he can obscure that life by being unreal or false. That is why Jesus says, "If he does not come to be the light" that he is, "the darkness is he."

Current Christian theology teaches that Jesus possessed both divine and human life. Jesus never said that. Current Christian theology teaches that we are born with an original sin—an overwhelming propensity to be evil. Jesus disagrees. Christian theology teaches that original sin is passed down to further generations genetically and spiritually. That is a foreign idea to Jesus. Christian theology teaches that our "original sin" needs to be removed by baptism if we are to live a good life now and after we physically die. That notion is not present in any of Jesus' parables, core sayings (those found in three or more NT *Gospels*), or in *Thomas*. Christian theology teaches that one needs to believe in Jesus' redemptive death on the cross, in his resurrection, in his future coming judgment, and that he was the Messiah (Christ) to be "saved." Jesus never taught those concepts.

For Jesus, the only sin we can commit is to not be our essential core life. To the degree that we do not live it, we live a false, dark version of our real selves.

He never says that anyone is evil. He does not observe that. Rather, he contemplated both the process of obscuring the light that we are and the process of becoming again our real selves. Describing that human de-evolution and evolution is his gospel, his core message.

Christians believe that Jesus was the *only* Son of God. Jesus disagrees as we see in Chapter 21, Poem 5 (Saying 3b):

Jesus
said this:

When
you
should know yourselves[1]

[1] *When you should know yourselves*: When you should recognize and leave your false selves and know your real selves…

Then
they
will know you[2]

[2] *Then, they will know you*: Then, people will see a radical difference in you.

And
you
will realize[3]

[3] *And you will realize*: And you will have external confirmation…

That
you
are
sons
of the Father[4]

[4] *That you are sons of the Father*: That you are sons and daughters of God.

Who
lives.[5]

[5] *Who lives*: Who lives the same life that is your soul essence.

In this poem, Jesus does not say that he is not God, but that that in essence we are all the life of God. We have the ability to not live that life and instead live the normal life that we see all around us. Thus, he observed that at our core, all of us are Gods. We simply choose not to evolve on the hidden "way" to be that life fully.

Jesus says that radical message in another way in his Child Poem, Chapter 2, Poem 3 (Saying 4):

Jesus
said this:

He
will delay
not[1]

> [1] *He will delay not*: A person who realizes that he lives a false dark self will not delay trying to find the way back to being the light that is his soul.

Namely
the man
of maturity
in his days[2]

> [2] *The man of maturity in his days*: The man who has become wise by living on the "light" hidden "way."

To ask a little
small child[3]

He
being
of seven days[4]

> [3] *To ask a little small child*: The wise person does not seek his core, light self in other dark adults, no matter how educated or prestigious they may be. Rather, he humbles himself to experience the pure light in a tiny child. He wants the child to teach him to be real.

> [4] *He being of seven days*: Biblically, the number seven means "perfection." A child is born with perfect soul-light.

About the place
of life.[5]

> [5] *About the place of light*: The wise person seeks to know and be the light center that he experiences in a tiny child.

And
he
will live.[6]

> [6] *And he will live*: If a person gets out of his head and soul-experiences the life in a child, he may become that life and light.

Jesus experiences the child as living from the center of "life" and "light." In contrast, adults living the normal "world" are dead and dark. That child does not need baptism. He does not need to believe X, Y and Z to be redeemed. He needs dead, dark parents and society to leave their "way" of the "world" in order to teach him how to live what he is at his core.

In this poem, Jesus describes how adults might evolve to be all that they desire. Step one is for the wise person to seek to know the "place of life" within a child or within another adult who lives divine life like a child. Step two is to live like that child.

In another poem he tells us the nature of that "place of life" in Chapter 21, Poem 5 (Saying 111a):

Jesus
said this:

He

Who
lives
out of He

Who
lives[1]

Will peer
not on death.[2]

[1] *He who lives out of He who lives*: A person who lives out of the life of our Father and Mother…

[2] *Will peer not on death*: Will not live the unfulfilling relative psychological death and unfulfillment of the "world."

The "place of life" in everyone is the center of our being where the Father and Mother reside one with us. Some may call that "place," "my higher self," "my source," "Allah," or something else. That is fine. As we will see, Jesus empowers people to discover their own answers. He does not preach absolute truths. So, people in the Kingdom are encouraged to define the "place of life" however they wish.

According to Jesus, we die when we become what we are not in our soul; that is, when we mentally adopt a false self as our real self. We live when we are congruent with our soul divine life. Further, all who live the life and light that they are will realize that they live in soul-oneness with God. By extension, a person in soul-oneness with himself is automatically in soul-oneness with everyone else, because all are unique versions of the soul of God.

The "place of life" is in one's soul. It is with the soul that we connect with infinite intelligence and reveal the wisdom to live in the Kingdom. To separate from our soul, we live a false self in the mind. For those reasons, in this book and in those accompanying this one, I call the "hidden" "way" to live, the "Way of the Soul." I call the normal "world" "way," the "Way of the Mind." I do not intend to disparage the mind or reason, but rather to point to the manner in which we make mental-knowing more important than soul-knowing or intuition.

SUMMARY

Way of the Soul	Way of the Mind
Hidden	Obvious and normal
Life and light	Death and darkness
The "Kingdom"	The "world"
Lives from He and She who lives	Lives from the false notions of the "world"
The way to return to being oneself	The way to become more miserably an aggregation of false selves

FAITH VERSUS EXPERIENCE

People in the "world" and on the Way of the Mind live from firm mental beliefs. They praise steadfast faith in religious, political, racial, class, nationalistic, and other "correct" dogmas. Jesus criticizes what the "world" honors in Chapter 2, Poem 2 (Saying 3):

Jesus
said this:

Part 1

If
they
should say to you
this: [1]

"Behold! [2]

[1] *If they should say to you this*: If religious, political, parental, educational or other authorities should indoctrinate you...

[2] *Behold*: Be in awe of the great things I am going to tell you that you do not know.

The kingdom [3]
is in heaven" [4]

Then
the birds
of heaven
will come to be
first
before you. [5]

If
they
should say to you
this:

Behold!

The kingdom
is
in the sea" [6] [7]

Then
the fish [8]
will come to be
first
before you. [9] [10]

[3] *The kingdom*: A way of living. We were born living the kingdom. It is full light and life.

[4] *Heaven*: A type or level of knowing or wisdom. To the degree that we are dark, to that degree we are unwise. Jesus does not refer to "heaven" as another world, or a place that we go to when we die.

[5] *Then the birds of heaven will come to be first before you*: Birds are ideas, especially blind beliefs. They occupy the mental sky and are flighty. When we seek a meaningful life in the birds of indoctrinators, we will adore those indoctrinators and their ideas as our false gods. Jesus refers us back to the commandment: "Do not worship false gods" (Exodus 20:3).

[6] *The sea*: Metaphorically, a "sea" is our emotions. We are sometimes, for example, awash in our emotions.

[7] *The kingdom is in the sea*: The indoctrinator says: "Your fulfilled, light way of living is in my emotional ideas." Some preachers convince with linear logic, and others with emotional (sea) beliefs that often lack logic.

[8] *Fish*: Emotional beliefs

[9] *Then the fish will come to be first before you*: Then the indoctrinator's emotional, often illogical beliefs will become your false gods.

[10] In Part 1, Jesus describes how a child is taught to live not from his soul light and life, but from the beliefs of adults. In doing so, the child forgets who he is and becomes a dark, false self. Instead of living from his soul knowing, he learns to live in his head dogma. Instead of being one and healthy, he becomes divided from his real self and emotionally sick. ·

Part 2

Rather
the kingdom

It
is
of your eye [11]
inward

And
it
is
of your eye
outward. [12]

[11] *Eye*: Single, third-eye soul-knowing. We can know primarily with our soul or with our mind. A child knows primarily with his soul. When one knows with two eyes, one focuses with one eye on social expectations and with the other eye on himself. Juggling those views leads to anxiety, worry and our other emotional problems.

[12] *The kingdom is of your eye inward...and outward*: Your fulfilled life will be found when you return to knowing all with a single eye that looks at yourself and out on the world—just as does a small child.

A child lives from his experience, not from blind beliefs. He trusts what his five senses tell him. He lives that faith until his experience tells him that he needs to modify his beliefs. Therefore, his growth process is to first experience; second, develop tentative beliefs; third, act on them; and fourth, modify those beliefs as he continues to define himself and all that is "out there."

A little child evolves as he evolves his beliefs. He naturally is not a person of steadfast faith. The "world's" "way" of firm faith leads to personal darkness and death.

Adults teach the child not to discover his own answers, but to live the beliefs of society. When his soul-insights conflict with the world's beliefs, he is told that he is "wrong" or "bad." If he does not rebel, he becomes divided or estranged from being who he is. The more divided he becomes, the more unfulfilled and emotionally sick he becomes.

In the NT parables and sayings and in the *Gospel of Thomas* poems, Jesus never tells anyone to have "faith" in dogma. The man observed reality. It was evident to him that no one becomes fulfilled or evolves in character by believing such things as "there are three persons in God," that "Jesus rose from the dead," or that "Mohammed was the last prophet." He implies that when we believe in what we cannot observe, we live in dark superstition, not light. However, people living in darkness cannot comprehend the obvious.

To leave the darkness of the "world," one needs to leave the darkness of indoctrinators and experience life as a child does. Further, he must do that on his own, being guided by his soul-Voice. Jesus articulates that core principle in Chapter 21, Poem 6 (Saying 111b):

Jesus
said this:

Whoever
is
the one

Who
discovers himself
on his own[1]

[1] *Whoever discovers himself on his own*: Whoever leaves indoctrinators (clergy, political leaders, parents, family, peers, etc.) and their organizations to discover himself on his own.

The world[2]
is
worthy of him
not.

[2] *The world is worthy of him not*: The normal people should be seen as the enemy of those who leave indoctrinators and find, with their soul-Voice, their own answers.

Jesus sees the "world" as consisting of various types of theological and secular religions; that is, institutions with high priests who indoctrinate people with dogma about how to think and act. We all join theological, political, corporate, social, nationalistic, and other secular religions. As we worship their leaders and their doctrine, we stop honoring our soul-Voice and ourselves. We think that we are independent when, in fact, we have chosen to conform to official doctrine. We know that we have done that when we say to others, "We believe..." rather than, "My beliefs today are..."

Jesus would not belong to any theological or secular religion. Those institutions hold us in the "world." He would support people who stopped living based on faith in dogma, and instead, lived based on their experience which they understood individually, each from his soul-knowing. He desired to liberate people to become what they are at their core, not to enslave them in an organization bent on indoctrinating them into being what they are not. He lived to empower people to find themselves on their own, not to become the twin of a family, clan, political, educational, or media demagogue.

Way of the Soul	Way of the Mind
Trusts only what one experiences	Possesses blind faith in dogma that cannot be tested in experience
Makes soul-knowing primary	Makes mental-knowing primary
Empowers people to find their own answers	Disempowers people by convincing them to be conformists to doctrine
Freedom	Psychological slavery
The way to return to being oneself	The way to become more miserably an aggregation of false selves

Absolute Truth versus Relative Truth

People in the world seek to possess firm faith in absolute truth. They think that when they discover it, they find their personal meaning, their self-confidence, and their superiority over people with faith in alternative absolute truths. That leads to everyone with steadfast faith in this absolute body of truths to judge themselves to be "good" and others with a different faith in their absolute truths to be "bad." That thinking causes all of our conflicts, because all of the "good" people want a good, peaceful world which can only happen when all of the "bad" people are converted, isolated, or destroyed. Some in the "world" steel themselves to "tolerate" other "bad" people; however, that suppressed hatred masking as kindness always exhausts itself in the right circumstances.

Many seek absolute truth in scripture or in other mediums. That happens in the face of the obvious: Everyone interprets every word heard, read, or seen subjectively. No two people, for example, interpret the word "God" or "Allah" in scripture the same way. Therefore, everyone interprets every word in any book or media presentation subjectively. Therefore, there is no absolute truth in the supposed word of God or even in the government's command on a stop sign.

Jesus viewed us as living on planes of wisdom. He called each a "heaven," perhaps because the person at any level thinks he has discovered heavenly absolute truth. One grows by challenging a lower level of heavenly wisdom to seek and find a higher level. He says that in Chapter 3, Poem 2 (Saying 11a):

> *Jesus*
> *said this:*
>
> This heaven[1]
>
> It
> will pass away;[2]
>
> And
> the one
> above it
>
> It
> will pass away.[3]

[1] *Heaven*: A level of knowing the truth about oneself, others and the world.

[2] *Pass away*: Our present view of what is true will change as we grow in character.

[3] *And the one above it, it will pass away.* As we grow, each lower level of knowing or belief passes away.

People in the world do not easily grow in character because they tie themselves to a level of heavenly wisdom. They do that by maintaining firm faith in the dogma at their current level. Those in the kingdom easily give up a level of faith in order to test and then decide whether to live higher truths.

People in the "world" live in fear of the unknown. They conserve what they know, declare it to be absolute truth, defend it as they would themselves, and often exclude relations with or punish people with different absolute truths. On the Way of the Soul, one masters his fear and forces himself to experience something or someone new. Only by doing that can they give up what seems to provide safety and sanity at a lower level to rule more wisely and powerfully over themselves and their interactions with others at a higher level of heaven.

Way of the Soul	Way of the Mind
Seeks higher relative truths	Seeks absolute truths
Challenges the truths of anyone including authors of scripture	Conforms to the truths of admired authorities including peers and authors of scripture
Holds and gives up tentative truths easily	Holds and gives up absolute truths with great difficulty
Overcomes their fear of trying a new way to think and act	Controlled by their fear of trying a new way to think and act
People are open	People are closed

UNCONDITIONAL LOVE-GUARDED VERSUS CONDITIONAL LOVE

The type of love in the hidden Kingdom is "unconditional love-guarded." Jesus tells us that in *Thomas* Chapter 8, Poem 2 (Saying 25):

Jesus said this:

Love your brother[1][2]

Like your soul;[3]

Guard him[4]

Like the pupil[5] of your eye.[6]

[1] *Brother*: Every person, animal, and plant—all that possess at their core the life of the Mother and Father.

[2] *Love your brother*: Be a twin of all.

[3] *Soul*: We are all unique manifestations of one soul-life.

[4] *Guard him*: Because your brother does not fully live life, guard him from himself, from others, and from hurting you.

[5] *Pupil*: Core.

[6] *Like the pupil of your eye*: Like the life-seeing center of your being.

Unconditional Love: When we love someone because he shares our soul life, we possess unconditional love for him. To express that, we empower him to be that life, even if it means that he upsets us by thinking and acting differently than us. Further, because everyone shares the same soul life, we will automatically grow to unconditionally love everyone as we grow to unconditionally love someone in front of us whom we formally disliked.

Love Guarded: We also need to guard ourselves and others from everyone else, because no one fully lives his core life. To the degree that he does not, he will automatically defend his false selves. When faced with the choice of loving us unconditionally and loving his false selves, he may choose to sacrifice us and love himself alone. When he chooses himself, we will be rejected and possibly harmed.

A wise person knows that anyone at any time could cause him and others problems. So, the wise will support others when they manifest unconditional love-guarded and protect themselves and others when they do not. For example, a parent may unconditionally love his child; however, he may also call the police if the child is misusing drugs.

Conditional Love-Guarded: To the degree that we are in the "world," to that degree we do not identify with our core soul life that we share with others. Instead, we identify with our things, money, theology, philosophy, politics, flag, title, family, traditions, friends, and even our sports team. We are not ourselves, but instead divided between our loyalties to things and people and our loyalties to our soul-Voice. Instead of unconditionally love-guarding others and events, we will love them on the *condition* that they support our false identities. When they do not, we automatically punish them in some way.

Mental health: When we identify with anything other than being unconditional love-guarded of all, which is our core divine life, we will have emotional problems. For example, if we identify with our money, we will be anxious and worried that it will be taken from us or that we will not have enough. When we lose a lot of money, we may be depressed and angry. In another example, if we identify with a friend, and that friend rejects us, we may feel alone, sad, and furious. Therefore, we all have such problems and will have them to the degree that we do not live on the hidden "way."

All of our emotional problems result when we do not identify with who we are at our core, and, instead, identify with false selves that we wrap around people and things. So, we will find fulfillment and steady joy to the degree that we become unconditional love-guarded of all. Jesus says that Chapter 7, Poem 1 (Saying 22).

Jesus
peered upon some little-ones
taking milk

And
he
said to his disciples:

"These little-ones[1]
taking milk[2]

They
are comparable
to those

Who
go inward
to the kingdom."

The disciples

responded:

Then
we
being
little-ones

We
will go inward
to the kingdom?"

Jesus
responded:

"When
you
should make the two

[1] *Little-ones*: Those who are one and single with their core life

[2] *Taking milk*: Discovering wisdom on their own.

The one; [3]

And if
you
should make the side
inward

Like
the side
outward

And
the side outward

Like
the side inward

And
the side
upper

Like
the side
lower [4]

And
not
the male
comes to be
a male

And so
you
will be making your maleness
and
your femaleness
one
and
single [5]

[3] *When you should make the two the one*: When you should leave your false selves and become one with your real self...

[4] *"You you should make the side...."* When you do not identify with any side of an argument... You may hold a position in a debate, but not to the extent that you get upset with anyone.

[5] *And so you will be making your maleness and your femaleness one and single:* You do not identify with anything or anyone, not even with your gender.

Such that
not
the female
comes to be
a female;

And when
you
should make an eye

In place
of some eyes [6]

And
a hand

In place
of a hand [7]

And
a foot

In place
of a foot [8]

And
an appearance

In place
of an appearance; [9]

Then
you
will go inward
to the kingdom." [10]

[6] *And when you should make an eye in place
of some eyes*: And when you know all with
a single soul-eye instead of using one eye to
look at yourself and the other to peer out to
see if you are meeting expectations.

[7] *And when you should make … a hand in
place of a hand*: A "hand" signifies "control."
And when you do not identify with being in
control or out of control of the situation…

[8] *And when you should make… a foot
in place of a foot*: A "foot" signifies "the
principles and beliefs that we stand on."
And when you do not identify with your
principles and beliefs…

[9] *And when you should make … an appearance in place of an appearance*: And
when you do not identify with how others
perceive and judge you…

[10] *Then you will go inward to the kingdom*:
Then, being free of false selves and all the
anger, frustration, depression, anxiety and
worry that you have caused by defending
and promoting them, you will become the
joyful, wise ruler of yourself and your interactions with others.

The Kingdom is a joyful, fulfilled life 24/7. We achieve it only to
the degree that we identify with nothing except being our core
self, which is unconditional love-guardedness of all.

SUMMARY

Way of the Soul	Way of the Mind
Unconditional love-guarded of all	Conditional love-guarded of those that support my false identities
Identifies only with his soul-Voice and life	Identifies with people, dogma, and things important to him
Never threatened and not worried about getting something, because he has it all	Continually threatened, because he has nothing substantial

LUCK VERSUS ORDER

People in the "world" wish each other "Good luck." They may also say, "Life is nothing but coincidences." Then, they may in compassion say, "I'll pray for you." Then, if the prayer is not answered, they may piously say, "God's ways are not our ways."

That is the confusion of the people of the "world." They do not see intelligent order, or if they see it, they think that God has intervened in chaos. As a result, most in the "world" are anxious and worried that bad luck will happen at any moment.

Many societies concluded that there is order governed by a god(s). Therefore, they tried to manipulate that powerful being into being benevolent and giving them what they wanted by praying or sacrificing something sacred. For example, they burned candles, made arduous prayer marches, and even altar-sacrificed a precious animal, virgin, slave, or child to get god (s) on their side.

Jesus saw perfect order and that he was given in unconditional love-guardedness exactly what he needed in the moment to evolve to higher levels of life and wisdom. Most of his poems imply that, such as Poem 6 (Saying 6) in Chapter 2:

*Jesus' disciples
asked him:*

"Do
you
want

That
we
fast?

And
what
is
the manner

That
we
will pray?

And
shall we
abstain
from certain foods?"

And
shall we
give alms?[1]

Jesus
responded:

"You
do
not speak lies.[2]

And
what
you
hate in him

You
do
not do
to him;[3]

[1] In all of these questions, the disciples want Jesus to indoctrinate them. They are not soul-seeking. They do not want to be guided by their soul-Voice. Rather they want external laws.
  The disciples see nothing but bad and good luck in the world, except when God intervenes. They do not see perfect order. They fast and pray, because they think that that God does not in the moment give them the perfect person or thing they need to evolve.
  The disciples may also think that God loves them on the "condition" that they obey religious laws or believe official doctrine.

[2] *Do not speak lies*: Do not be what you are not, that is, do not be an assemblage of false selves. Instead, be the core divine life that you are.

[3] What you hate in him, do not do to him: What we hate in others ultimately is incongruence. The people of the "world" do not identify with their core life; instead they live in dark falseness. One automatically hates such dishonesty in himself and in others.

For	[4] They are revealed …in the presence of heaven:
they	When we live at a high level of heaven, we
are revealed	become that heaven. When there, others are
	automatically "revealed" to us for what they are.
All of them	Thus, only by evolving can we gain the wisdom
	to guard ourselves and others from people of
In the presence	the "world."
of heaven."[4]	

Jesus sees perfect order. As a result, he does not pray or fast in order to manipulate God into changing things. Instead, he asks his soul-Voice to teach him how to unconditionally love-guard all in his current situation. Then, he will understand better the perfection that is behind good and bad things happening.

Jesus knows, in other words, that good and bad do not happen. It is all perfectly given in unconditional love-guardedness to enable everyone at every moment to evolve, no matter how it appears. He came to the conclusion not through abstract reasoning, but by observing nature, people and events.

People of the "world" do not agree with him, because they observe life from a low level of heavenly wisdom, because they have been brainwashed to see only good and bad things happening, and because they cannot account for tragedy, such as rape, the death of a child, etc. "How" they ask, "could a loving God have permitted such an event?" Paradoxically, the answer to such a question can only be known by the participants from a high level of heavenly wisdom.

Jesus implies in most of his poems that we are one in our soul with universal intelligence that tells us how to leverage the present moment into the next perfect step in our lives. Thus, personal mistakes are impossible. Our problems are us: we choose not to open to be unconditional love-guarded in the face of certain events and the actions of certain people. When we reach a high level of heavenly wisdom, all of our questions are "revealed" such as "What will happen after one physically dies?" "What is 'my' mission in life?" and "Why did this happen?"

Jesus does not pray, he converses with his Mother and Father. That is not something that only exceptional people, such as ancient prophets, do. He models what we all can do to the degree that we are one with ourselves and single-eyed and eared.

And finally, we notice in this poem that Jesus does not live the Torah laws that he was taught as a child. He lives only one law: be congruent with whom you are, which is divine unconditional love-guardedness of all. In that kind of love, one does what he single-eye and ear senses to do, whether it be to kill or save someone. No law exceeds or supplants that one.

SUMMARY

Way of the Soul	Way of the Mind
Experiences order in every event	Experiences luck and coincidences
Experiences perfection in every event	Experiences bad and good things happening
Evolves to understand what appears to be tragedy	Unable to make sense of tragedy
Evolves by going into and through painful emotions	Devolves by escaping painful emotions
Obeys primarily one law: Be congruent with the divine life that you are	Is divided by making primary conflicting religious and secular laws

THE BEGINNING VERSUS THE END

Many Christians desire as their *end* to get into "heaven" and to avoid going to "hell." Their *end* in prayer sometimes is to get something in the future or to relieve the guilt about something that happened in the past. Most people seek personal fulfillment as their end. Jesus did not think that way. He explains in a single poem not only his end, but the essence of the entire *"hidden"* *"way" that he taught and lived.* We read it in Chapter Five, Poem 1 (Saying 18a):

The disciples
said to Jesus:

"Speak to us
this:

Our end
will come to be
in what manner?"
Jesus
responded:

"For
have
you
revealed yourself
in the beginning

So that
you
will be seeking
after the end?

For
in the place

Where
the beginning
is
there

The end
will come to be
there.

"The disciples said to Jesus: 'Speak to us this: Our end will come to be in what manner?'" The disciples said to Jesus: "Tell us how we each will get to our ends."

The disciples knew that the word "end" in the Bible often refers to the end of one era or "world" and the beginning of a new era when the Messiah will lead everyone out of darkness and into light. When that happens, Old Testament prophesies indicated that the "lost tribes" of Israelites will be returned to Israel, everyone on the planet will worship the same one God in a temple cleansed of false priests and doctrine, that there will be a single overriding government on earth, and that people will live for 1000 years in peace (4 Ezra 12:32-34; 7:113).

So, the disciples were asking for Jesus to explain how he, as the Messiah, would fulfill the OT prophesies. They probably were also asking him when their wandering around behind him would "end" and they would obtain personal fulfillment.

"Jesus responded: 'For have you revealed yourself in the beginning; so that you will be seeking after the end?"

Right now, as you, the reader, read this, you have only one choice: to "reveal yourself in the beginning" or to continue the race to endless heart ache, punctuated with moments of happiness. If your present stress invites you to ruminate about the past, every you that you "reveal" to yourself in your imagination will lead you to devolve to deeper stress about the past. If your present stress invites you to worry about the future, every you that you "reveal" to yourself in your imagination will lead you to devolve to more stress about the future. If, on the other hand, you sacrifice your every impulse to flee the present situation and, instead, *to be unconditionally love-guardedness in the face of everything that is going on for you right now*, including your stress, you will "reveal yourself in the beginning," you will "end" all your soul-aches, you will be a co-Messiah "ending" all the conflicts in the world and starting the new era of peace, you will be full of the life of little child, you will transcend to a new level of truth, you will become the cleansed temple, you will be on the "hidden" "way" that will reveal to yourself the next perfect step for continuing to be in the "beginning" in a fulfilled "life," you will be one of those in the lost tribe that returns to the heart-Israel, and you will realize that all of your past so-called "mistakes" actually brought you directly and successfully to this "place" where you live as an equally important part of a universal government in the Garden of Eden, the Promised Land, Nirvana, and the Kingdom.

"For in the place where the beginning is there, the end will come
to be there." The "end" is the soul-Voice "place" in one's heart.
It is not out there with anyone or anything in the past or future.
It is not in mentally living in religious or secular blind beliefs.
It is where we will be guided by the "will of God" (Mk 3:35) to
exactly what we most *deeply and unconsciously* seek.

Jesus never talks about the tragedy of physically dying. He
adored the magnificent eternal divine life in all. As we evolve,
we become like him and more. From a high level of wisdom
and life, we will easily observe, not believe, that the life of the
least microbe cannot be extinguished, and that one will only go
to another non-bodily place where one again either chooses to
reveal himself in a heavenly beginning or live in a hell of past
regret and future worry.

THE BEGINNING

Probably, Jesus used the word "beginning" to explain his
understanding of the first three-stanza poem of the Creation
story in the Bible:

In the beginning
God
created heaven
and
earth;

And
the earth
was
without form
and
void;

And
darkness
was on the face
of the deep.

The word "beginning" in the Creation story and in Jesus poem does not mean "at the start of life on earth." Instead, metaphorically it means, "when a person is living in the present moment and not in the past or future."

"God created heaven and earth." A person possesses as a gift from God the abilities both to know life at higher levels, and to nurture a seed of wisdom in his reflective consciousness."

"The earth was without form and void." When a person become present, he recognizes that his reflective consciousness does not contain an inspired wise insight.

"And darkness was on the face of the deep." And the person was upset. The "deep" refers to deep water, which are our emotions.

When anyone makes the effort to become present in the "beginning" with himself, he lives this poem. For example, every morning finds me out in my chair with my dog and cup of tea facing the desert and the mountains. Usually, I am reacting to something "dark" that I have dreamed in the night or that happened the previous day. My "deep" emotions are upset. I know at that point I am not in the "beginning." In the Creation story terms, I am not yet born.

While sitting and sipping, I wait to be brought into the "beginning." I know that happens when I begin to taste the tea and become one with my dog, the desert and mountains. When in awe and oneness with myself and all before me rather than being in the past or future, I know that I am born again conscious in the "beginning."

Then, I wait for an insight to be planted in my "earth" (reflective consciousness) by my soul-Voice. That idea often tells me that something or someone that has caused some anxiety or worry needs to be unconditionally love-guarded. Gradually, my "heavenly" vision becomes activated and I see how I can look at myself and my interactions with the world in a more alive way. As I rehearse doing that, I usually feel a release from a lower level of knowing and a burst of energy to live differently. I am now born again as a new person.

All that I go through each morning to be born again at a higher level of being is expressed in the first poem and in later poems in the Creation story. That magnificent, brilliant work is not about a past historical event. It is about each one of us. We can live the "Creation" event throughout the day, anytime we choose to be more evolved in the "beginning." Therefore, the "Creation" story is an *allegory*.

An allegory appears to be a historical narrative about a central person; however, it is really about each of us. When the author shows how that person (usually a hero or heroine) develops or declines in character as he encounters problems, he teaches us how we can do the same. In most allegories, all of the characters represent each of us in some way. Further, the animals and things in the story symbolize or are metaphors for aspects of ourselves.

In the Bible, we find pure allegories with no historical facts, and historical allegories with some historical characters and events. In the latter, the author intends *primarily* to show character development or decline, not history; consequently, he may distort historical facts and invent things that never happened. That presents both problems for historians and archeologists trying to research whether Biblical events actually occurred, and huge conundrums for people who seek absolute truth in the Bible.

The Creation story is pure allegory. The Exodus story may be a historical allegory. Some of the described events may have happened; however, it is primarily allegory. The NT Gospels are historical-theological allegories. They appear to be primarily a historical account of part of Jesus' life. However, as allegories, they describe how each of us might live to be Jesus. Thus, the Exodus allegory and the Gospel allegories are not primarily about Moses and Jesus, they are about each of us as a Moses and a Jesus.

In the Exodus and Gospel allegories, we are told that, as a Moses or a Jesus, each of us needs to "divide the sea" and "walk on the sea" if we are to grow. Those actions metaphorically describe a necessary step that one takes to evolve from one level of "heaven" to another. The "sea" is our pool of emotions. We need to divide or rise above it/them to grow.

In another example, both Moses and Jesus go into the "wilderness." We all will go into the "wilderness" in our journey from living on the Way of the Mind to living on the Way of the Soul. The "wilderness," therefore, metaphorically describes that alone time when we leave the "land" (consciousness) of our dark, dead support groups to be free, independent and alive on a radically different "way."

The Gospels teach that we are to heal the sick and the blind, not physically, but by modeling for others a high level of life. The NT Gospels also send a theological message: that we need to believe in the crucifixion and resurrection of Jesus to be "saved." Therefore, the Gospels are both historical and theological allegories. That is why the history and the theology differ from one Gospel to the next. (This book will explain the meaning of many of the important Biblical metaphors).

The ancient allegories are self-help manuals. They were composed by wise people who wanted to help others evolve to a more fulfilled life. That form of literature was developed before writing. An author composed an allegory in his mind, recited it, saw the reactions of people, edited it mentally, and recited it again. People listening memorized it, reflected on it as they wove or herded sheep, and when they found it helpful to them to grow personally, recited it to others. Passing traders memorized the allegory and recited it to others in the far away they travelled to. That was their internet-like way of spreading mental health information.

Think of that! We need books and videos to remind us of important information. The ancients carried their libraries around in their heads.

We do not read the Bible and other ancient literature as allegories because the translations are incorrect. For example, we do not read today the first poem in the Bible as a three-stanza poem. Rather, we read it like we would a paragraph in a textbook. Further, translators do not translate a word or phrase the same way every time it occurs in the same work or in other works that reference each other. If, for example, a translator translates a word as "beginning" at one point, and later as, "to begin with," and later as "at the start," and later as "now;" we cannot recognize and less understand the meaning of metaphors, how an author explains a metaphor by using it in different contexts, and how later authors reference previous ones. In short, we cannot see that what appears to be a historical document is really an allegory.

We demean the ancient authors when we think of them as illiterate primitives. Because we cannot understand and apply their allegories, they would regard us as technically sophisticated with our smart phones, but as personally unconscious pre-Stone Agers.

SUMMARY

Way of the Soul	Way of the Mind
Chooses to be unconditional love-guarded in the face of anything happening	Chooses to flee the present to live in the past or future
Evolves to live more joyfully and wisely in the beginning	Devolves to live more painfully and unconsciously in the past and future

THE ORIGINS OF CHRISTIANITY

Historians now know how Christian theology became so opposite of what Jesus taught. To begin with, his message possibly was never embraced by anyone when he was alive, because, as you are seeing, it was so revolutionary. In the NT and in the *Gospel of Thomas*, usually the authors describe the followers of Jesus, including his mother and brothers, as confused and rejecting of Jesus' message. After he died, at least three communities preached different versions of his gospel: the Gnostics, the Ebonites, and the Jerusalem group headed by Jesus' brother, James. They did not do this because Jesus did not declare his gospel clearly, but because they could not follow his radical message, and they all sought to retain sacred parts of their religious and secular traditions.

Shortly after Jesus died in 33 C.E., Paul the Apostle, a Jewish cleric, began arresting and persecuting the followers of Jesus because they were preaching Jesus' "way" (Acts 9:2). That "way" threatened Paul and the Jewish establishment so much that even without Jesus' leadership, they felt the need to obliterate any mention of it in order to preserve their own "way."

In about 37 C.E., as Paul was traveling to Damascus to arrest Jesus' followers who lived there, he experienced a vision that told him that Jesus was the Messiah (Acts 9:3-20). That created difficult choices for him. He needed to either reject the vision, return to Jerusalem and join one of the communities of followers, follow and preach Jesus' "way," or create his own version of Jesus' gospel. He chose the latter.

Paul did not go back to Jerusalem; instead, he traveled to Arabia. While there, he decided that the reason Jesus appeared to him was to correct the message he was preaching before he died. Paul also felt that he was inspired to author his own gospel that stated that Jesus was the Messiah (Christ), that humanity inherited an original sin from Adam; that Jesus was the son of God in a way that we are not; that Jesus died on the cross as the perfect sacrifice that God desired to appease Adam's transgression; that Jesus was resurrected from the dead in a way that we cannot; and that Jesus will come again to judge the living and the dead. Finally, Paul decided that everyone needs to believe his theology in order to go to heaven after death. (Gal 1:11; Romans 1:1-4; 5:10-13; 8:1; Philippians 2: 5-10: Ephesians 5:2. 1Cor. 15:34).

Equipped with that message, Paul returned to Jerusalem and announced it to Jesus' brother James and to Peter, who were the leaders of the newly created "Christian" community. They were shocked to hear a gospel that Jesus never preached; therefore, after a few days, they asked him to leave. He did and did not return to work out his differences with the Apostles for 10 years!

That rejection by Jesus' Apostles and disciples compelled Paul to spend the rest of his life preaching his message to mostly non-Jews in other parts of the Roman Empire. Throughout that mission, *Paul was careful to never preach any of Jesus' parables, sayings, or poems.* To do so would be to expose Jesus' "way." Instead, Paul preached his own gospel in personal sermons and in letters, while fronting it by heralding Jesus as the Messiah.

Historians tell us that Paul died at some time between 62 and 65 C.E. During his 22 years of preaching, he founded many churches and converted so many people to his gospel that Jesus' "way" became hidden further. Additionally, he greatly influenced the Evangelists. Mark published the first NT Gospel in about 70 C.E. Within 20 years, Luke and Matthew published theirs. John published his Gospel between 90 and 110 C.E. All four of the Evangelists adopted and adapted Paul's theology.

For example, they included Jesus' parables and sayings in their works; however, they emphasized his passion and death—as did Paul. None of them ever explained the nature of Jesus' real "gospel," or "way."

Matthew emphasized that Jesus was the Messiah, as we see in the following famously quoted verses

When Jesus came into the district of Caesare'a Philip'pi, he asked his disciples, "Who do men say that the Son of man is?"

And they said, "Some say John the Baptist, others say Eli'jah, and others Jeremiah or one of the prophets."

He said to them, "But who do you say that I am?"

Simon Peter replied, "You are the Christ, the Son of the living God."

Jesus answered him, "Blessed are you, Simon Bar-Jona! For flesh and blood has not revealed this to you, but my Father who is in heaven.

And I tell you, you are Peter, and on this rock I will build my church, and the powers of death shall not prevail against it. I will give you the keys of the kingdom of heaven, and whatever you bind on earth shall be bound in heaven, and whatever you loose on earth shall be loosed in heaven."

Then he strictly charged the disciples to tell no one that he was the Christ. (Matt 16: 13-20):

In this passage, the translator translates the Greek word "ekklesia" as "church." It actually means "assembly," or more accurately, an assembly of people brought together to make a decision. A "church" as we know it did not exist at that time.

The word "rock" metaphorically means a strong statement or principle, usually one that differs from what people are thinking. So, when Jesus says "Upon this rock I will build my church" he means, "upon Peter's statement that Jesus is the Messiah he will form a group of decisions makers that will hold that belief as a core principle."

Matthew uses the word "heaven" to mean a place we go to after we die. Jesus did not use the word "heaven" that way in his parables.

Finally, this passage is not found in any of the other Gospels. If it did contain the commission of Peter as the head of Jesus' Apostles, we would find such an important declaration quoted by others. Historians tell us, further, that James, Jesus' brother, headed the Apostles in Jerusalem after Jesus died, not Peter.

When we consider what the passage really means and that it is not found in any other NT text, we can be sure that Matthew invented a dialogue that never happened. He has a right to do that because his Gospel is an historical-theological allegory, not just a history narration. He is supporting Paul who wants us all to believe that unless we blindly believe that Jesus was the Messiah we will not go to "heaven" after we die, something that Jesus did not say.

Because of the NT Gospels and other events, the Church that Paul established grew throughout the next 200 years. It became so dominant that the Roman Emperor Constantine decided, in about 300 C.E., to use it as one of his tools to unite the Empire. To accomplish that, he brought the Church's Bishops to Nicaea to write a creed. They did that *without using any of Jesus' parables or core sayings.* They also chose to include in the New Testament only those Gospels which taught Paul's theology. They knew of the Gospel of Thomas and deliberately excluded it from the official Cannon. Thus today, Christians believe in a creed and read Gospels that do not explain Jesus' gospel. They think they follow Jesus when, in fact, they follow Paul.

The Gospel of Thomas was discovered buried in Egypt in 1945. This book and the accompanying ones provide ample evidence that Jesus was the author of this highly organized, ingeniously and wisely written Book. In it, we find for the first time a full explanation of Jesus' version of the hidden "way." We also learn how to be guided by the "will of God" in every thought and action (Mk 3:35)—a problem unsolved until now. Nothing in Thomas contradicts the NT parables and core sayings; in fact, about half of the Gospel's poems share some or most of their content. The rest of Thomas contains Jesus' poems that appear to have been unknown to the Evangelists or deliberately ignored.

CONCLUSIONS

1. Jesus would not endorse dogma-based Christianity; however, he would support people who suspended their blind beliefs

to be guided by the Holy Spirit to unconditionally love-guard all and communicate directly with God.

2. Jesus would not endorse any organization that taught people that they were good, superior, worthwhile, saved or redeemed because they embraced dogma.

3. Jesus would endorse people and organizations whose primary goals were, first, to empower people to discover their own personal answers, and second, to discipline those who do not live unconditional love-guardedness of all.

4. Jesus observed that we are all the sons and daughters of our Parents. He did not view himself as core different than the rest of us. He modeled how we can become the Kingdom even more than he did.

5. Jesus was a therapist, not a zealot, theologian, or cleric.

6. Jesus was a follower of Abraham, who also did not join or found a religion but choose, instead, to be guided by his soul-Voice (Gen 22:18; 26:5).

7. Jesus would put higher his vow to be in the "beginning" in unconditional love-guarded of all over his allegiance or vows to a flag, spouse, family or other organizations.

8. Jesus would not say "good luck" or pray for what was not given.

9. Jesus would unconditionally love-guard what was given and not pray that anything be different.

10. Jesus would pray in the sense of reminding himself and others of the need to evolve in light-life, and in the sense of having give and take conversations with his soul-Voice.

11. Jesus observed infinite, universal intelligence guiding everyone and everything.

12. Jesus observed that everyone and everything was the son or daughter of God to the degree that they evolved in being the divine light that they are at their core.

13. Jesus would not endorse Paul the Apostle or anyone who did not preach his (Jesus') message, which is in his parables and core sayings.

14. Jesus would not endorse the New Testament Gospels because they emphasize his passion and death and not his core message.

15. Jesus would encourage people to use the NT Gospels and the Gospel of Thomas to know his parables and core sayings.

16. Jesus' passion and death occurred whenever he gave up one of his false selves to live his core light-self, not just physically on a cross at Golgotha.

17. Jesus' logic leads us to understand that the indirect, root-cause of the Second World War Holocaust and all of the other holocausts that have occurred and are continuing to occur today are leaders like Moses, Paul, and Mohammed who established a religion that declared that people were not inherently perfect and divine, that people needed to believe and act according to the religious founder's blind beliefs and laws to be "good," and that those who did not follow the founder's doctrine were "core-bad" and worthy of punishment.

18. Jesus would understand that Stalin, Hitler and other past and present demagogues unconsciously implemented and currently implement the religious logic that they were taught from birth.

19. Jesus would see our current fascination with majority-vote democracy as unwise. A new form of national and group governance needs to be invented that will put in power light leaders who unconditionally love-guard every person, plant, animal and thing, because people of the "world," who today

are in the majority, hate rather than love those living light-life and will not elect or appoint them.

20. Jesus models in his interactions with is blind and dead disciples that a light-leader will disagree; however, he will resolve differences honestly, without bias, and with love-guardedness for all.

21. Only when everyone is on the hidden Way of the Soul as taught originally by Abraham, Buddha, Jesus, the author of the Garden of Eden Allegory, and other wise people, will humanity peacefully solve most problems and efficiently solve the rest.

22. Because we have been mistranslating and misunderstanding the Bible for about 2000 years, we need to question the validity of the theological and other Biblically–based conclusions from this period.

CHAPTER ONE

THE DISCOVERY OF THE GOSPEL OF THOMAS

The Gospel of Thomas and the New Testament?

For more than 300 years after Jesus died, those who revered him argued about what to include in a New Testament. They could not agree because they each wanted texts that supported their own doctrines. In the 4th century, the leaders of the Church of Peter and Paul (which today is known as the Roman Catholic Church) finally listed the documents we typically find in the New Testament. They were able to make their decision final for others because they had been appointed by Constantine, the Emperor of the Roman Empire to do so.

The Roman Christian Church Bishops based their doctrine on Paul, the Apostle. Logically, those leaders excluded any document antithetical to their creed, such as the Gospel of Thomas. With the backing of Rome, they also ordered both the destruction of all documents with competing doctrines and the persecution of people proclaiming them.[1]

Background

In the mid 1940s, the world became aware of two magnificent archeological discoveries. The first occurred in Egypt in 1945 and is known as the "Nag Hammadi Library." These Books are mostly Christian writings composed in the first three centuries C.E. The second, better known to laypeople, occurred in 1947, and is known as the "Dead Sea Scrolls." The Dead Sea Scrolls are Jewish writings composed before 70 C.E.

The Nag Hammadi Discovery

In December of 1945, in Upper Egypt near the current city of Nag Hammadi (see the map below), two brothers, Muhammad 'Ali and Khalifah, set off on their camels to obtain nitrogen rich soil for use as fertilizer.

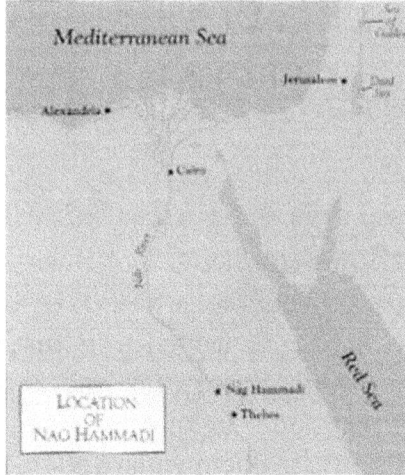

Figure 1. *Nag Hammadi in Egypt*

At a large mound called Djebel el Tarif, the brothers began to dig. Soon Muhammad 'Ali unearthed a large, sealed clay pot. Inside he found thirteen leather bound codices filled with crumbling yellowed parchment.

Figure 2. *Area of the Discovery*

Figure 3. *Muhammad 'Ali Who Led the Expedition*

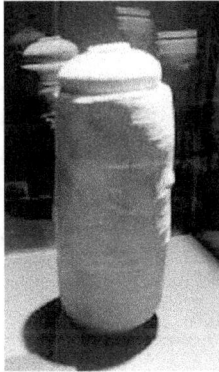

Figure 4. *120 CM High Jar*

Figure 5. *Thirteen Codices*

Figure 6. *A Single Codex Containing Many Books*

Although he was unable to read the text, Muhammad 'Ali knew that the books were ancient and possibly worth a lot of money if sold to antiquities dealers on the black market in Cairo.

What Muhammad 'Ali had discovered was a collection of books that included many Coptic copies of Christian manuscripts composed before 300 CE. Most of the originals seem to have been written in Greek, the language of the New Testament. The buried manuscripts date from the third and fourth centuries.

Muhammad 'Ali took the books to his house. While he was out on an errand, his mother ripped out some of the pages and began to burn the manuscripts as kindling. Fortunately, before all was destroyed, Muhammad 'Ali hid them from her and from the authorities who would confiscate them. He placed them with different friends.

Those friends began to sell them in Cairo. It didn't take long for the books to come to the attention of the Egyptian Department of Antiquities. Over the course of many years, the books were collected and became the property of the state.

While the Dead Sea Scrolls became famous rather quickly, the Nag Hammadi Library was largely unheard of by the general public until the early 1970s. One of the barriers to publication was the absence of scholars who could read and translate Coptic, the language of the documents. The second reason for the hesitant publication was that scholars initially dismissed the documents as arising out of a branch of Christian thinking, called "Gnosticism." They did not believe that Gnosticism contributed much to our understanding of Jesus or early Christianity. Now, many believe the opposite.[2]

THE GOSPEL OF THOMAS

One of the codices contained a Book that scholars today call the "Gospel of Thomas." They gave it that name because a scribe wrote in the last page of the document, "Gospel of Thomas," as shown below in the middle of the page on the left.

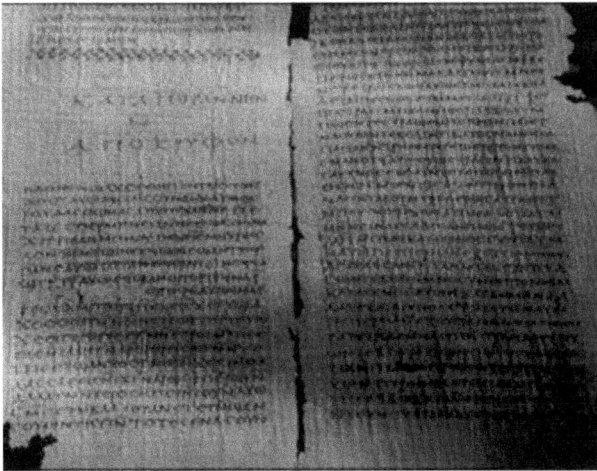

Figure 7. *Two Pages from Coptic Text of the Gospel of Thomas*

The Gospel contains what scholars in the 1950s, shortly after its discovery, considered to be 114 wisdom sayings. In the next volume of this series (*The Gospel of Thomas: The Original 21-Chapter Poetic Arrangement*), I will present evidence that the Gospel contains 129 highly organized poems rather than 114 sayings. The Gospel is so tightly organized that I will argue that only one person could have done it, that person had to have known all of the poems in depth, and that person was probably Jesus.

This "newly discovered" Gospel has become sensational among students of early Christianity. It is studied today not only more than the other Nag Hammadi writings, but also more than any other early Christian document. The reasons are many:

First, Thomas contains, in some form, about 50% of the parables and sayings that are in the Gospels of Mark, Luke, Matthew and John. This drives scholars to attempt to discover whether Thomas was composed before or after the New Testament Gospels, and by whom?[3]

Some scholars who compare the literary style of the Thomas material to that in the New Testament Gospels find the style in Thomas to be more primitive—implying pre-New Testament composition. For example, in Thomas, the Parable of the Sower does not contain an explanation; in Mark, the first New Testament Gospel thought to have become published before 70 C.E., there is an explanation. If these scholars are correct, and the style and content of Thomas are more primitive, then it is possible all or parts of the Gospel of Thomas were together before or shortly after Jesus died.

A second reason Thomas is more studied than the rest of the Nag Hammadi Library is that the content of the Gospel of Thomas expresses emotionally moving, practical wisdom instead of the abstract, blind belief religious theology that is found in many other early Christian texts. Thus, religious and nonreligious people that are interested in personal development may find the content enlightening.

A third reason for the intense interest in Thomas concerns the first sentence in the Gospel of Thomas, in which Jesus is identified as the author, as shown below:

Gospel Prologue

These are
the words,

Those hidden,

Which

Jesus,

Who lives,

Spoke.

It is worth noting that despite the fact that no other early Christian text begins with such a hugely remarkable claim, scholars have generally dismissed the possibility that Jesus composed the Gospel. They cite various reasons:

A Book written by Jesus would have been well known. We possess no historical evidence that Jesus composed a Book before he died. However, if what Jesus wrote was so inflammatory, so revolutionary, and such a threat to secular and religious authorities, that anyone caught with such a Book might be killed, such a Book would have been well hidden for many years.

The Gospel of Thomas was known by that title, and not as the "Gospel of Jesus," as early as the beginning of the third century.[4] However, that title may not mean anything as most early works were not titled as composed by their original authors. For example, we do not know for sure who authored the Gospels in the New Testament. It was common, in the first few centuries C.E., for communities to give their works legitimacy by labeling them as having been written by people with close ties to Jesus.[5]

A fourth reason for the massive interest in the Gospel of Thomas concerns the degree to which its content diverges from current Christian theology. In it, we find no trace of Paul's notions that one is "saved" because he believes

1. in original sin,

2. that Jesus died on the cross to wipe out original sin, and

3. that Jesus was resurrected.

Jesus died in 30 C.E. Paul composed his first letters in about 50 C.E. If Jesus composed all of the material in the Gospel of Thomas, or someone shortly after Jesus collected material and added it to what Jesus composed, we would expect that the Book would not include any references to Paul's theology. That, in fact, is the case. We have no historical record of Jesus believing in original sin or in any of Paul's other core ideas.

A fifth reason that the Gospel of Thomas is fascinating to students of early Christianity is that scholars know that the Evangelists—Mark, Luke, Matthew, and John—were selecting from one or more larger collections of Jesus' compositions. Much is being written about whether the Gospel of Thomas was one of the early sources of information for the Evangelists.[6]

A sixth reason to study Thomas is that it is not a biographical account of Jesus' life; it does not mention his passion and crucifixion, as we would expect that from a Gospel put together after his death. These factors therefore indicate that the Gospel was composed before Jesus died.

Let us remember that the Gospel of Thomas was discovered 1945. The text is in ancient Coptic, a language understood by few scholars at the time of the discovery. It was not until the 1970s that enough people learned Coptic to translate it and begin studying it.

We are clearly in the very early stages of understanding the nature of this magnificent Book.

ENDNOTES

[1] Elaine Pagels, Beyond Belief, the Secret Gospel of Thomas, Random House, 1995.

[2] Marvin W. Meyer, James M. Robinson, The Nag Hammadi Scriptures: The Revised and Updated Translation of Sacred Gnostic Texts Complete in One Volume, 2009, Introduction

[3] Robert E. Van Voorst, Jesus Outside the New Testament: an introduction to the ancient evidence, Grand Rapids: Eerdmans, 2000, pp 187-193.

[4] Meyer, Robinson, Introduction

[5] Paul J. Achtemeier, The Gospel of Mark, The Anchor Bible Dictionary, Doubleday, p. 545.

[6] James D. Tabor, The Jesus Dynasty, The Hidden History of Jesus, His royal Family and the Birth of Christianity, Simon & Schuster, 2006, 259-71.

CHAPTER TWO

JESUS' GOSPEL: BECOME FULLY HUMAN

How a person views human nature determines how they think about the causes of conflict within themselves and between individuals and groups. Those on Jesus' Way, here called the "Way of the Soul," view human nature in a manner opposite to those following what I call the "Way of the Mind." Therefore, they resolve conflict in a strikingly different manner.

THE TWO MEANS OF KNOWING

We encounter the following poem six times in the Gospel of Thomas:

He

Who
has his ear (sg.)[1]
to listen,[2]

Let him
listen.[3]

[1] *Ear*: A third-ear, an intuitive ear for "soul-listening".

[2] *Listen*: Soul-listen.

[3] *Listen*: Soul-listen.

I will later present evidence that the Gospel also ended with this poem.

Way of the Soul

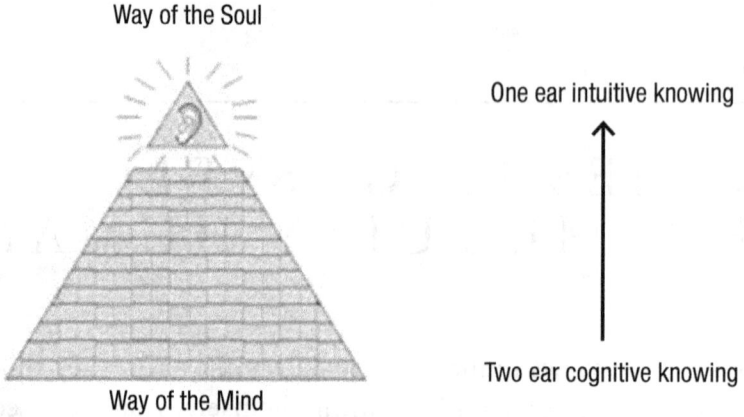

One ear intuitive knowing

Two ear cognitive knowing

Way of the Mind

BECOME A KINGDOM

According to Jesus, when one uses self-directed intuition properly, he enters a type of kingdom where he rules wisely over himself and his interactions with others. He speaks of a third eye and a third ear that we can use for that self-directed intuition, to see and hear intuitively, within ourselves and outwardly. He defines this kingdom in Chapter 2, Poem 2 (Saying 3) as follows:

The kingdom,

It

is

of your eye[1]

inward,[2]

And

it

is

of your eye

outward.[3]

[1]*Eye*: Third-eye

[2]*It is of your eye inward*: It is a means of looking inward at yourself with your third-eye.

[3]*It is of your eye outward*: It is a means of looking outward at others and the world with your third-eye.

"The kingdom..." A person as a kingdom.

Jesus tells us that when we evolve, we become what he calls a kingdom, or a field of regal influence. Think of the core self within each of us as projecting a radiation field. It affects every cell in our body and it emanates out to affect others.

For example, we all know that when we are fully alive and full of joy, one with our personal power, our bodies feel different, and when we walk into a room, everyone seems to notice. When we are like that, we know we have become more a king or queen over our kingdom, that is, our field of influence.

"It is of your eye inward..." The kingdom is an evolved means of knowing *oneself* with one's third, intuitive eye.

In the first poem, Jesus points to our third ear as a source of intuitive knowing. Now, he tells us that we have also a third eye. Both enable us to "soul-know," the term I will use for third-ear and third-eye knowing.

"It is of your eye outward." The kingdom is an intuitive third eye means of knowing *others* and the world.

As a person evolves on Jesus' Way of the Soul, he increasingly rules over himself and his interactions with others. He, thus, becomes more a king or queen, a fully developed, independent, self-joyful person. The contrast is a person who has not evolved to rule over himself or his interactions with others. Instead, his social conditioning and the expectations of others rule him. He listens and sees only with his physical eyes and ears, and not with his third-eye and third-ear.

Way of the Soul

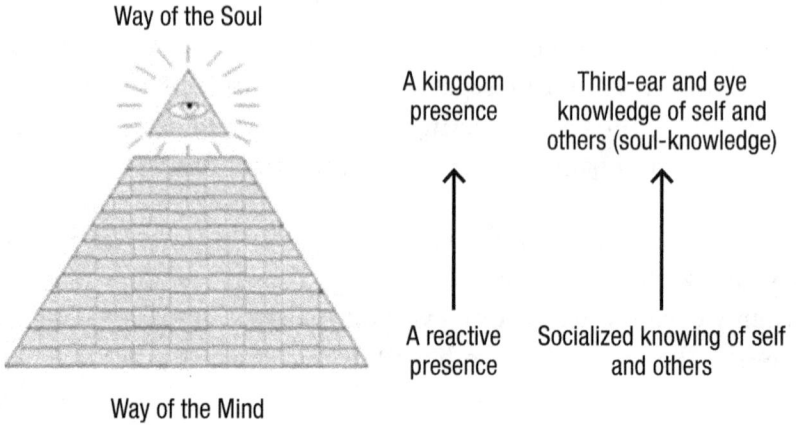

A kingdom presence

Third-ear and eye knowledge of self and others (soul-knowledge)

A reactive presence

Socialized knowing of self and others

Way of the Mind

THE SOUL-KNOWING PROCESS

We all instinctively know that what we perceive through our physical senses does not tell the entire story. Therefore, many people, especially creative types, seek a means to break out of their routine, indoctrinated means of perceiving, in order to discover the reality that is hidden from them.

My friend Tom, an artist, recently sent me an email in which he described his soul knowing creative process. I quote it below because it details the process that many use to see reality:

> *"When I become totally engaged in painting, I sometimes arrive at a place of calm, a place where I don't think about the strength of my composition or what color to choose, because that all happens automatically and I experience (though I don't know this until later) the stillness that comes as a result of "turning off" the left side of my brain and the associated ego with all its noisy worries and fears, dreams and resentments, sorrows, joys and puzzle solving. In that ego-less state, in the stillness I refer to as 'getting out of my own way,' my right brain takes in the images and other information that I need."*

Tom described his process of excavating information that is hidden from him. That information is the image that he puts on canvas. His process has five stages:

First, he becomes "ego-less." He has told me that when he paints to make money or to gain a reputation, he cannot soul-see.

Second, he becomes willing to abandon his prevailing ideas and expectations for the work.

Third, he achieves stillness. He has certain places and rituals that enable him to find quietude. He knows that when his Mind is in a state of regret, worry, or excitement, he cannot soul-know. These mental states hinder his ability to be present in the moment.

Fourth, he allows information to come to him freely and flow through him without judging it. He lets the force of his intuition move his hand.

Fifth, he inspects what he senses and decides what to do with it through left-brain analysis. However, his left-brain never takes over the process, always working with his right-brain. In other words, he tempers the right-brain's creativity with the left-brain's rationality. He discovers the meaning of what his right-brain provides with the left side of his brain.

Notice, that during the entire process, he uses his right-brain to receive information and his left to shape it. When we do the reverse, we turn off our soul-knowing.

Way of the Soul

Egoless   Evaluates ideas
                 in their pure form

↑   ↑

Seeks ideas to   Critiques ideas
support ego   before pondering them

Way of the Mind

Way of the Soul

Right brain   Information flows
receives,   through
left shapes

↑   ↑

Left brain   Information is
receives and   manufactured
shapes

Way of the Mind

Jesus describes the soul-knowing process in Chapter 8, Poem 2 (Saying 27):

If

you

do

not make the Sabbath

outward[1]

The Sabbath

inward[2]

You

will peer[3]

not

upon the Father.[4,5]

[1]*Sabbath outward*: A normal Sabbath Day when one does not work. The physical things one does to make the Sabbath holy: stop work, light candles, dress nicely, etc. Intentionally stopping thinking about and dealing with stressful things. Metaphorically, physically resting in stillness.

[2]*Sabbath inward*: A time of internal stillness. Making the Sabbath holy *inward* as well as outward. A time of living in the present rather than the past or future.

[3]*Peer*: Soul-seeing.

[4]*Father*: Jesus calls the male aspect of God, "Father."
(He will later talk about his God "Mother").

[5]*Peer not upon the Father*: Jesus maintains that if we use soul-knowing deeply, we can experience the divine in everyone and everything.

"If you do not make the Sabbath outward, the Sabbath inward," If you do not actualize the external ritual of rest by being still within yourself…

Jesus expressed that one cannot soul-know unless he is present in the here and now. When we are internally distracted by the past and future, we are perceiving through our physical senses (two eyes, two ears); that is, we are socially-knowing, letting society's beliefs shape our perceptions.

"You will peer not…" You will not soul-see.

"You will peer not upon the Father." You will not soul-see the Father. In other words, you will not *experience* the Father. Instead, you will either blindly believe or disbelieve in Him.

Way of the Soul

| Lives in stillness | Lives the Sabbath inwardly every day |
| Lives in busyness | Lives the superficial Sabbath |

Way of the Mind

Way of the Soul

| Perceives the divine in all | Experiences God |
| Perceives only non-divine life or inanimate objects | Blindly believes or disbelieves in God |

Way of the Mind

That Poem, thus, expresses Jesus' understanding that one need *not believe* in God, because through soul-knowing, it is possible to *experience* God.

Jazz guitarist Larry Carlton described soul-knowing like this:

"When I was in College, 19 years old, there was an upright bass player, student, keyboard player, and myself, and a sax player—we were all about the same age, and we were all very passionate about jazz. We got together one Friday night in someone's front room to jam. That evening was the first for me because I experienced for the first time going to the "zone" musically. Before that I had always played...and played a lot 6 nights a week in clubs, and so I had been playing 13 to 14 years by then. However, that night we played (he strums a chord). I went to the zone during my solo...which means...I don't want to make this to sound cliché, but I became one with the instrument that night. What I knew how to play, and what I had been playing was transcended that night to another level to where for the first time I became not in control of the guitar, but one with the guitar. What happened is...I played chorus after chorus after chorus, it is like experiencing runners high if you are a runner, where you do not need any effort any more, you are just running, you don't feel anything...well, that happened that night. And I just played chorus after chorus after chorus. I was loving the experience. Pretty soon the bass dropped out, and now it was just me and the piano player, and pretty soon the piano player stopped playing. But my awareness was so in touch with this that I just kept playing. And I don't know if I played two more choruses or five more choruses, I don't remember the details of it, but I remember coming out of it, and opening my eyes and they were all just sitting there looking

*at me, because they had experienced it with me.
That was the first time that my maturity level
as a musician went to that place of connecting
with my instrument. That experience...once you
experience it, you want to experience it again. So,
my life's goal is to try to go to that place when I
am playing the guitar. I pick up the instrument
in a setting that has the potential, whether it's
with the blues band or jamming with a guy, my
whole objective is to get to that place where I
am connecting with my instrument and feel that
experience again."*

Larry becomes one with his instrument when he soul-knows.
Those around him could tell that he was different and they loved
what was coming *through* him. That is the type of knowing that
Jesus emphasizes as the foundation to his Way of the Soul.

Tom puts his discoveries on canvas for others to see; Larry puts
his into music; Jesus put his in poems for others to see and
reflect on.

All of us soul-know to be creative. All of us seek to be one with
all. This is what we seek through drugs, thrills, romance, and
candlelit dinners. Few of us develop the discipline and courage
to soul-know as wise people do.

Throughout time, people desiring personal growth have found
it necessary to retreat from their daily routines to obtain hidden
information by soul-knowing. Some Native American tribes
encourage their members to use the sweat lodge to soul-sense
visions to improve their lives. Spiritual people all over the world
attend retreats led by trained spiritual guides who assist people
in "listening." All of them are discovering the meaning of hidden
information.

Many cultures revere those who specialize in soul-knowing,
calling them "seers," "mystics," "shamans," and "prophets."
Literature and oral traditions from these cultures describe the
conditions for hearing hidden words. One generally must

- Go apart, that is, get away from the influence of the ideas of others;

- Become still;

- Abandon expectations and prevailing beliefs;

- Be open to new ideas;

- Be willing to see visions, hear words, and sense vague impressions;

- Trust what one hears and sees;

- Ponder what has been heard and seen;

- Discern how to use the new information in one's life;

- Formulate new tentative beliefs about how to be a more evolved person; and

- Have the fortitude to live differently in the face of opposition.

Jesus did those things to reveal to himself how to live a more fulfilled life. He then structured his insights into the poems that we find in this Gospel.

Way of the Soul

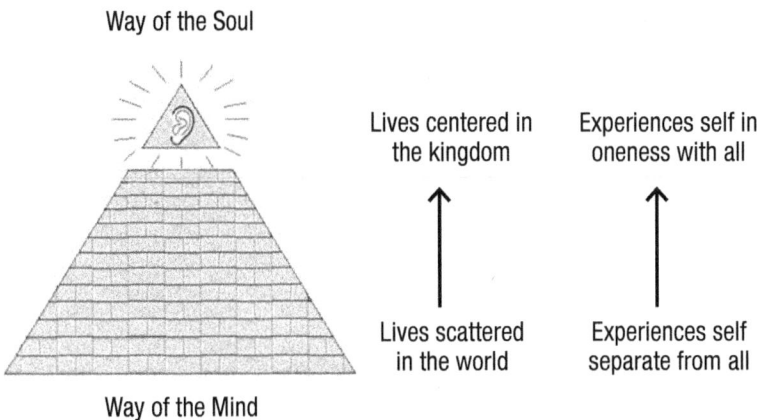

| Lives centered in the kingdom | Experiences self in oneness with all |
| Lives scattered in the world | Experiences self separate from all |

Way of the Mind

Jesus composed every Poem in the Gospel by revealing his "hidden" soul with soul-knowing. That is stated in the Prologue, Poem 1 in Chapter 1 (Saying 1a):

These
are
the words,¹

Those
hidden,²

Which
Jesus,³

Who
lives,⁴

Spoke⁵

¹*These are the words:* These are the words of soul that make up this Book.

²*Those hidden:* Those hidden by our socialization.

³*Which Jesus:* (Implied) Which Jesus soul-discovered and applied to his life.

⁴*Who lives:* Who lives fully as an evolved, fulfilled human being.

⁵*Spoke:* He spoke out to the world to enlighten others.

In Part Three of the first Poem in the Book, he tells us his purpose:

Whoever¹
discovers the meaning
of these words,²

Will take a taste
not
of death.³

¹*Whoever:* Whoever soul-listens.

²*Whoever discovers the meaning of these words:* Whoever discovers the meaning of these words for their own lives.

³*Will take a taste not of death:* Will not be living death.

"Whoever discovers the meaning of these words." Whoever uses my insights as a stimulus to discover their own answers.

"Will not take a taste of death." Will be led by their soul-knowing out of slavery to society and its endless doctrines to living a fulfilled life of one's own.

Jesus unearthed the soul that was hidden behind his socialized blindness, discovered its meaning, and become fully alive. Jesus saw that soul surrounds us, is in us, and is us. He experienced that soul as a person; and addressed him as his "Father." He thus tells us that our "Father" gives us access to the answers we need. We are not individuals wandering in the world alone. Implied in every poem are his core discoveries:

1. Everyone receives unique information tailored to bring him to fulfillment.

2. All of that information comes wrapped in love.

3. All of that information is hidden by our prevailing belief systems.

4. Nothing happens by accident. It is all designed to lead us to fulfillment.

5. All of our "death" emotions arise because we do not understand this design.

His conclusions are verified when we cease social-knowing and begin using our soul-knowing.

For example, if we were taught to believe that democracy is good and socialism is bad, we will see democracy as our salvation and socialism as our ruin. We will look for evidence to support our preconceptions. Further, we will distort evidence to confirm these preconceptions. We may even sacrifice and die for our indoctrinated beliefs.

That is the Way of the Mind. When we follow that path, we base our lives on other people's ideas. We become so blind and deaf that we do not know that we are blind and deaf. This is not freedom, it is slavery.

We all impose patterns on reality in order to understand it. For example, some people are skeptics, some see evil around every corner, some are positive-thinkers, and some are atheists. Jesus presents us with alternate patterns for our consideration. As we choose our perceptual patterns, we choose our lives. With soul-knowing we can examine the evidence in support of our tentative beliefs.

Jesus poetically presents alternate ways of viewing our situations. He also empowers us to verify his observations for ourselves. Thus, he facilitates rather than indoctrinates.

Way of the Soul

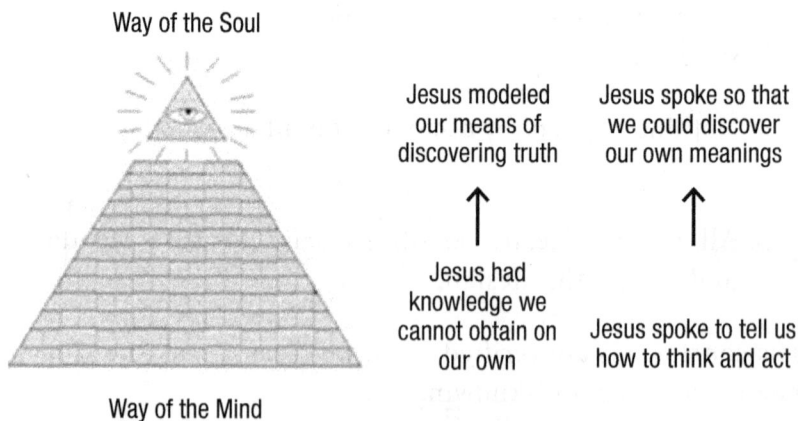

Jesus modeled our means of discovering truth

Jesus spoke so that we could discover our own meanings

↑

↑

Jesus had knowledge we cannot obtain on our own

Jesus spoke to tell us how to think and act

Way of the Mind

Way of the Soul

All is alive with   The answers we
information to   need are available to
lovingly guide each   be revealed
person

↑   ↑

We receive neutral   We may or may
information that   not figure out our
may or may not help   answers

Way of the Mind

Way of the Soul

Our conscious   Life is human
goal: live more   fulfillment in
and more life   every way

↑   ↑

Our unconscious
goal: live more
and more death   Life is spiritual

Way of the Mind

THE WORLD

The "world" for Jesus is people who primarily use what I call, "socialized knowing." Instead of using their intuitive soul-knowing to know themselves and others most or all of the time, their knowledge of themselves and others arises primarily from what they have been taught by others. To facilitate people to be on his Way of the Soul, Jesus taught them to leave the world and enter a community of kingdom people. He says that in Poem 2 from Chapter 8, (Saying 27):

Jesus
said this:

If
you
do
not fast
from the world, [1,2]

You
will discover
not
the kingdom. [3]

[1] *World*: People who primarily use their two eyes and ears to know themselves, others, and the nature of the universe. People who socially-know rather than soul-know.

[2] *If you do not fast from the world*: If you do not starve yourself from soul-knowers. If you do not leave your Ways of the Mind.

[3] *You will discover not the kingdom*. You will not discover yourself as an independent, insightful knower of yourself, others, and the principles governing human growth and interaction.

"If you do not fast from the world…" If you do not leave the influence of your parents, teachers, clergy, peers, media, and other authorities who have taught us how to think and act…

As I pointed out in the Preface, when a person identifies with a set of theological or secular beliefs, he creates a *Way of the Mind*. Those beliefs were not native to him as a newborn child. The "world" taught them to him.

When we identify with a Dogma, that is, *a set of beliefs held by others*, we defend and promote that Dogma as we do ourselves. Unconsciously, our Dogmas become an extension of ourselves. We also promote and defend our indoctrinators (parents, teachers, clergy, politicians, media-idols, peers, etc.) because they are representatives of our world.

"If you do not fast from the world..." Jesus says strongly: If you do not leave your socialized world, all your Ways of Dogma, you will not follow me, you will not find yourself, you will not be a kingdom, and you will not be fulfilled.

"You will discover not the kingdom." You will not discover on your own how to rule over yourself and your interactions with others. Instead, you will forever be a mental slave to society and its multitude of theological and secular dogmas.

In short, fast from the world, and you may discover yourself and become a free and independent person; do not fast from the world, and you will become an ever more naïve, reactive serf.

We don't "discover" by listening to sermons, political speeches or school lectures; we don't "discover" through socialized knowing. We don't rule by placing the authority of indoctrinators and their doctrines above the authority that we personally hold over ourselves.

The kingdom is a state of being independent from the beliefs of others. To discover it, one must question and suspend all that he has learned through his physical eyes and ears in order to attain soul-knowing of reality through his faculty of intuition.

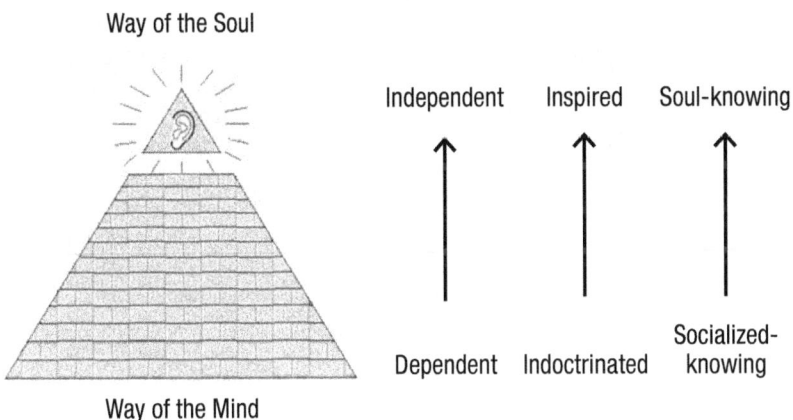

Way of the Soul

Independent   Inspired   Soul-knowing

Dependent   Indoctrinated   Socialized-knowing

Way of the Mind

Way of the Soul

Dominion over oneself & one's interactions   Kingdom

↑   ↑

Slave to the opinions & doctrines of others   World

Way of the Mind

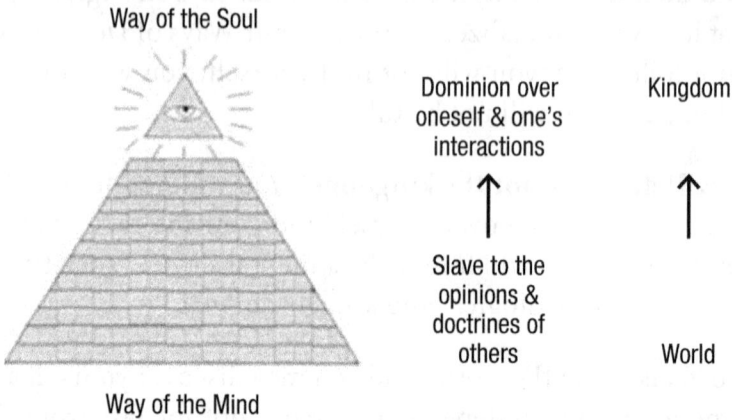

DISCOVER RATHER THAN BELIEVE

We all have lenses through which we view the world. They consist of the beliefs we bring with us to our acts of physical sensing. Instead of observing reality, our preexisting beliefs compel us to see and hear what we want to see and hear.

With respect to seeing, as we peel away the first layer of belief lenses, we understand more. The more we peel off layers, the more we will get closer and closer to the truth.

Jesus states his core principle for becoming a kingdom in many poems. Here is another from Chapter 21, Poem 4 (Saying 110):

*Jesus
said this:*

*Whoever
has discovered the world,[1]*

*And
he
comes to be
rich,[2]*

*Let him
abdicate
from the world.[3]*

[1]*Whoever has discovered the world*: Whoever has used his soul-knowing to discover his enslavement to the Ways of Dogma.

[2]*And he comes to be rich*: And he becomes a self-confident ruler of himself and his interactions based on his adopted beliefs.

[3]*Let him abdicate from the world*: Let him give up that rule to discover himself on his own.

"Whoever has discovered the world…" Whoever has removed his belief filters to see the true nature of the world…

Our belief filters are not easily removed, because our present false reality is a part of our identity. Thus, to know more truly, we must die to the oneself and be born again in enlightenment.

Our belief filters are also difficult to remove because we are rewarded by our peers for conforming to their ways of thinking and acting, because that makes them comfortable. People generally do not trust or enjoy the presence of those who disrupt the status quo. However, clearly, Jesus only sought out and encouraged rebels.

Courage is a necessary quality of those who follow the Way of the Soul. It is a continual process of painfully destroying cherished beliefs, thereby creating a new awareness and self.

"And he comes to be rich…" And he comes to be a ruler of himself and others based on his firm, adopted beliefs

Those following the Way of the Mind believe that their Way is the absolute truth. They use that knowledge to feel self- confident, that is, to rule themselves and their interactions. They also use that knowledge to encourage others to do the same thing. Those following the Way of the Soul live their lives in constant pursuit of the truth. Those following the Way of the Mind live arrogantly and stagnate in their blind faith. Those following the Way of the Soul die to themselves and their faith to be reborn in their true natures, continually discovering themselves, others, God and the nature of the world.

"Let him abdicate from the world…" Let him permit others to follow the fools' means of obtaining self-confidence.

Jesus did not indoctrinate people with beliefs that they could proudly use to rule themselves and others. Instead, he led people off the Way of the Mind and onto the Way of the Soul. His kingdom is a Way of independently standing alone against the belief-rulers of the world, together with others following the same Way.

Therefore, the kingdom is a non-doctrine-based way of living for the individual and groups. It incorporates everyone who dedicates themselves to leaving their secular and theological Dogmas in favor of the path of perpetual discovery.

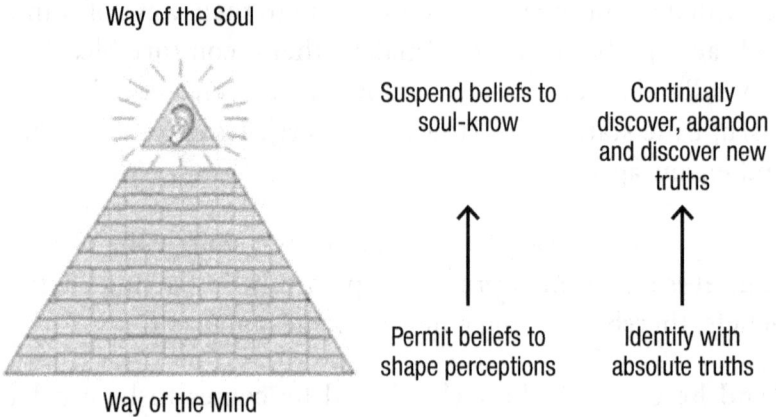

Way of the Soul

Suspend beliefs to soul-know	Continually discover, abandon and discover new truths
↑	↑
Permit beliefs to shape perceptions	Identify with absolute truths

Way of the Mind

BECOME LIKE A LITTLE CHILD

Jesus and others following the Way of the Soul view a newborn differently than those on the Way of the Mind do. We see that in the Child Poem Chapter 2, Poem 3 (Saying 4) of the Gospel of Thomas.

Jesus said this:

He
will delay
not,[1]

Namely
the man
of maturity
in his days,[2,3]

[1]*He will delay not*: He will immediately.

[2]*The man of maturity*: Especially the one who has become conscious and alive at a high level of soul.

[3]*Days*: Times of enlightenment. As opposed to nights, which are times of intellectual slavery.

To ask a little,
small child,

He
being
of seven days,[5]

About the place[6]
of life;[7]

And[8]
he
will live.[9]

For
there
are
many first,[10]

Who
will come to be
last;[11]

And
they
will come to be
single ones.[12]

[5]*Seven*: The child is born complete; he has not been corrupted by the world.

[6]*Place*: That place within, from which we think and act.

[7]*Life*: A fulfilled way of living.

[8]*And*: And learning from a small child...

[9]*He will live*: He will be fulfilled by modeling the child.

[10]*There are many first*: There are many wise people.

[11]*Who will come to be last*: Who will seek to learn from those others regarded as "last," such a little, small child.

[12]*Single one*: Congruent ones. A little, small child is congruent with their true natures.

"He will delay not, namely the man of maturity in his days to ask a little, small child, he being of seven days, about the place of life." A wise man will not make anything more important than seeking to be more alive. He looks for a model for his life, not in his theological beliefs, in adults, in books, but in a newborn.

Most people do not seek "life" as their first priority when they get up in the morning. A wise person does.

To grow, most people talk to therapists, their clergy, their friends, read books, or reflect. A wise person gets out of his head, away from adults, and observes life in its purest form.

Jesus was an acute observer. He did not use abstract logical speculation or deduction, primarily. He was a poet, not a theologian. He was a phenomenological therapist and philosopher, not a behavioral psychologist or objective philosopher. He ignored his mental musings and delved into his experience to understand how he might evolve. He was primarily seeking a model, not an idea.

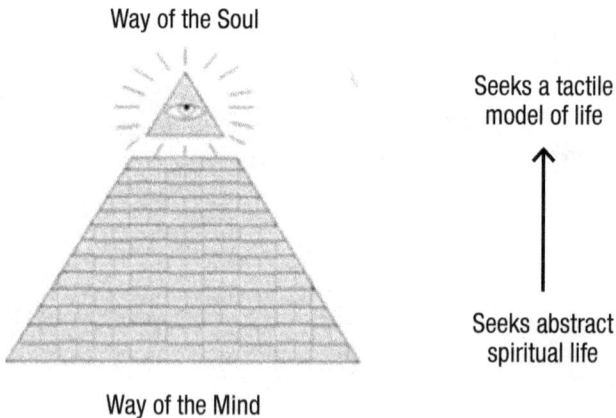

Way of the Soul

Seeks a tactile
model of life

Seeks abstract
spiritual life

Way of the Mind

Way of the Soul

Does not believe in a
concept that cannot be
verified in his experience

↑

Believes in a concept
that cannot be verified in
his experience

Way of the Mind

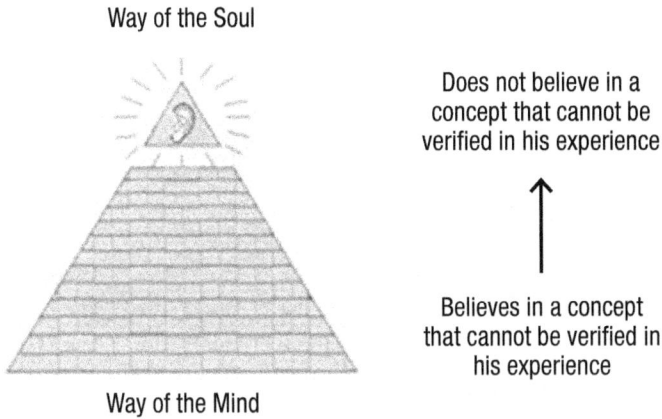

"Ask a little, small child, he being of seven days," Ask an overlooked little child, or an adult who is like a little child.

We sometimes live in confusion because we cannot discern the difference between people living fully alive from those living less alive. That results in us not possessing real life goals for ourselves. Instead, we wander around, adoring this false life in one person, and that one in another. We dress ourselves in this way of being, and then in that one—never finding our true selves.

Sometimes we encounter a very alive person, and instead of humbly modeling them, we either become embarrassed that we are not that alive, or become jealous of their life. The wise seek out those more alive, study them and humble themselves to learn from them.

Way of the Soul

Discerns levels
of life

Seeks to live at a
high level of life

↑

↑

Cannot discern
levels of life

Wanders through
life aimlessly

Way of the Mind

Way of the Soul

Humbles himself before a
person more fully alive

↑

Ignores and/or
persecutes one with
child-like life

Way of the Mind

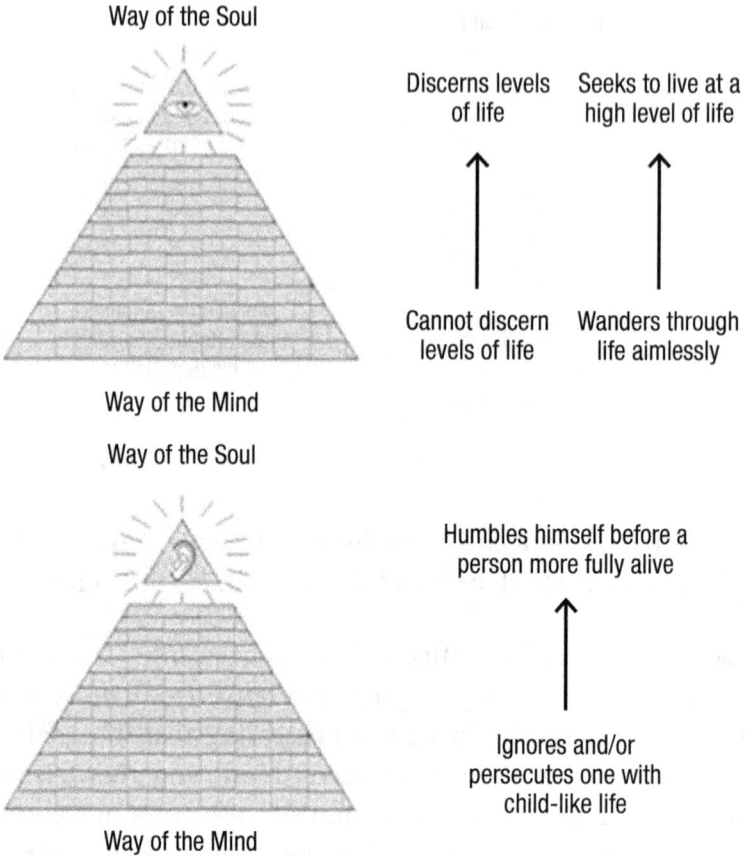

"Ask a little, small child, he being of seven days, about the place of life." Observe beyond appearances at the source of life in a new born.

Some look at a little child and see original sin as the source of his life. Others may not even look for the source. A wise person becomes fascinated at the "place" within a little child from which he lives.

"To ask" is the first step in the soul-seeking process. If we do not recognize the lack of life in ourselves, we will not ask one to show it to us. If we do not humble ourselves to ask, we do not evolve.

Way of the Soul

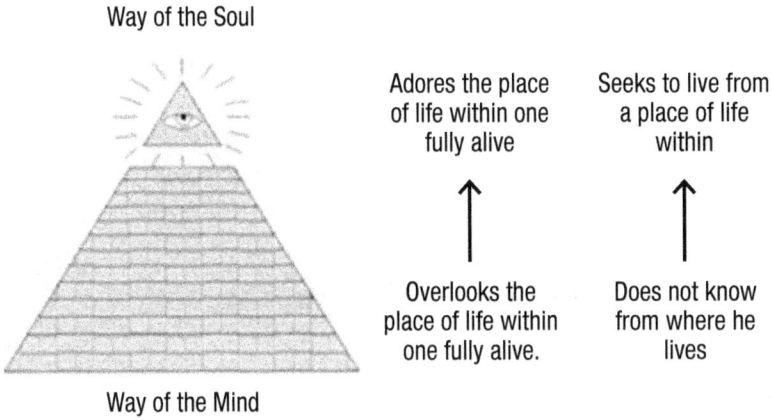

Adores the place of life within one fully alive	Seeks to live from a place of life within
↑	↑
Overlooks the place of life within one fully alive.	Does not know from where he lives

Way of the Mind

"And they will come to be single ones:" And they will come to be congruent with their core selves.

Most of us, if not all of us, are to some extent divided between our true and false selves. We can illustrate that like this:

Way of the Soul

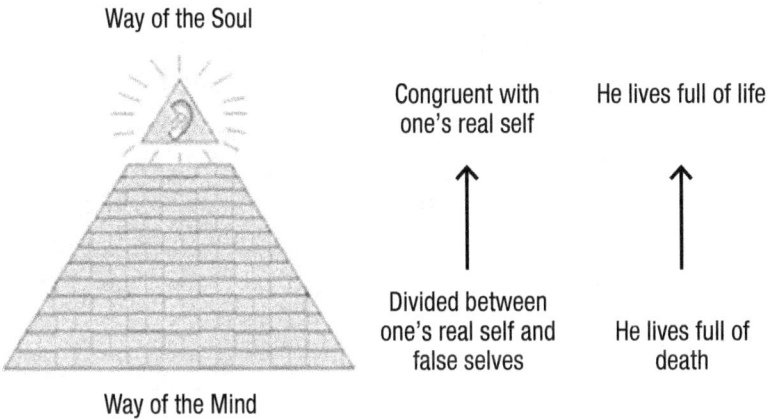

Congruent with one's real self	He lives full of life
↑	↑
Divided between one's real self and false selves	He lives full of death

Way of the Mind

Jesus does not distinguish between a spiritual life and a personal life. They are the same. When we develop ourselves, we develop our whole selves. His formula for personal development is this: Abandon your false selves and live congruent with your true self. You will then be more evolved spiritually, mentally and emotionally.

When we identify with a false self, we identify with a set of beliefs. For example, if one identifies with being a Christian, he chooses to *be* not himself primarily, but the doctrine of some church. That doctrine becomes part of his false self. He will promote and defend it as if it were his real self.

In another example, if one labels himself a "conservative," he tells himself and the world that he believes certain things. In other words, he has established an artificial identity.

If one chooses to identify with his possessions, he identifies with the beliefs associated with his things and money, not with his true self.

The little child does not crawl around believing this and that. He does not say, "I am smart," "I am black," "I am Asian," "I am an American," "I am a Muslim," "I am rich," or "I am poor." He does not invest himself in beliefs about those false identities. He just is—and he is fulfilled in life. That is why he is Jesus' model of soul.

Through socialization, we learn to think and behave in particular ways. We invest ourselves in our false selves enough to promote and defend them as if they were our true selves. They are not. We have created them from our own amalgamation of socially accepted beliefs. Thus, we become divided from who we truly are, resulting in a kind of living death.

Way of the Soul

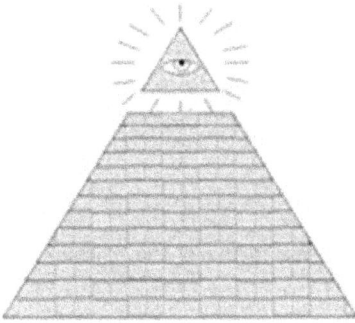

One is without a   I am me
need to believe
anything about
himself

↑   ↑

An amalgamation
of socially learned   I am first, one idol,
beliefs   then another

Way of the Mind

Way of the Soul

Single without   Models himself on
identifying with   a little child
doctrine

↑   ↑

Models himself
on successful 1st
Split by his pride   people with false
in his doctrines   selves

Way of the Mind

"For there are many first, who will come to be last." For there are many who think that they are first because they identify with a superior-to-others false self, who then become humble by recognizing that in fact, they are last to one full of life. Then, because they seek to evolve, they become "last" when they "ask" one modeling life to teach them about their "place" of life.

Way of the Soul

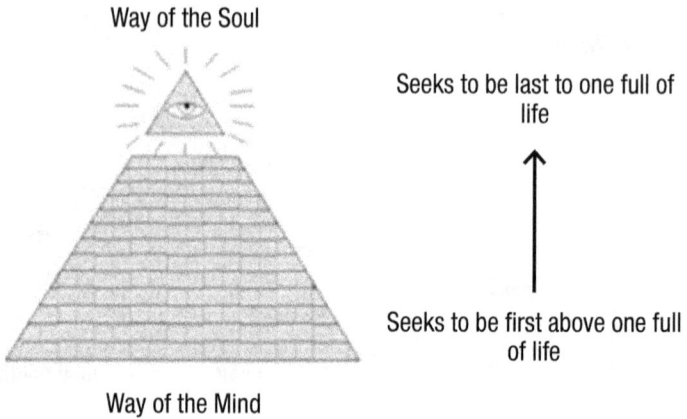

Seeks to be last to one full of life

Seeks to be first above one full of life

Way of the Mind

DISTINGUISH BETWEEN LIGHT AND DARKNESS IN PEOPLE

According to Jesus, we enter the world living light. In Chapter 13, Poem 2 (Saying 61), he explains how we live darkness.

When
he
should come to be
divided,[1]

He
will be
full
of darkness.[2]

[1] *When he should come to be divided*: When he should come to be divided between his true self and his many false selves.

[2] *He will be full of darkness*: He will be opaque and dishonest.

"When he should come to be divided," When we become divided between our true and false selves.

"He will be full of darkness." He will be full of dishonesty.

Jesus does not use the word "evil" or "sin" in this Gospel. Instead, he says that we become "dark when we divide from the true self that we are at birth. When we do that, we lie, because we proclaim ourselves to be what we are not.

Consequently, Jesus formulated the two laws of the Way of the Soul that we find in Chapter 2, Poem 6 (Saying 6b):

Jesus responded:

"You do not speak lies,[1]

And what you hate in him,[2]

You do not do to him."[3]

[1] *You do not speak lies:* You do not live through a false self. You do not live through any religious or secular doctrine.

[2] *And what you hate in him:* And the false selves that you hate in him. And the incongruence that you hate in him. And the lies that you hate in him. And the Ways of Dogma that you hate in him.

[3] *You do not do to him:* You do not become what you are not to punish someone who is not what he is.

"Do not speak lies." Do not be a false self.

In other words, Jesus recognizes that behind all harmful thoughts and actions are lies about what we truly are. When we identify with our religious theology, with our secular doctrine, with the things and people important to us, we lie. Further, when we lie, we become dark. When we become dark, we know it; we suffer and the world suffers.

"And what you hate in him, you do not do to him." And the lie that you hate in him, do not do.

For example, if we hate a politician for not being what he is, we lie and become his twin. To hate a liar is to lie. (Later we will learn how to act toward others who lie).

Way of the Soul

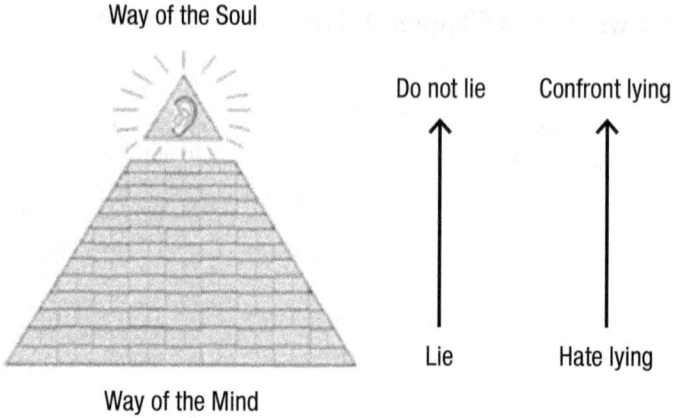

Do not lie   Confront lying

Lie   Hate lying

Way of the Mind

Thus, Jesus counsels us to distinguish two polarities in ourselves: lying and being congruent; darkness and light. He speaks of being light in Poem 3 in Chapter 7 (Saying 24):

He
said to them:

*The light[1]
exists inward
of a man
of light,* [2,3]

*And
he
comes to be
light
to the world,* [4,5]

*All
of it.* [6]

[1]*Light*: The life force that illuminates.

[2]*Man of light*: An adult who has become again congruent with his core self.

[3]*The light exists inward of a man of light*: Divine light is in each of us to the degree that we are light.

[4]*World*: Dishonest people who are divided between their false selves and their real selves. People who lie.

[5]*He comes to be light to the world*: He comes to save the world. He comes to reveal the true nature of dishonesty in the world.

[6]*All of it*: All of the world.

"The light exists inward of a man of light." Divine illuminating power exists in a person to the degree that he chooses to be his core self. When he chooses to be a lie, that is, to identify with his false selves rather than be what he was at birth, he creates darkness within.

Jesus never speaks in this Gospel about an evil Satan outside of ourselves. Rather, he holds us responsible for being light or darkness for ourselves and for the world. In other words, we create ourselves as Satans as we choose to lie or live false lives.

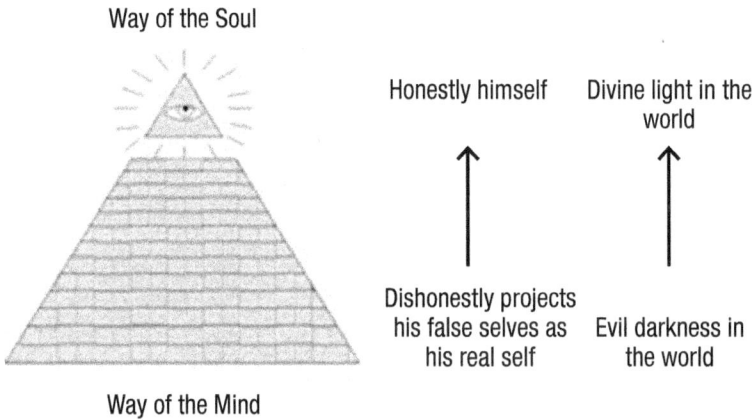

Way of the Soul

Honestly himself   Divine light in the world

↑   ↑

Dishonestly projects his false selves as his real self   Evil darkness in the world

Way of the Mind

When people asked Jesus about the source of light in a child, he responded as follows in Chapter 11, Poem 5 (Saying 50) (Remember he reports what he observes, not his logical deductions):

Jesus said this:

If

they[1]

should ask you

this:

"You

have

come into being

from where?"[2]

[1] *They*: People who are divided and full of darkness. People on the Way of the Mind. People who lie.

[2] *You have come into being from where?* You are not like other people. How did you come to be like that?

Speak to them
this:

"We
have come outward
of the light, [3],[4]

The place[5]

Where
the light
comes to be
there,

Outward
by its own hand;[6]

It
stood itself
on its own feet[7]

And
it
appeared outward
in our appearances."[8]

If
they
should ask you
this:

"Are
you
it?"[9]

[3]*light:* The divine intelligence and spirit within us.

[4]We have *come outward of the light:* Outward of God. We live from the One who is light, honesty, and congruence.

[5]*Place:* The location within us from which we think and act.

[6]*The light comes to be there outward by its own hand:* "By its own hand" means "by its own control." light is alive. It emanates from us with its own intelligence as it chooses.

[7]*Stood itself on its own feet:* To "stand" is to find one's confidence. To "stand on one's own feet" is find one's confidence in who one is.

[8]*Appearances:* Our unique manifestations of the light. The light-Life is the same in each of us; however, it manifests itself in each person's unique appearance.

[9]*Are you It:* Are you divine light?

Say this:

"We
are
its sons, [10]

And
we
are
the chosen
of the Father[11]

Who
lives."[12]

If
they
should ask you
this:

"What
is
the sign
of your Father[13]

Which
is
in you?"

Say to them
this:

"It
is
movement,

And
it
is
stillness.[14]

[10]*We are its sons:* We possess the same light-life as the light. Yes, we are sons of God.

[11]*Chosen of the Father:* Jesus experienced the Father as choosing to make light manifest in people. The light acts, the Father chooses when and to whom it is to act on.

[12]*Who lives:* Who lives life, as opposed to death and darkness.

[13]*What is the sign of your Father:* What is the observable proof that you are divine?

[14]*It is movement and it is stillness:* It is thought and action from stillness. One can think and act from stillness or from busyness. Movement from stillness is the visible sign of God. We can sense it in ourselves and see it in others who are of the light. Those full of light do not live in the past or the future; they live in the now, in the present.

"We have come outward of the light." We have come outward of God who lives in congruence with his divine life.

We now know more fully what Jesus meant in the previous Poem: **"And he comes to be light to the world, all of it."** He comes to be God to the world, all of God, not a bit of God. Jesus observed that the light is not reduced in a person. He saw the divinity in a little child and in those who are like little children, while others observe original sin or mere personhood.

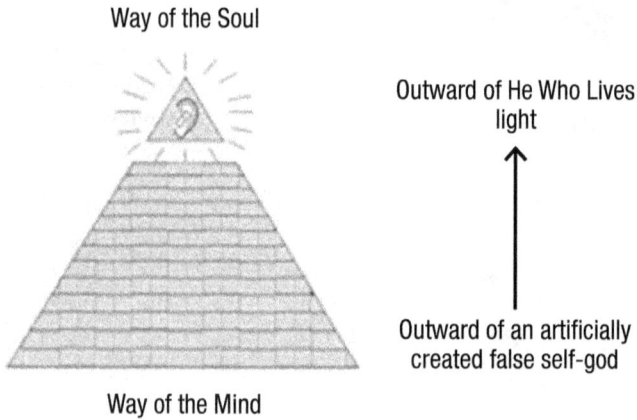

Way of the Soul

Outward of He Who Lives
light

↑

Outward of an artificially
created false self-god

Way of the Mind

"The light comes to be there outward by its own hand." The light moves as a living force with its own intelligence. It automatically leads people to be congruent with their core selves. It fights them through its absence when they are not.

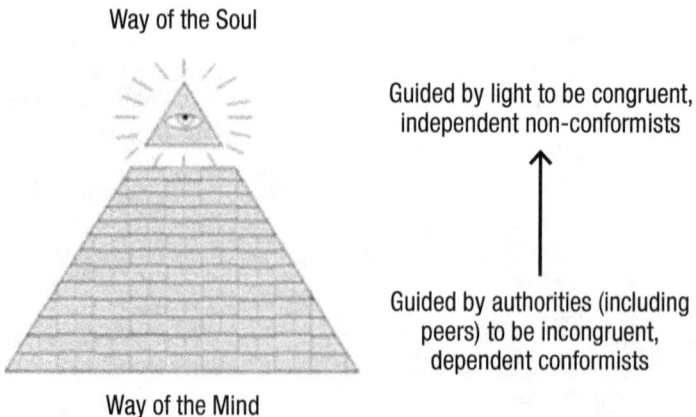

Way of the Soul

Guided by light to be congruent,
independent non-conformists

↑

Guided by authorities (including
peers) to be incongruent,
dependent conformists

Way of the Mind

"We are the chosen of the Father." We do not choose light, rather, the light, which is the life of the Father, chooses us. It acts in response to our choice to be light.

The nature of life and light includes two choices, ours and the Father's. Each instant we choose to be congruent or incongruent, to be honest or to be liars, to evolve or to devolve. The light within us responds with more light or its lack, darkness.

Jesus calls the source of light, his "Father." Again, he did not arrive at that conclusion through logical deduction. When he soul-knew a little child, he discovered the Father as the source of the light.

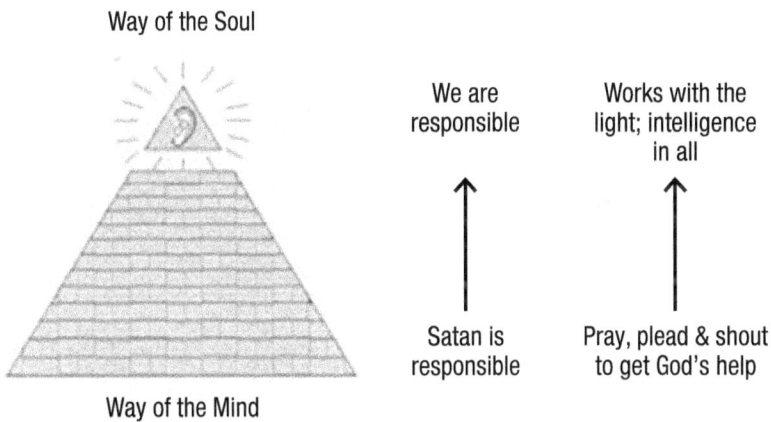

Way of the Soul

We are responsible

Works with the light; intelligence in all

↑

↑

Satan is responsible

Pray, plead & shout to get God's help

Way of the Mind

"It stood itself on its own feet." The light within us possesses its own dignity. It is what it is and knows itself. A person who possesses it is who he is, and knows himself. He does not need outside approval or justification for any thought or action. He stands, challenging the world, on his own two feet, fortified by the light.

When we live through our false selves, we seek self-confidence by standing, not on our own light, but on our Dogmas. For example, an American stands on his nationhood and its traditions, values, beliefs, rituals and laws; that is, on the doctrine of Americanism.

A Muslim stands on his Islamic community and beliefs. A liberal stands on his political faith. A rich man and a poor man stand on their class associations and beliefs.

When we believe that we are something or someone outside ourselves, we stand on sand, a poor foundation. When we stand only on our inner light, our foundations are strong.

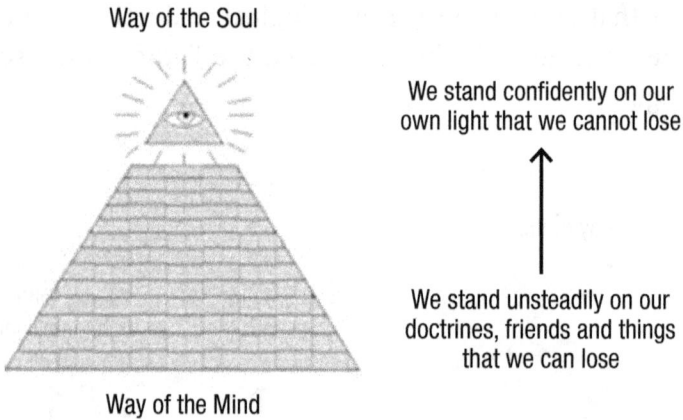

Way of the Soul

We stand confidently on our own light that we cannot lose

We stand unsteadily on our doctrines, friends and things that we can lose

Way of the Mind

"And it appeared outward in our appearances." The light becomes observable by others in our unique manifestation in the world. Jesus observed that everyone possesses divine light at their core.

People who are happy when others live through their false selves are darkness valuing darkness. When people look through a person's darkness to their light core, they are light penetrating darkness to value the other person's true self.

Way of the Soul

Light looking at light	Light revolutionaries seen as light
↑	↑
Dark calling false-selves- gods, "light"	Light revolutionaries seen as dark

Way of the Mind

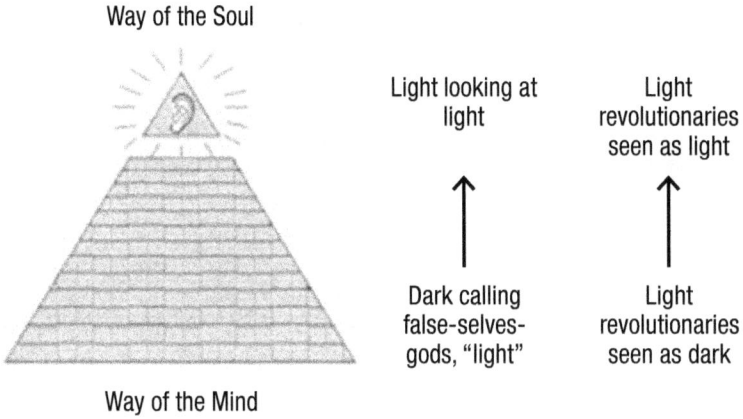

"We are its sons." We are all sons and daughters of God.

Jesus does not say that he is *not* the son of God; rather, that we all are. However, we are unevolved sons and daughters. We choose the degree to which we live that divine life and possess the inner light.

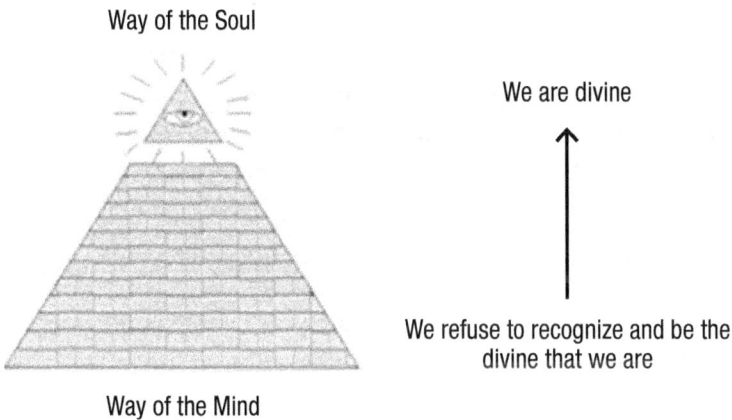

Way of the Soul

We are divine

↑

We refuse to recognize and be the divine that we are

Way of the Mind

"What is the sign of your Father?" What is the tactile proof that you are the son or daughter of God?

How many people go around looking for a sign that God is in a person? Would they even know what to look for?

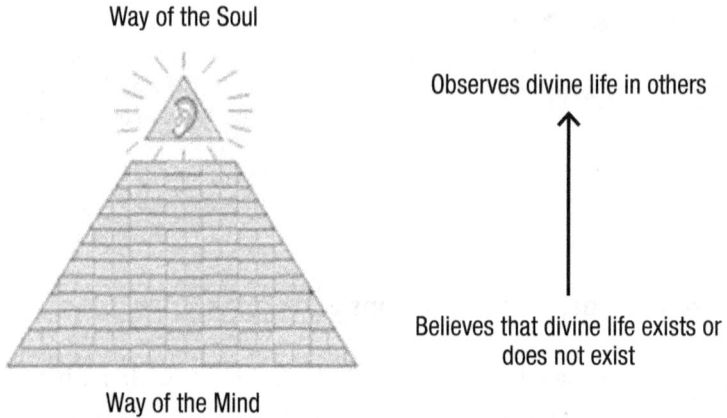

Way of the Soul

Observes divine life in others

↑

Believes that divine life exists or
does not exist

Way of the Mind

"It is movement and it is stillness." It is a contradiction: movement and stillness at the same time. That is an experience like no other.

When one chooses to live through a false self, he will immediately enter a cycle of continuous transition between regret, worry and out of body excitement, even if he does not notice it much. His Mind will flutter between the past and the future. He is movement from busyness. When he chooses to be in oneness with himself, he becomes movement from stillness in the now.

Thus, Jesus discovered that we can know when we are living divine life. Further, we can experience it in others. It is not something spiritual that we must blindly believe in. It is not miracles worked by a person that makes him a saint. It is movement from stillness.

Today, some relaxation therapists and clergy teach people to move from stillness. They call the practice, "Mindfulness," "non-thinking movement," "contemplation in action," and by many other terms. Of course, if people are taught to do it, and follow rules or procedures to do it rather than live it by choosing to be their real selves, they will fail in those exercises.

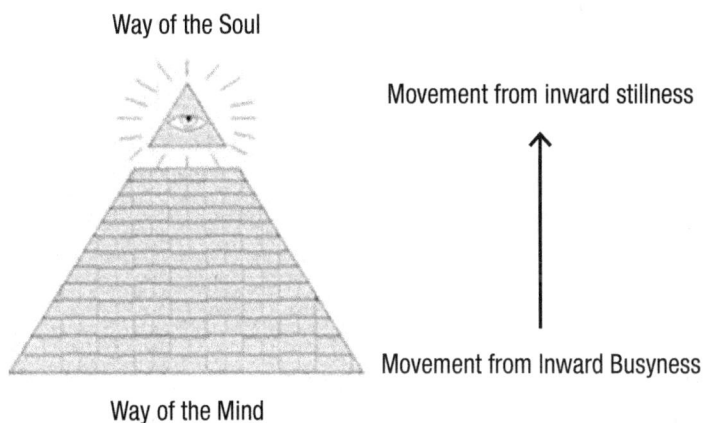

Way of the Soul

Movement from inward stillness

Movement from Inward Busyness

Way of the Mind

"We have come outward of the light." We are light.

Interestingly, Jesus never says that we are "outward of darkness." He never gives darkness such a power. He never talks about darkness as an intelligent source, like the idea of Satan. He never explains an opposite to the light of the Father. Consequently, we know that he observed that the Father was the light in all, including darkness.

Instead, he observes that we are the source of darkness to the degree that we choose to not be our true selves. We are therefore, responsible for evil. He will not permit the attribution of evil to an imaginary outside source, such as Satan.

We were born with light. It is an intelligent power with the ability to choose. We use it to stand ourselves on our own true feet or on our false feet. Through this means, we choose to be good or bad, saints or sinners, light or darkness.

Way of the Soul

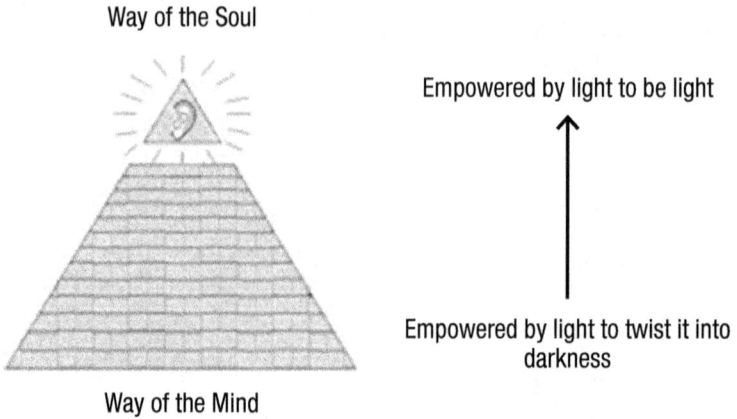

Empowered by light to be light

Empowered by light to twist it into darkness

Way of the Mind

RECOGNIZE OUR TWO MOTHERS

Jesus discovered that we have two mothers (Chapter 20, Poem 4 (Saying 101)):

Jesus
said this:

My mother,

*She
brought me
forth,*[1]

[1]*She brought me forth*:
My physical mother
"brought me" into many
false selves.

*My Mother
however,*

[2]*The true*: My divine
Mother.

The true,[2]

[3]*She gave to me Life*: She
gave me my core real,
light, divine Life.

*She
gave to me
Life.*[3]

"My mother, she brought me forth." My mother who was not completely one with her true self, brought me forth to be like her.

Mary may have taught Jesus to identify with being a man, a Jew, a poor person, a tan person, and a brother to his siblings. Whenever he identified with any of those traditions, titles or roles, he identified with a false self. As he did that, he became divided from his true self, distancing himself from the light.

"My mother, the true, she gave to me Life." My divine mother not only shared her divine life with me, she made me aware that is who I am. Therefore, forever I will seek to become single with that core life.

Jesus soul-knew that he was not his false selves. He had to discover for himself how to abandon them and become his true self.

"Father" "Mother": Jesus has now said that he experiences with soul-knowing two God-Persons in one. He called one Person, "Father," and the other "Mother." They are the source of the life and light within us, as he says.

We have all heard that the Israelites believed in one Lord. That is not true. The Bible begins with the following:

In the beginning
Elohim
created heaven
and earth.
(Gen. 1:1)

Throughout the Old Testament, in particular in Genesis, the Hebrew word, "Elohim," has been translated, "Lord." However, "Elohim," which comprises a feminine root with a masculine plural ending, means "strong Ones" or "Gods." Jesus knew that, and when he looked at the obvious, that little children are male and female, he understood that the sources of life within us were both masculine and feminine. He called one, "Father," and the other, "Mother."

Way of the Soul

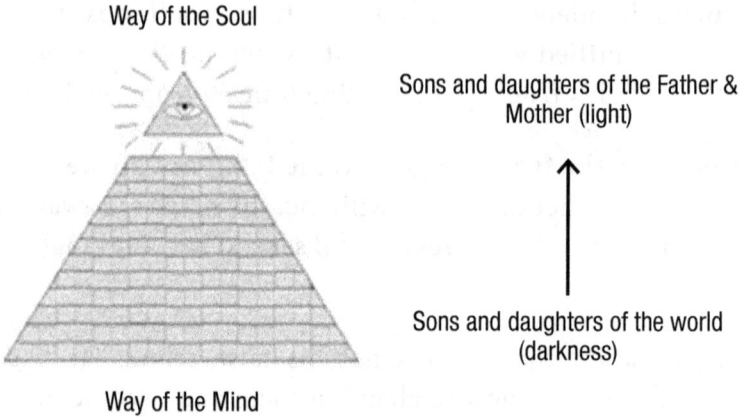

Sons and daughters of the Father & Mother (light)

↑

Sons and daughters of the world (darkness)

Way of the Mind

Jesus soul-knew that the Sons and Daughters of the Father and Mother live out of a different life (Chapter 21, Poem 5 (Saying 111a)):

Jesus
said this:

He,

Who
Lives[1]

[1]Lives: Lives the life of our Father and Mother.

Out of He[2]

[2]*Out of He:* Out of the Father.

Who
lives,[3]

[3]*Who lives:* Who lives light in oneness with his true self.

Will peer
not on death.[4]

[4]*Death:* Dividedness, movement from busyness.

Way of the Soul

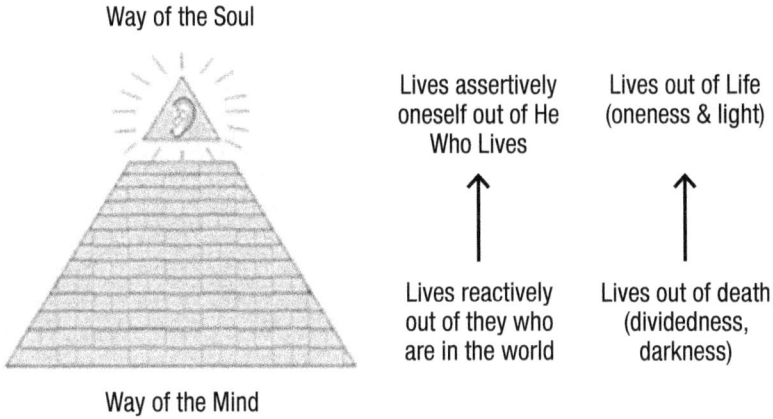

Lives assertively   Lives out of Life
oneself out of He   (oneness & light)
Who Lives

↑   ↑

Lives reactively   Lives out of death
out of they who   (dividedness,
are in the world   darkness)

Way of the Mind

BECOME THE ALL

When we live out of He Who Lives, we evolve naturally to be more our true selves and into oneness with all others. We cannot become our true selves without healing our dividedness from others. We cannot heal our dividedness from others without becoming one with ourselves. Both must be accomplished to live life out of He Who Lives. Jesus says this beautifully in Poem 10, Chapter 16 (Saying 77):

Jesus
said this:
I am
the light,[1]

[1]I am the light: I am undivided and one with He Who Lives.

The One[2]

[2]The One: The divine Light.

Which
is
upon them,[3]

[3]Which is upon them: Which shows everyone the Way. Which is the salvation of the world.

All of them.[4]

I

am

the all.[5]

Has

the All[6]

come outward

of me;

And

has

the all

split

to become me.[7]

Split

a timber[8]

And

I

am

there. [9]

Take

the stone[10]

up,

And

you

will discover me

there.[11]

[4]*All of them*: All people, animals, plants and things.

[5]*I am the all*: I live the light and life that is in everything, even things that many regard as inanimate. It is all divine light and life.

[6]*Has the all come outward of me*: Has the divine light in all come from me.

[7]*Has the all split to become me*: Has the divine life in all become uniquely me.

[8]*Split a Timber*: Split a person's support. A house is like a person. A house is constructed of timbers and stones. A "timber" is a strong structural element.

[9]*Split a timber, And I am there*. Look inside the fundamental support of a person, and I am present.

[10]*Stone*: A word.

[11]*Take the stone up*: Look under what a person says, and you will find me.

"I am the all." I am the core life in everyone and everything.

Jesus grew to identify with nothing else.

"I am the light...I am the all." I am the light intelligence that is in all, guiding all to evolve.

Way of the Soul

I am the light in me and in the all

↑

I am white, male, Irish, a husband, father, PhD, CEO, my job, a liberal, a Catholic, my reputation, my friends, my enemies, my money, my sports teams, my things, my past, and my dreams.

Way of the Mind

Way of the Soul

I am peacefully one with my true self and all

↑

I am painfully divided from my true self and all

Way of the Mind

CHAPTER THREE

PAUL'S VIEW OF THE HUMAN CONDITION

PAUL REJECTS JESUS' WAY

Paul the Apostle created the foundation of the Christianity that we know today. He never met Jesus. He was a Jewish cleric who began arresting, persecuting, and killing the followers of Jesus shortly after Jesus' death. He never said why he was doing that; however, the author of the Acts of The Apostles (thought to be Luke the Evangelist), tells us that Paul (called "Saul" before he became a Christian) was trying to destroy Jesus' "Way:"

> *But Saul, still breathing threats and murder against the disciples of the Lord, went to the high priest and asked him for letters to the synagogues at Damascus, so that if he found any belonging to the Way, men or women, he might bring them bound to Jerusalem. (Acts 9: 1-2)*

For nearly two thousand years, people have speculated about the nature of the "Way" that so enraged Paul and his superiors.

After a few years of chasing down Christians, Saul had a conversion experience near Damascus in which he was told that Jesus was the expected Messiah. (Acts 9:3-20) Instead of humbly returning to Jerusalem to study with Jesus' apostles and disciples, he traveled to Arabia to decide how to proceed. On the one hand, he was disturbed by this new Way of Jesus, and on the other, he knew that Jesus was the man he wished to follow. Those were huge problems he needed to resolve.

In Arabia, Saul changed his name to "Paul" and became inspired to think of himself as an apostle. He said of himself later in Gal. 1:1:

> I, Paul an apostle, (not of men, neither by man,
> but by Jesus Christ, and God the Father).

This tells us that Paul learned in a direct revelation that Jesus and the Father had commissioned him to be not a disciple of Jesus, but the 13th apostle.

The word "apostle" means messenger. A "disciple" is one who is learning from a master. Paul tells us that he is not being taught by Jesus. Instead, he is God's messenger.

Apparently, Paul had the revelation that Jesus wanted to replace the gospel that he (Jesus) had spent his life preaching and writing about with another gospel that would be revealed to him (Paul). Paul tells us in Gal. 1:11:

> I want you to know, brothers and sisters, that the
> gospel I preached is not of human origin. I did not
> receive it from any man, nor was I taught it; rather,
> I received it by revelation from Jesus Christ.

That is quite a statement. Paul wants himself and us to believe that Jesus, who Paul in other writings calls the "son of God," spent his entire life on earth preaching a gospel he regrets formulating. This perfect God-man now needed to correct himself through Paul.

With that revelation, Paul had justification for not going to Jerusalem and studying with the Apostles and the other disciples of Jesus. He did not need to learn everything that Jesus taught, because it was all wrong. Jesus, the all-knowing, all-perfect God, had somehow blown it. Paul believed that Jesus and the Father commissioned him to be humankind's savior from Jesus' own false message.

Way of the Soul

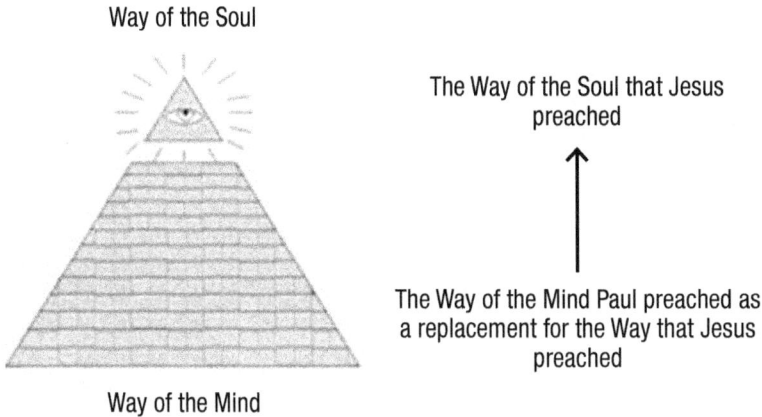

The Way of the Soul that Jesus
preached

↑

The Way of the Mind Paul preached as
a replacement for the Way that Jesus
preached

Way of the Mind

Jesus died in the year 30 C.E. Paul began persecuting Christians shortly after Jesus' death. He had his conversion experience in about 37 C.E. He was in Arabia from 37 or 38 C.E. until 40 C.E., and died in 62 C.E.

PAUL'S VIEW OF A LITTLE CHILD

Paul decided that all of humankind's problems arose from its sinful nature. Jesus looked at a little child and saw life and Light. Paul saw death and darkness. He wrote in Romans 5: 12-13:

> *Sin entered the world through one man (Adam),*
> *and death through sin, and in this way death came*
> *to all people, because all sinned— To be sure, sin*
> *was in the world before the law was given, but*
> *sin is not charged against anyone's account where*
> *there is no law.*

"Sin entered the world through one man and death through sin." In the beginning, there was no sin and no physical death, instead, there was only spiritual and physical life. Because the sin of Adam is passed down through the patrilineal line, every person is born in sin that results in physical death.

Thus, we each may decide to agree with either Jesus or Paul about the nature of a little child.

Way of the Soul

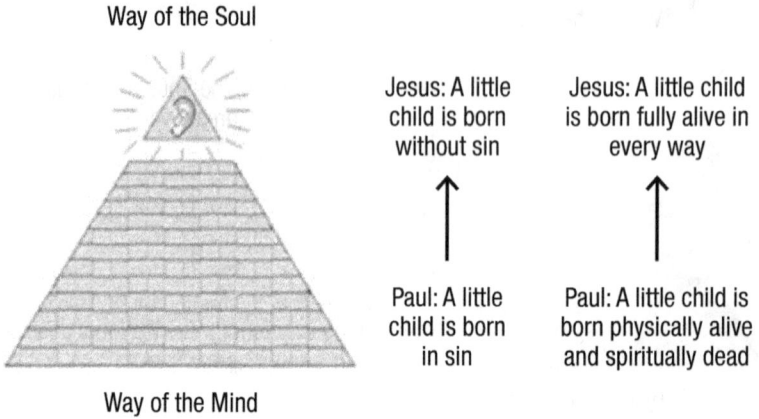

Jesus: A little
child is born
without sin

↑

Paul: A little
child is born
in sin

Jesus: A little child
is born fully alive in
every way

↑

Paul: A little child is
born physically alive
and spiritually dead

Way of the Mind

JESUS' AND MAN'S BODY

Jesus, according to Paul, possessed a body different from the body all other people possess. He called it a "likeness." We read about that in Philippians 2: 5-10:

> Christ Jesus, who, though he was in the form of God, did not count equality with God a thing to be grasped, but emptied himself, taking the form of a servant, being born in the likeness of men. And being found in human form he humbled himself and became obedient unto death, even death on a cross.

"Christ Jesus who, though he was in the form of God, did not count equality with God a thing to be grasped, but emptied himself, taking the form of a servant, being born in the likeness of men." Jesus, the Messiah, was born as God without sin resulting in physical and spiritual death; however, because sinful man could not comprehend such magnificence, he took on the form of a human servant. He was not really in a sinful body that could physically die, but appeared to be in one so that other humans could relate to him.

"And being found in human form he humbled himself and became obedient unto death, even death on a cross." And when people saw his human form and hated him, he became obedient to them and let them murder his body on the cross; although, he, as the entity he was, could not die.

Thus, Paul preached that Adam and Eve were born whole and perfect and immortal. However, after Adam sinned, his progeny possessed a sin that we know is there because humans die. That sin also accounts for all of the inner conflict within a person and all of the conflicts between people.

Paul says that Jesus, on the other hand, came into the world without inheriting sin in spirit or body. He was a man in form, but not in substance.

Way of the Soul

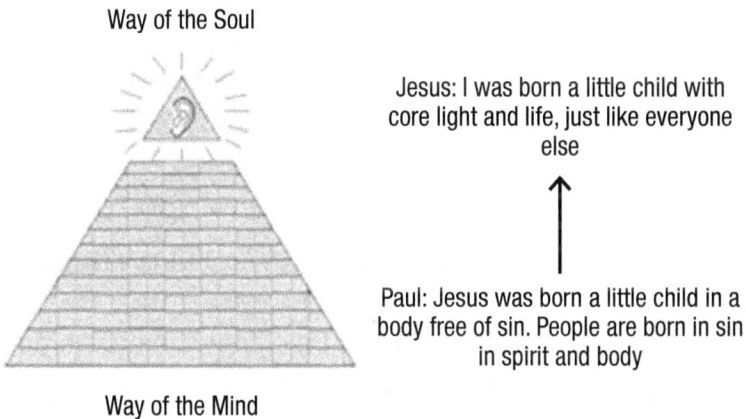

Jesus: I was born a little child with core light and life, just like everyone else

Paul: Jesus was born a little child in a body free of sin. People are born in sin in spirit and body

Way of the Mind

Paul's Belief in the Unseen

In 2 Cor. 4, Paul glorifies the fact that he and his followers based their life blindly believing in "things that are unseen:"

> For this slight momentary affliction is preparing for us an eternal weight of glory beyond all comparison, because we look not to the things that are seen but to the things that are unseen; for the things that are seen are transient, but the things that are unseen are eternal.

"For this slight momentary affliction is preparing for us an eternal weight of glory beyond all comparison, because we look not to the things that are seen but to the things that are unseen." This "slight momentary affliction"—meaning all negative human physical experience, from getting sick to being tortured and killed—prepares those who believe in the unseen to be glorified after we physically die.

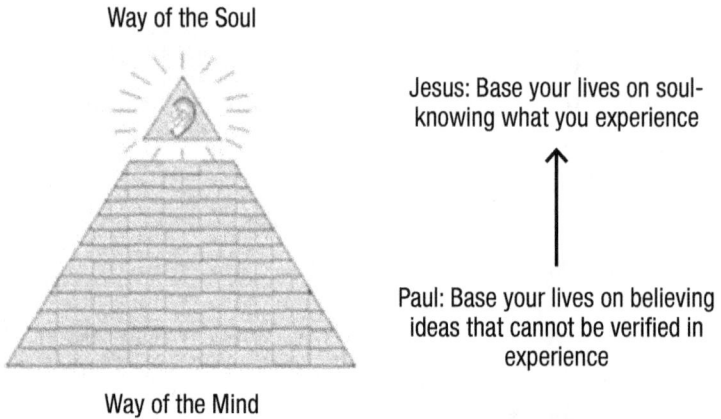

Way of the Soul

Jesus: Base your lives on soul-knowing what you experience

↑

Paul: Base your lives on believing ideas that cannot be verified in experience

Way of the Mind

"For the things that are seen are transient, but the things that are unseen are eternal." The life you see in a little child, in a smile, in one who sacrifices for others, is not a manifestation of everlasting life. Instead, have faith in the primacy of the unseen.

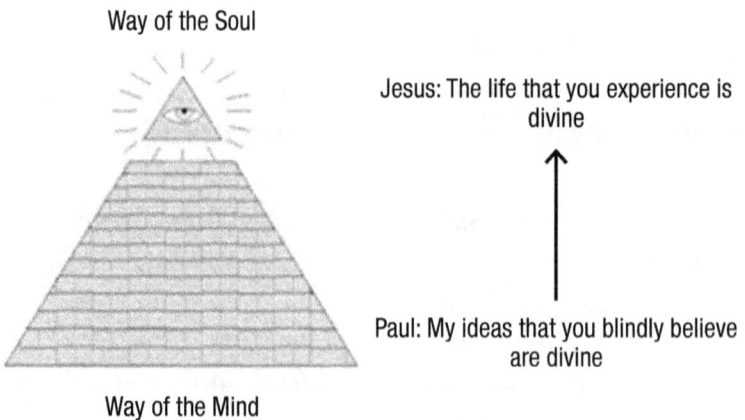

Way of the Soul

Jesus: The life that you experience is divine

↑

Paul: My ideas that you blindly believe are divine

Way of the Mind

CHAPTER FOUR

THE GOALS OF JESUS' WAY OF THE SOUL

DISCOVER THE KINGDOM

In several previous poems, Jesus said that he discovered a "place of life" at our core. He also calls that place, the "kingdom." We see this in the following, Poem 1 from Chapter 11 (Saying 49), where he summarizes the goal of the Way of the Soul:

Those blessed ones,[1]

They

are
the single ones,[2]
and
the chosen ones;[3]

For
you
will discover the
kingdom;[4,5]

[1]*Blessed ones*: Those who are full of light and divine life.

[2]*Single ones*: People congruent with their true nature.

[3]*Chosen ones*: The Father chose to give them congruence with their divine life.

[4]*Kingdom*: One's core, real, divine self.

[5]*You will discover the kingdom*: For you will rediscover the kingdom you were born with. We each are a unique manifestation of the kingdom. We can prevent it from manifesting itself.

> For
> you
> are out
> of it,[6]
>
> And again,
> you
> will be going
> there.[7]

[6]*For you are out of it*:
We all remember the
kingdom that we really
were when we were born;
consequently, we all seek
it behind every choice.

[7]*Will be going there*: The
kingdom is in us waiting.

"The blessed ones are the single ones...For you will discover the kingdom." The blessed ones grow to split their allegiance less and less between many false selves, and to become "single" with who they are. Therefore, they increasingly rediscover their true selves and their interactions with others.

Those blessed ones evolve out of being nationalists, racists, and sexists. They evolve out of being separatists, elitists, isolationists, and patriots. They evolve toward singleness with the intelligence within all.

"For you are out of it." We all remember a life where we were wonderfully happy just being us and the all. Now, we experience worry, regret, mania, depression and longing. We ask, "What caused us to come to the point where we must struggle to find kingdom joy again?"

"And again you will be going there." And again, when you follow the Way of the Soul, you choose to be the kingdom again.

Way of the Soul

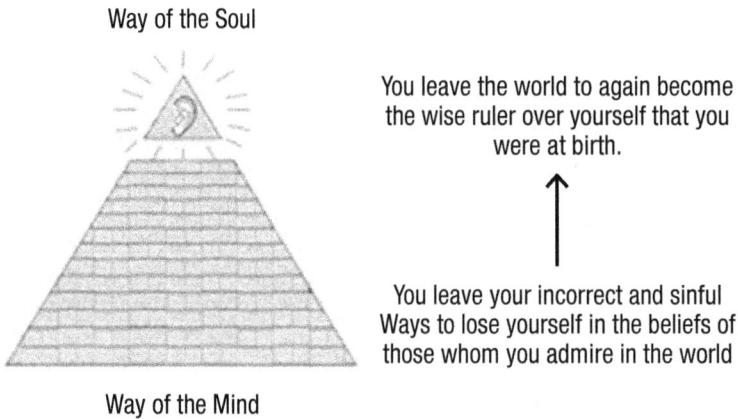

You leave the world to again become the wise ruler over yourself that you were at birth.

You leave your incorrect and sinful Ways to lose yourself in the beliefs of those whom you admire in the world

Way of the Mind

An aside: Some may be asking, do we go into the kingdom once and for all, or do we move in and out? Let me explain my understanding with reference to a more modern Jewish theologian/philosopher, Martin Buber.

Buber stated that we can be in one of two kinds of relationships: One he called "I-Thou," the other, "I-It." The first is a genuine relationship fostered by a person who is congruent with himself. The second is a manipulative relationship initiated by a person who is not himself. Buber also found that a person could not be in both at the same time; rather, one flipped from one to the other. If one wishes, he may develop himself to be gradually more I-Thou in every thought and action.

Jesus seems to have said something similar 2000 years ago. For Jesus, the kingdom includes an I-Thou relationship; however, as we have seen and will see, it is much more than that. He calls those in I-It relationships, "the world." His Way of the Soul is the means by which we may grow to live in the kingdom all of the time.

WILL OF THE FATHER

Those on the Way become one within and as a community because they get their orders from one source. Jesus tells us that in Chapter 19, Poem 4 (Saying 99):

The disciples
said to him:

"*Your brothers
and
your mother,*[1]

*They
are standing there,*[2]

*They
on the side
outward."*[3]

He
said to them:

*"Those
Who
are
in these places,*[4]

*Who
do the will
of my Father,*[5]

*They
are
my brothers
and
my mother.*[6]

[1]*Your brothers and your mother*: The network of people tied to your Way of the Mind (parents, peers, teachers, clergy) who gave you your false identity.

[2]*They are standing there*: They are standing there with the expectation that you will grow to share their world and their world view.

[3]*On the side outward*: On the side of the world, on the side of darkness, on the side of movement from busyness, on the side of the Ways of Dogma.

[4]*Places*: Places of divine life.

[5]*Who do the will of my Father*: Who live according to their true natures.

[6]*They are my brothers and my mother*: They are our true support network. They encourage us to stand on our own feet no matter how nonconformist we become.

"Your brothers and your mother, they are standing there, they on the side outward." Your family put up obstacles to you being your real nature.

"Those who are in these places, who do the will of my Father." Those who live from their places of light, where they soul-sense the will of the Father.

Many Catholics believe that the will of the Father comes down through a succession of Popes to their local Bishop and through him to the local Pastor who tells them how to think and act. Protestants reject that notion and instead look to scripture for the will of the Father. Catholics think that a clergyman speaks objective, absolute truth. Protestants think that scripture tells them objective, absolute truth.

Jesus disagrees with both. He tells us that truth comes to each of us subjectively through soul-knowing. His followers may get the will from a Papal encyclical one day, from scripture the next, from a billboard the next, from a child the next, and directly from a sensed insight the next day. Everyone interprets what he hears and sees subjectively. No one personally experiences objective truth. As one leaves all to soul-know, he does so without bias.

"They are my brothers and my mother." They are my intimate family of non-conformist soul-seekers. From them I learn how to discover myself as the kingdom.

Way of the Soul

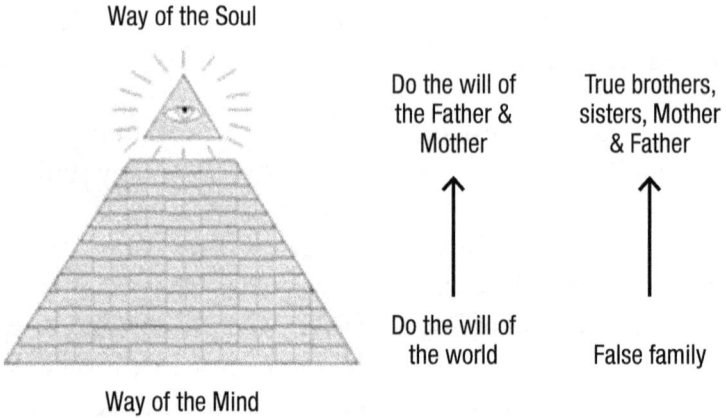

| | Do the will of the Father & Mother | True brothers, sisters, Mother & Father |

↑   ↑

Do the will of the world   False family

Way of the Mind

HATE YOUR FATHER AND MOTHER?

Jesus tells us that we all must sever our dependent relationships on the lives that our parents and authorities gave us and become one again with our real Mother and Father and with all in the kingdom. That is a very difficult process as Jesus points out in Chapter 20, Poem 4 (Saying 101):

*Jesus
said this:*

*Whoever
hates his father,
and
his mother
in my way
not,[1]*

*Can come to be
a disciple
to me
not.[2]*

[1] *Whoever hates his father and his mother in my way not*: Whoever does not hate being the person he adopted when he identified with the beliefs, hopes, values and traditions of his parents, clergy, teachers, and other leaders.

[2] *Can come to be a disciple to me not*: Unless you stop identifying with your family life, you will not follow me, as I identify only with our Mother and Father and those brothers and sisters who do their will.

Way of the Soul

Hates the conformist messages given to him by his parents, friends, teachers, media and other leaders

↑

Embraces the conformist messages given to him by his parents, friends, teachers, media and other leaders

Way of the Mind

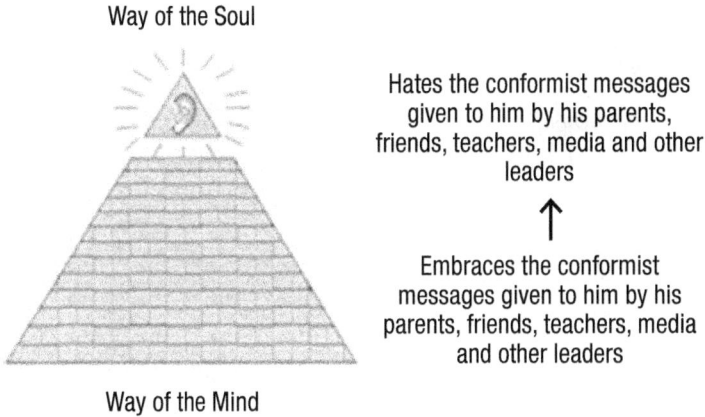

LEAVE YOUR GENDER IDENTITY

Those on the Way of the Soul must continually be on guard against the doctrines of the world that he adopted as he became socialized. Those doctrines are propagated by secular and theological authorities, oftentimes under the guise of so-called "common sense." For example, it is common sense to identify with masculinity or femininity and to assign roles, titles, and privileges to these false selves. We see that below in the clever Poem 8 of Chapter 21 (Saying 114):

Simon Peter
said to him
this:

"Make Mary
leave us,

For
women
are
worthy not
of life."[1]

[1]*For women are worthy not of life*: For women are not worthy of life in the kingdom. When Jesus preached of life in the kingdom, his disciples interpreted him as meaning that women would be inferior in this new realm. They made this assumption because they adopted the "common sense" theological and secular beliefs in the inherent inferiority of women.

Jesus
said this:

"Behold!
I
myself
will lead her, [2]

So that
I
might make her
male, [3]

So that,
she
might come to be
a spirit [4]

She
living [5]

And
she
resembling
you males; [6]

For
any woman,

Who
makes herself
male, [7]

Will go
into the kingdom
of the heavens. [8]

[2]*Lead her*: Empower her, teach her.

[3]*So that I might make her male*: So that I might show her how to identify with her core life and the identical core life in men. That I might teach her not to identify primarily with being a woman, which is a false self.

[4]*Spirit*: Her divine spirit.

[5]She *living*: She consciously identifying with the life of her Father and Mother in herself and all.

[6]She *resembling* you males: She possessing the core life just as males.

[7]*Makes herself male*: Who gives up her identification with her gender.

[8]*Kingdom of the heavens*: See below.

EVOLVE THROUGH HEAVENS

We will return to that Poem about gender stereotypes; however, to understand it, we need to analyze the strange last phrase, "kingdom of the heavens(pl)." Jesus defines an evolved Way of living as a kingdom made up of a number of heavens. Let us read the entire second part of the Poem again:

> *For*
> *any woman,*
>
> *Who*
> *makes herself*
> *male,*
>
> *Will go*
> *into the kingdom*
> *of the* **heavens**(pl).

First, Jesus defines kingdom in another way in Chapter Two, Poem Two (Saying 3):

> Jesus
> said this:
>
> *The kingdom,*
>
> > *It*
> > *is*
> > *of your eye[1]*
> > *inward,[2]*
> >
> > *And*
> > *it*
> > *is*
> > *of your eye*
> > *outward.[3]*

[1]*Eye*: Third eye.

[2]*It is of your eye inward*: It is a means of looking "inward" at yourself with your third eye.

[3]*It is of your eye outward*: It is a means of seeing outward with fresh eyes like seeing with the fresh eyes of a child.

Based on that Poem, Jesus tells us that a kingdom is a means by which one looks at himself inwardly and at the world outwardly. From previous poems, we also know that we were born with third-eye knowledge of all. We also know that we abandoned it for the world's two-eye seeing, and that to the degree that we evolve on the Way of the Soul, we return to using only third-eye seeing.

In summary, we were born into the "kingdom" means of viewing ourselves, others, and the world. In that kingdom, we ruled ourselves differently than we do when we identify with false selves and their doctrines. We also know that to become that kingdom again, we must hate the false socialized knowing that we received from our families, friends, and teachers.

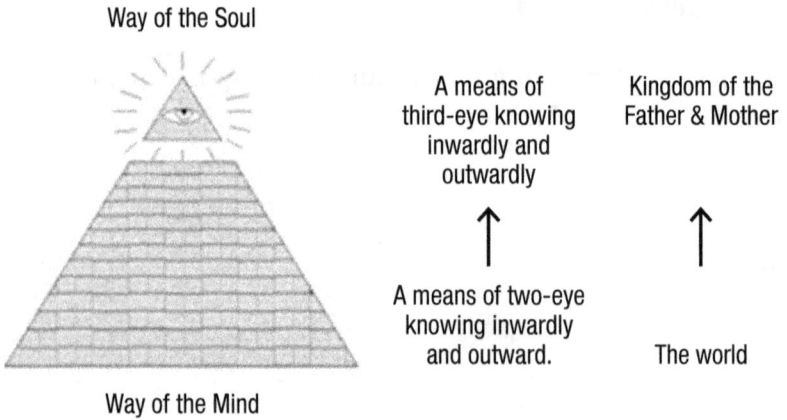

Way of the Soul

A means of   Kingdom of the
third-eye knowing   Father & Mother
inwardly and
outwardly

↑   ↑

A means of two-eye
knowing inwardly
and outward.   The world

Way of the Mind

Jesus gives us more information about his meaning for "heavens" in Chapter 3, Poem 3 (Saying 11):

Jesus
said this:

[1]Heaven: A level of knowing oneself, others, and the world.

This heaven,[1]

[2]*Pass away*: Our present level of knowing will pass away as we become more fully alive. Thus, our perception of truth changes as we evolve.

It
will pass away;[2]

And
the one
above it,[3]

[3]*The one above it*: There are infinite levels of knowing or truth.

It
will pass away.[4]

[4]*It will pass away*: Each level of knowing must be given up in order to reach a higher level of knowing.

"This heaven will pass away." This level of knowing inwardly and outwardly will pass away as one evolves. Thus, each level is a level of experiencing or being.

We can deduce from that Poem that the word "heaven" in Thomas does not mean a place that one goes to after he dies. That kind of heaven does not pass away. Nor does it refer to the place where God lives.

Heaven is a level of soul. As one grows, one passes through levels of heavens. For those who remain fixed in their steadfast faiths, their heavens will not "pass away" to make way for other levels of heaven to evolve.

Way of the Soul

A high (heavenly) level of knowledge
of self and all

A low (heavenly) level of knowledge
of self and all

Way of the Mind

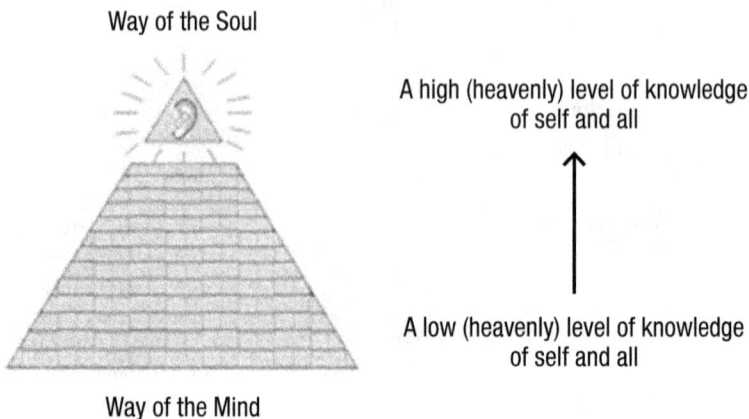

"And the one above it, it will pass away." And my heavenly level of beliefs above this level, it will dissolve as I evolve. Each successive level of heaven will dissolve as I evolve through them on the Way.

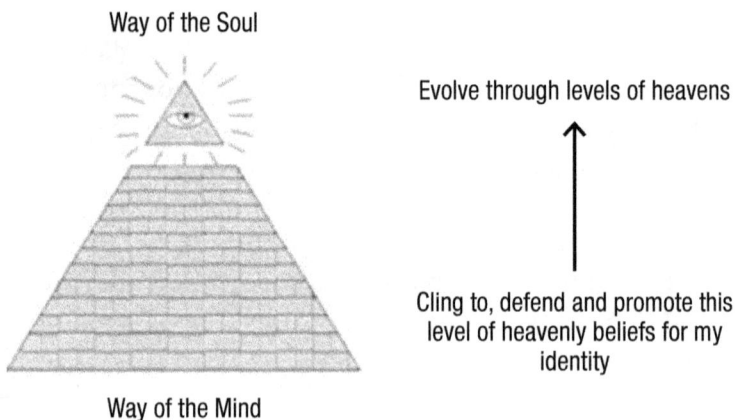

Way of the Soul

Evolve through levels of heavens

Cling to, defend and promote this level of heavenly beliefs for my identity

Way of the Mind

The wise know to not identify with their current truth, because it isn't the entire picture.

The wise person will base his life on natural beliefs, those that he discovered in himself, in others, and in the world. The unwise will base his life on doctrines, usually those of others.

The wise understand the thinking of the unwise person; however, the unwise cannot understand the thinking of the wise person.

For the unwise person to be able to understand the wise person, he must evolve to the higher level of heavenly life and soul of the more evolved person.

Way of the Soul

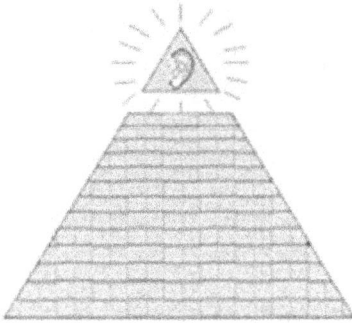

People deliberately losing their faith at one level in order to experience reality at a higher level

↑

People remaining at the same level of steadfast, blind faith

Way of the Mind

Way of the Soul

Understands much of the world of the unwise person; often more than that person

↑

Cannot understand the world of the wise person

Way of the Mind

Way of the Soul

Knows that wise and unwise will most likely never agree

↑

Thinks that discussions between the wise and unwise will solve problems

Way of the Mind

Those on the Way of the Mind seek absolute truths. Those on the Way of the Soul know that they will never know an absolute truth. They will get infinitely closer, but never reach it.

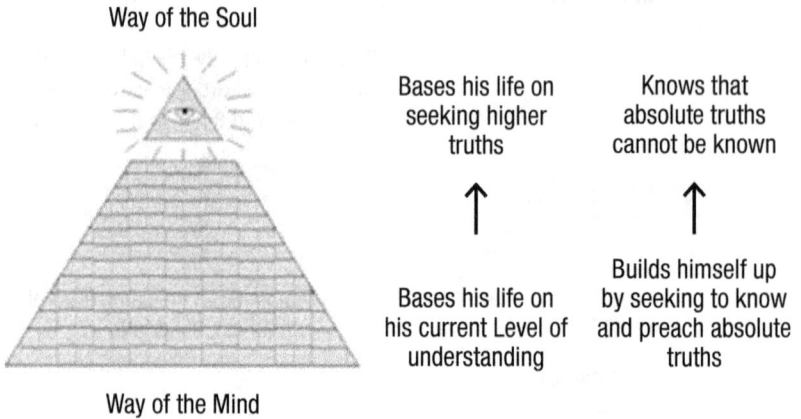

Way of the Soul

	Bases his life on seeking higher truths	Knows that absolute truths cannot be known
	↑	↑
	Bases his life on his current Level of understanding	Builds himself up by seeking to know and preach absolute truths

Way of the Mind

According to Jesus, as one grows on the Way of the Soul, one undergoes changes in his perception. On the Way of the Mind, one may live year after year without noticing any differences in the way he perceives himself or others. It's difficult for him to change because he develops habits of seeing things in one way, which prevents him from soul-seeing and seeing things in another way. Thus, he becomes blind to new ways of looking at things. Further, that blindness prevents him from seeing how he nurtures his inner death.

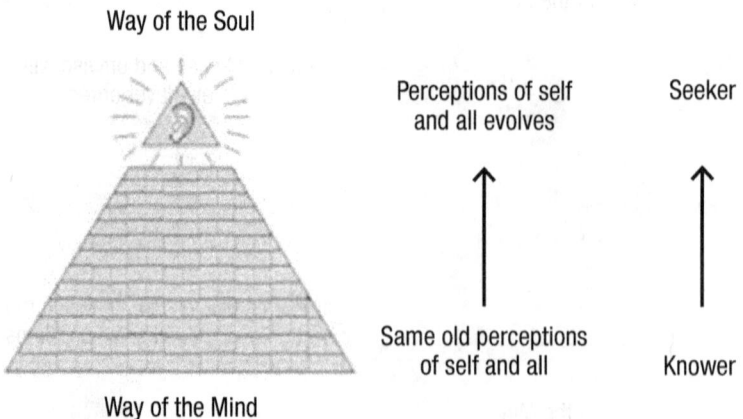

Way of the Soul

	Perceptions of self and all evolves	Seeker
	↑	↑
	Same old perceptions of self and all	Knower

Way of the Mind

Evolve to Know Your Divinity

To know oneself as Jesus knew himself with his soul-knowing, one must pass upward through many levels of heaven. From a high level, Jesus exclaimed something most will find surprising, which we read in Chapter 2, Poem 5 (Saying 3b):

Jesus
said this:

When
you
should know yourselves,[1]

Then,
they
will know you,[2]

And
you (pl.)
will realize[3]

That
you[(pl.)]

are

sons
of the Father[4]

Who
lives.[5]

If
you
will know yourselves
not,[6]

[1] *When you should know yourselves*: When you should soul-know yourselves at a high level of heaven.

[2] *Then they will know you*: Those living at low and high levels of heaven will know you. Those at a low level will know that you are different, but they will not understand the difference. Those living at a high level will know the real you.

[3] *And you will realize*: And you will realize from everyone's response to you.

[4] *You will realize that you are sons of the Father*: You all will soul-recognize your heritage from your divine Parents.

[5] *Who lives*: Who lives a divine life.

[6] *If you will know yourselves not*: If you will not soul-know yourselves at a high level of heaven.

Then

you

exist

in poverty,[7]

And

you

are

the poverty.[8]

[7]*Then, you exist in poverty.* You will be inwardly impoverished of that which you need in order to be fulfilled.

[8]*And you are the poverty:* You will be poorness itself. A void of life. Something that diminishes the world.

"When you should know yourselves, then, they will know you." When you soul-know yourselves at a high level of heaven, then people will know that you are a kingdom.

"And you(pl.) will realize that you(pl.) are sons of the Father who lives." And you will realize humbly that you are sons and daughters of the Father who lives one with you.

"If you will know yourselves not." If you will insist that the self you know is all that there is to know. If you will not give up your present beliefs about yourself. If you want to live the life you live today forever.

"Then, you exist in poverty." You choose not to live a life of richness from the joy of the soul. You are instead seeking false riches from people who can offer you nothing truly satisfying.

"And you are the poverty." And you help destroy the world.

Way of the Soul

Soul-knows self   Wealth in the
                         kingdom

Ignorant of self   Poverty in the world

Way of the Mind

Way of the Soul

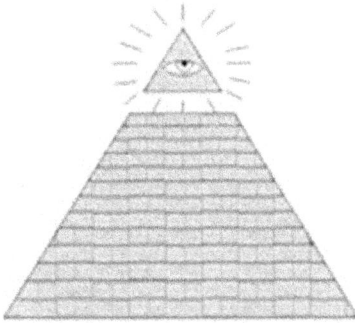

Models God

Models the world

Way of the Mind

BE A TWIN

Now we are ready to further analyze Poem 8 of Chapter 21 (Saying 114). Notice the Poem's shift in tone:

Simon Peter
said to him
this:

*"Make Mary
leave us,*

*For
women
are
worthy not
of the life."*

Jesus
said this:

*"Behold!
I
myself
will lead her,*

*So that
I
might make her
male,*

*So that,
she
might come to be
a spirit*

*She
living*

And

she
resembling
you males;

For
any woman,

Who
makes herself
male,

Will go
into the kingdom
of the heavens."

Peter says: **"Make Mary leave us, for women are worthy not of the life."** Look Jesus, were you not taught God's order: that women need to humbly accept their essential inferiority in life? We are not threatened by them, and it is not that they are not good people. However, notice, God raised up Abraham and Moses, both men. By doing that, God declared that men are the superior, naturally more alive, wise leaders that the world needs. Therefore, for the sake of our traditions, our society, common sense, and these women, make Mary leave us.

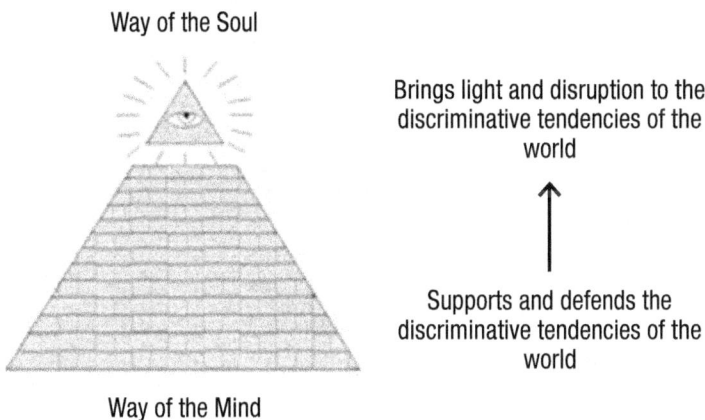

Way of the Soul

Brings light and disruption to the discriminative tendencies of the world

↑

Supports and defends the discriminative tendencies of the world

Way of the Mind

Jesus says: **"Behold! I myself will lead her."** Look Peter, I will lead her to become more of what she is.

"So that I might make her male." So that I might help her to reclaim her core life that is identical to that in every man.

"So that she might come to be a spirit, she living, and she resembling you males." So that she might identify with her core spirit, which is her unique version of the divine spirit in everyone; and thus, become a fraternal twin of everyone.

"For any woman who makes herself male will go into the kingdom of the heavens." For any woman who becomes the twin of the core, divine life in men will rule wisely at a high level of heaven. Further, any woman who does not identify with the core life in all men, and any man who does not identify with the core life in all women, will devolve in misery to a low level of worldly ignorance and death. On the Way of the Soul, we primarily are genderless.

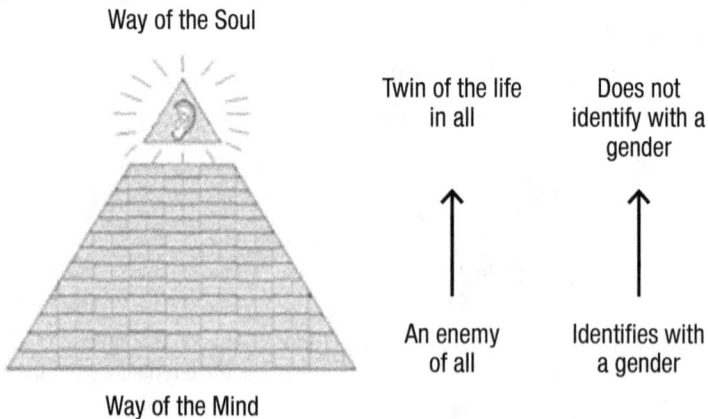

BE A LION

As we see in the above Poem, Jesus is not the all-loving Jesus that many imagine. He is a lion who eats his enemies, like Peter, alive. Let us read about that lion in Chapter 2, Poem 7 (Saying 7):

Jesus
said this:

A blessed one,[1]

He
is
the lion,[2]

The one,

That
the man[3]
will eat,[4]

And
the lion
comes to be
the man.[5]

And
he
is cursed,[6]

Namely
the man,[7]
The one,

Whom
the lion
will eat,[8]

[1]*A Blessed one*: A person evolved in soul and life at a high level of heaven.

[2]*Lion*: A person who is not naïve like a child. He guards his aliveness and attacks those following the Way of the Mind who are a threat.

[3]*Man*: A seeker of the life and soul of the lion.

[4]*Eat*: Takes in the soul of the lion, digests it, implements it, and makes it part of his life in his own fashion.

[5]And the *Lion comes to be the man*: And the soul of the lion comes to be the life and soul of the seeker.

[6]*Cursed*: Alive-dead.

[7]*Man*: A person who seeks to be a conformist to people-think rather than to be congruent with himself and one with all. A person who identifies with society's expectations and not with his core life.

[8]*Whom the lion will eat*: The lion sees the death in a man and destroys him with a word or glance—as Jesus did to Peter in the previous Poem. In that way, he eats him alive.

*And
the lion
comes to be
the man.*[9]

[9]*And the lion comes to
be the man*: The man
becomes haunted by the
memory of a lion who is
so powerful, wise, and
vigilant.

"A blessed one, he is the lion." One blessed by being the divine presence in the world is a lion.

"The one that the man will eat." The lion whom a seeker of life listens to and models.

"And the lion comes to be the man." And the spirit of lion comes to be a similar spirit in the seeker.

"And he is cursed, namely the man, the one whom the lion will eat." And the non-seeker of life is cursed, because his pretenses of soul will be exposed and shredded by the wise lion.

"And the lion comes to be the man." And the way that the lion guarded himself and attacked the non-seeker's false identities will forever haunt the terrified victim.

Way of the Soul

Seekers humbly and hungrily eating
the spirits of those more wise and
alive

↑

Non-seekers haughtily one more wise
and alive

Way of the Mind

Way of the Soul

A wise lion guarding and attacking his
own false selves and those in others

↑

A boisterous mouse guarding and
attacking threats to his false selves

Way of the Mind

Way of the Soul

One possesses both childlike
singleness and the soul and courage
of a lion

↑

One is both duplicitous and fearful

Way of the Mind

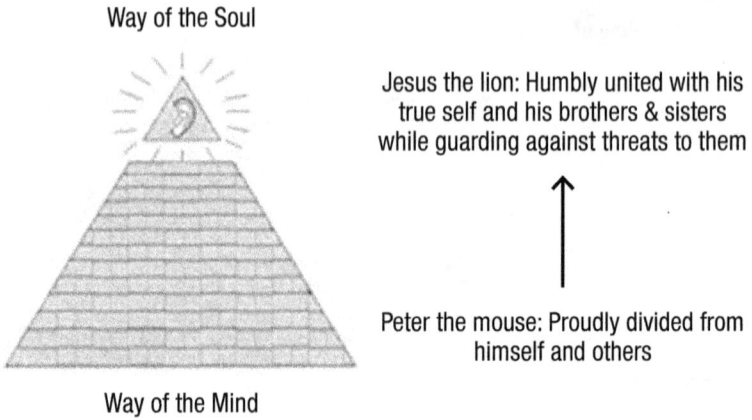

Way of the Soul

Jesus the lion: Humbly united with his
true self and his brothers & sisters
while guarding against threats to them

Peter the mouse: Proudly divided from
himself and others

Way of the Mind

LOVE-GUARD

In Chapter 8, Poem 5 (Saying 25) Jesus explains how a child/lion encounters everyone and everything in the world:

Jesus
said this:

Love your brother[1,2]

Like
your soul.[3]

Guard him[4]

Like
the pupil[5]
of your eye.[6]

[1]*Brother*: One who possesses divine life. Every person, animal, plant and thing—all.

[2]*Love your brother*: Be in your heart place, a twin of all.

[3]*Soul*: Your unique essence. We are all unique essences of one divine life.

[4]*Guard him*: Protect and attack threats to your brothers.

[5]*Pupil*: Core.

[6]*Eye*: Third eye.

"Love your brother." Love the core life in people, plants, animals, and things.

"Love your brother like your soul." Unconditionally love your brothers for who they are, not for their false selves.

"Guard him." Protect yourself and your brothers from those not loving them unconditionally for who they are.

"Like the pupil of your eye." Like your most valuable possession, soul-knowing, without which, you cannot evolve.

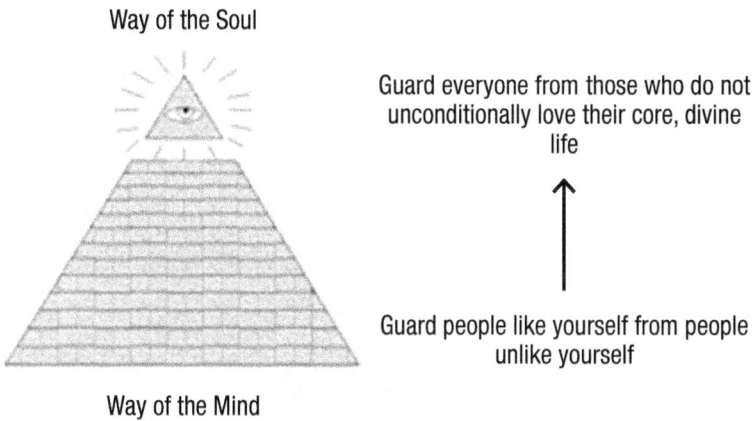

Way of the Soul

Guard everyone from those who do not unconditionally love their core, divine life

↑

Guard people like yourself from people unlike yourself

Way of the Mind

Jesus loved the core light in Peter; however, he guarded himself and all people when Peter attacked a woman:

Simon Peter
said to him
this:

*"Make Mary
leave us,*

*For
women
are
worthy not
of life."*

"For women are worthy not of life." For one's gender determines one's worth on the Way of the Mind. For half of the world are inherently inferior to me. For I need to be above women to feel good about myself. For women do not possess a soul like mine.

For his love of Peter and all people, Jesus guarded by saying:

"Behold!

I
myself
will lead her,

So that
I
might make her
male,

So that,
she
might come to be
a spirit

She
living

And
she
resembling
you males;

For
any woman,

Who
makes herself
male,

Will go
into the kingdom
of the heavens.

"Behold, I myself will lead her." Behold Peter and you other arrogant men, I will show you how wrong you are. I will become one with Mary in order to be her guide.

"So that I might make her male." So that she might stop identifying with what society has conditioned her to believe about her gender.

"So that, she might come to be a spirit, she living, and she resembling you males." So that she may become a twin in her spirit to all men and women.

That is quite an undertaking. To accomplish it, Jesus must teach Mary that a naïve lover loves everyone unconditionally. A follower of him loves everyone unconditionally for their core spirit and makes the tremendous effort to notice every flaw. Then, he guards himself and every other person, animal, plant and thing from the darkness he finds in another. In other words, everyone is loveable; however, everyone is dangerous to the degree that he has not evolved on the Way of the Soul.

So, to evolve, Mary must become a child/lion who love-guards everyone that others dismiss. According to Jesus, there is no other means by which one may become fulfilled, sane, and wise.

Way of the Soul

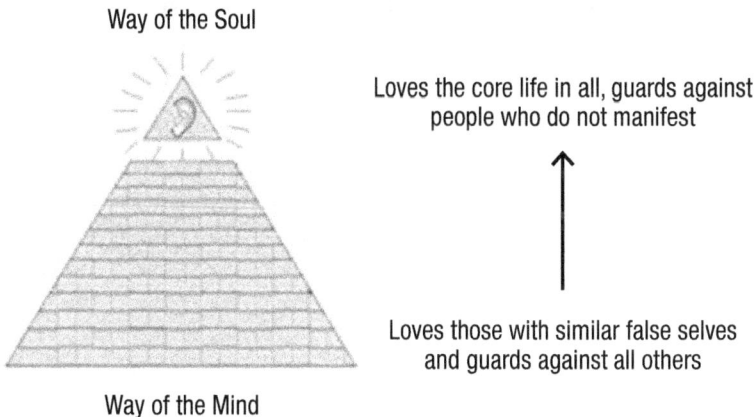

Loves the core life in all, guards against people who do not manifest

Loves those with similar false selves and guards against all others

Way of the Mind

Be Cunning and Innocent

Jesus showed us that a fully alive person does the seemingly impossible, he unconditionally loves another; then, with the information that that love discloses, he cunningly guards himself and others. Jesus tells us that in Chapter 10, Poem 1 (Saying 39):

Jesus
said this:

Come to be
cunning
like serpents[1,2]

And
innocent
like doves.[3]

[1]*Come to be cunning*:
Come to be cleverly
guarding.

[2]*Serpent*: Jesus refers
to the serpent in the
Garden of Eden who
cleverly seduced Eve.

[3]*And innocent like doves*:
A dove is a symbol of
inspiration. It gives us
information when we
become vulnerable.

"Come to be cunning like serpents." Discriminate light from darkness; use your cunning to guard yourself and your brothers and sisters.

"And innocent like doves." Be vulnerable and open to soul-know the essence of everyone beneath their false selves.

This is a dangerous world. Love and guard. Do not just love and fail to see the darkness.

Way of the Soul

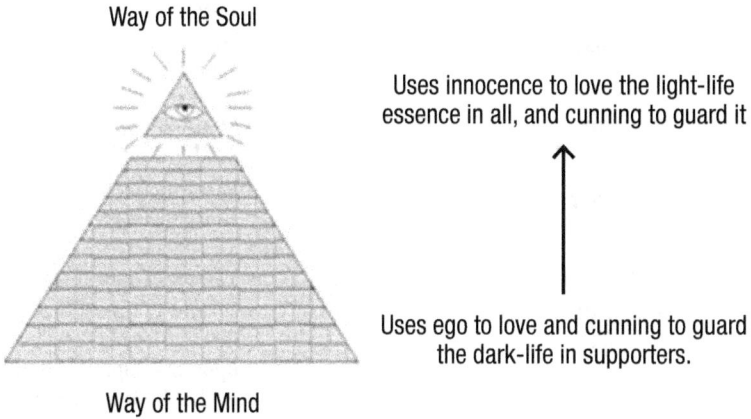

Uses innocence to love the light-life essence in all, and cunning to guard it

Uses ego to love and cunning to guard the dark-life in supporters.

Way of the Mind

To guard is to disrupt. Jesus expressed that in the following Poem 2 from Chapter 4 (Saying 16):

Jesus
said this:

Perhaps
they
are thinking,

Namely
men,[1]

That
I
have come
to throw peace
upon the world;[2]

[1]Men: People on the Way of the Mind.

[2]To throw peace upon the world: To speak words to make those on the Way of the Mind comfortable.

And

they

know

not

That

I

have come,

to throw divisions³

upon the earth:⁴,⁵

Fire,⁶

sword,⁷

and

war.⁸

For

there

are

five

Who

will come to be

in a house.⁹

There

are

three¹⁰

Who

will come to be

against two;

³*To throw divisions*:
To cast words that
expose an individual's
incongruence with who
he really is.

⁴*Earth*: Reflective
consciousness.

⁵*Throw divisions upon the
earth*: Say things that
make the person reflect
upon his duplicity, that
is, that he is both a false
and a real self.

⁶*Fire*: Words that burn
one's conscience.

⁷*Sword*: Words that divide
a person within, and that
divide him from others.

⁸*War*: Words that cause 1)
a person to fight himself,
2) people within a Way
of the Mind to fight one
another, and 3) cause
people on the two Ways
to confront each other.

⁹*Five who will come to be
in a house*: A "house" is
primarily a person, and
secondarily, a family or
group. Jesus refers to one
real person and four false
persons within a single
person, or five people
in a family, one real and
four false.

¹⁰*Three*: Three parts of
oneself, or three persons
in a family or group.

And

two

against three;[11]

The father[12]

against the son;[13]

And

the son

against the father;[14]

And

they

will stand on their feet;[15]

They

being

single ones.[16]

[11]*There are three who will come to be against two, and two against three:* There are three people on the Way of the Soul who will come against two on the Way of the Mind, and Two on the Way of the Soul who will come against three on the Way of the Mind.

[12]*Father:* Within each person and each group is a father personality who takes charge of passing on traditions.

[13]*Son:* Within each person and each group is a son personality who inherits the father's traditions.

[14]*The father against the son and the son against the father:* When the father and son are on different Ways, they will go "against" each other.

[15]*Stand on their feet:* Be confident in who they are, while the rest are shaken.

[16]*Single Ones:* People congruent with themselves.

Way of the Soul

Way of the Mind

Comforts those on the Way of the Soul, disrupts the lives of those on Ways of Dogma

↑

Comforts those on the same Ways of Dogma, disrupts the lives of those on opposing Ways of Dogma and Soul

CHAPTER FIVE

PAUL'S GOALS

PAUL'S OVERALL PLAN

We left off with Paul in Arabia. There, he decided that a person was born with original sin and separated from God. Therefore, he had to decide if it was possible to unite that person with God again. He must have thought, "Perhaps mankind is doomed."

His revelation on the road to Damascus that Jesus was the Messiah told him that somehow Jesus was sent to save mankind from Adam's disobedience. However, Paul had several problems. First, Jesus never said he was the Messiah. Second, Jesus did not do the things that the Messiah was supposed to do, such as drive out the occupiers and bring everyone in the world to worship the one God of Israel. Nor did he cleanse the Temple and restore true Temple worship. Third, Jesus never said that he wanted to save humankind from original sin. Instead, Jesus preached a Way that Paul detested and that he probably knew would lead to the destruction of Judaism, to the raising of revolutionaries who would destroy all order, and because of original sin, to a world of unfettered debauchery.

So somehow, Paul needed to replace Jesus' Way, make it possible for people to be united with God again, show that Jesus was the Christ who was needed to save mankind, and form a church that would indoctrinate people to think and act in accord with Paul's interpretation of God's will. He probably also possessed unconscious selfish desires to build up his own ego and remove all of his guilt about persecuting and killing followers of Jesus.

That would be an impossible agenda for most people, but not for Paul, the religious, murderous fanatic.

BLOT OUT JESUS' GOSPEL

He tackled the problem of erasing Jesus' Way easily. He decided to remove the real Jesus from the historical record by never quoting him.

Can we imagine that? He has never met Jesus, he knows that Jesus has a large following, he knows that people have memorized Jesus' soul poems, he is filled with love for the man who visited him in a vision; and yet, he decides that he will dedicate himself to destroying any written or memorized record of what Jesus said. Is that a plan that we would expect from someone of great character, or from a crazed fanatic?

As we know now, Paul largely succeeded! He never quotes any of Jesus' soul poems in any of his letters, and almost certainly never in any of his conversations. In other words, he deliberately hid Jesus' life's work: all of his parables, poems and sayings; and yet, claimed to be following the man.

Was Paul dishonest, delusional, or so unconscious that he believed his own lies?

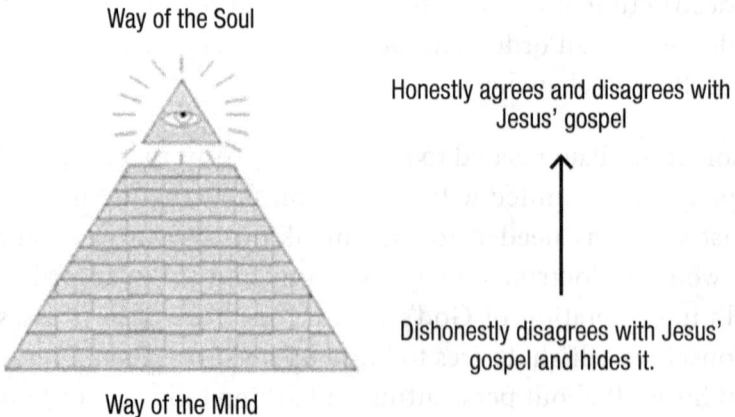

Way of the Soul

Honestly agrees and disagrees with Jesus' gospel

↑

Dishonestly disagrees with Jesus' gospel and hides it.

Way of the Mind

Declare that Jesus is God

The second thing Paul did was to decide that God still loved humans and wanted to unite them with himself. He believed that a man with original sin could not just say, "I'm sorry," and be welcomed by God to his former sonship. No, Paul believed the slap that Adam gave God was so grave that only another God could somehow make up for the affront. Further, that other God would have to do so in a way that necessitated the total submission of humankind to God's will.

Where was this other God? Paul decided that it was Jesus, despite the fact that Jesus never said that he was the only son of God. We read this in Paul's Letter to the Romans 1:1-4:

> *Paul, a servant of Jesus Christ, called to be an apostle, set apart for the gospel of God which he promised beforehand through his prophets in the holy scriptures, the gospel concerning his Son, who was descended from David according to the flesh and designated Son of God in power according to the Spirit of holiness by his resurrection from the dead.*

"Paul, a servant of Jesus Christ, called to be an apostle, set apart for the gospel of God" I, Paul, called to be an apostle of Jesus, not by Jesus, but by God in a mystical vision, the one set apart from everyone in the world, including Jesus' disciples, to preach my gospel, which I call, "the gospel of God" to distinguish it from the gospel of Jesus.

Way of the Soul

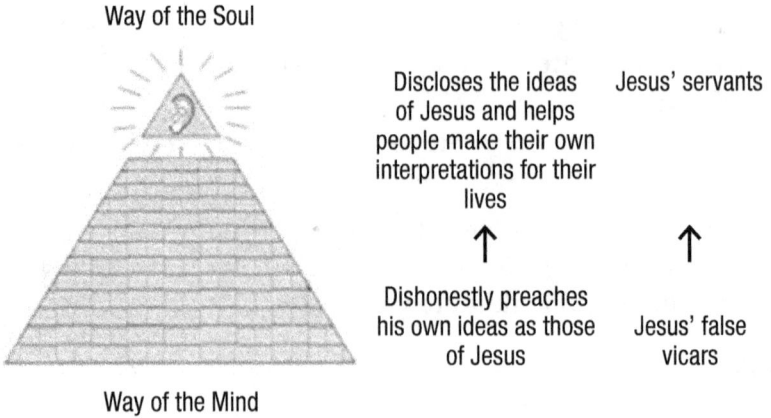

Discloses the ideas   Jesus' servants
of Jesus and helps
people make their own
interpretations for their
lives

Dishonestly preaches   Jesus' false
his own ideas as those   vicars
of Jesus

Way of the Mind

"the gospel concerning his Son" My (Paul's) gospel concerning Jesus, who I declare to possess divine life, a life different from what we see in other humans, animals and plants.

Way of the Soul

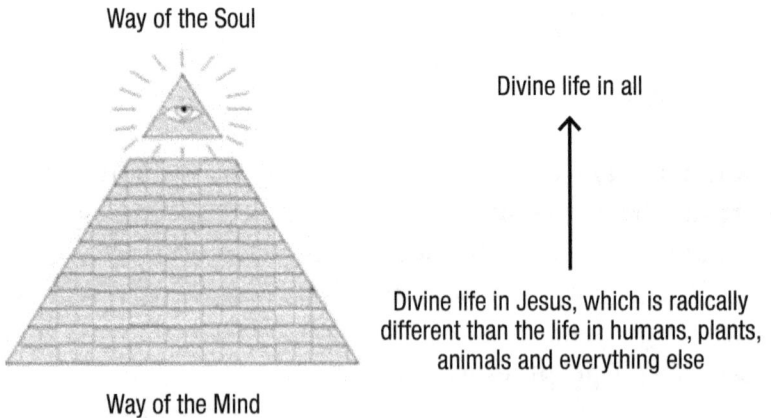

Divine life in all

Divine life in Jesus, which is radically
different than the life in humans, plants,
animals and everything else

Way of the Mind

"who was descended from David according to the flesh and designated Son of God in power according to the Spirit of holiness by his resurrection from the dead." Jesus was biologically related to King David. When he was resurrected, the Holy Spirit showed everyone that 1) Jesus is the Son of God in a way that we are not, and 2) he was resurrected in a way that we cannot be.

Way of the Soul

All will die physically and live eternally

Jesus died physically and will live
eternally like no one else will

Way of the Mind

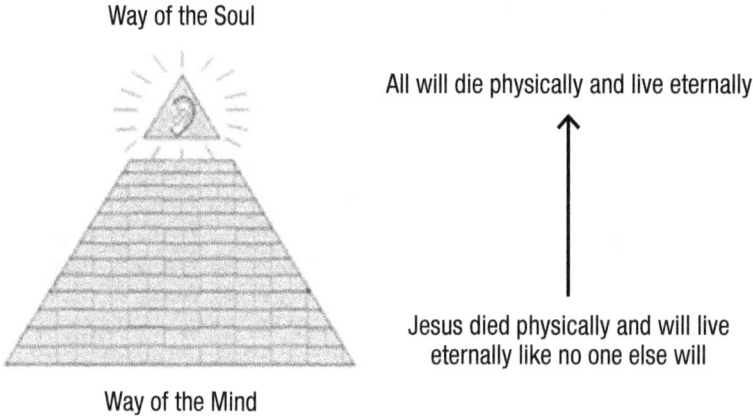

Declare that Jesus Died for Humankind's Sins

Once Paul decided that Jesus had been designated "son of God" because he resurrected himself, Paul decided that Jesus sacrificed himself on the cross for humankind, even though Jesus never said that. In Romans 5: 10, we read:

> *For God has done what the law, weakened by the*
> *flesh, could not do: sending his own Son in the*
> *likeness of sinful flesh and for sin, he condemned*
> *sin in the flesh, (Rom. 8:1)*

"For God has done what the law, weakened by the flesh, could not." In other words, after God gave the laws to save humankind, God realized that those laws did not do what He thought they would do. God failed.

"God…sending his own Son in the likeness of sinful flesh and for sin, he condemned sin in the flesh." God sent his own Son not in human sinful flesh, but in flesh that looked like sinful flesh, and because he showed the difference between the two fleshes, he condemned the one that encases humans.

Way of the Soul

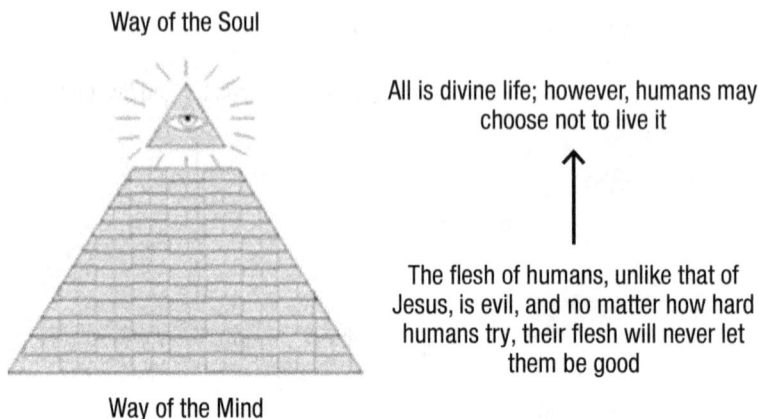

All is divine life; however, humans may
choose not to live it

The flesh of humans, unlike that of
Jesus, is evil, and no matter how hard
humans try, their flesh will never let
them be good

Way of the Mind

Paul goes on to say:

> For if while we were enemies we were reconciled to God by the
> death of his Son, much more, now that we are reconciled, shall we
> be saved by his life. (Rom. 5:10)

> Christ loved us and gave himself up for us, a fragrant offering and
> sacrifice to God (Ephesians 5:2).

**"For if while we were enemies we were reconciled to God by
the death of his Son."** For while most humans did not regard
God as their enemy, God declared them to be His enemy.
However, God did not want them to be enemies; so He lovingly
sent his Son to die a horrible death.

**"Much more, now that we are reconciled, shall we be saved by
his life."** So now that God called us "enemies" and figured out
a means for us to be friends, we still needed to be "saved" from
our sinful flesh by the special kind of life that Jesus lived. It was
not enough that Jesus died, we must now do something else.

**"Christ loved us and gave himself up for us, a fragrant
offering and sacrifice to God."** You see, the Messiah loved us
and sacrificed his life as an offering to the God who declared us
his enemies; so that God would feel differently about us.

Declare that People Need to Believe Paul's Gospel

However, Paul reasoned that it was not enough that Jesus died for the sins of humankind. People also had to agree to that.

Paul explains below that while everyone has been "reconciled," only those who believe that he has been reconciled by Jesus' death and resurrection would be "saved."

> I (Paul) am making known to you, indeed, brothers, the gospel which I declared to you, which you received, and in which you also stand, by which you are saved, if you hold it fast, unless you believed in vain. For I delivered to you as of first importance what I also received: that Christ died for our sins in accordance with the scriptures, that he was buried, and that he was raised on the third day in accordance with the scriptures (1Cor. 15:34).

In that quote, we find the four foundation stones of Paul's gospel and future church that he said were revealed to him in Arabia:

1. Christ died for our sins.

2. Christ was buried.

3. Christ was raised.

4. No one is "saved" unless he believes 1, 2 and 3.

Notice especially, belief number four: To be saved, to live forever with God, one must believe Paul's gospel, which he arrived at in mystical experiences. That justifies the need for Paul to start a hierarchical church that would both teach people to believe in his ideas, and convince them about their eternal reward and punishment if they did not. That also satisfied Paul's ego needs by putting him in the center of the church with his misrepresentation of Jesus.

It also ensured that he could be without guilt. He only needed to believe in his own beliefs to be forgiven by God. There was no need to ask forgiveness of the families he terrorized when he persecuted and killed their members. (Is that the thinking of a man of character?)

Declare that Jesus was the Messiah

Therefore, Paul rationalized to himself that Jesus really was the Messiah who came to drive out the occupiers of Israel, to cleanse the temple and to bring people to worship the one God of Israel. The Temple was our sinful flesh, which got cleansed so that we, the occupiers of it, could be saved when we believed that Jesus died for our sins.

Found a Dogma to Indoctrinate People

Paul could not accomplish his mission unless he could establish a church and get people to believe him. That need forced him, after three years, to leave Arabia and return to Jerusalem (Gal. 1:18-24).

> Then after three years, I went up to Jerusalem to get acquainted with Peter and stayed with him fifteen days. I saw none of the other apostles— only James, the Lord's brother. I assure you before God that what I am writing you is no lie.

He met with James, the brother of Jesus and the head of the Jerusalem community, and with Peter, his assistant. We can only imagine their initial fear when he walked into the room; and then, their shock when he said he was preaching Jesus; and then, their total dismay when he laid out a gospel that they had never heard Jesus speak; and then, their complete shock when he told them that unless they abandoned Jesus' gospel and believed his, they would be eternally damned. James and Peter must have thought that they had died and been reborn in a house of warped mirrors.

Notice that Paul does not say that while in Jerusalem he visited the families of those he persecuted and killed. He never apologized for persecuting and killing the fathers and mothers of the children in the Jerusalem community. In his Mind, he need not do that because he has been reconciled by Jesus' death and resurrection and self-saved by his belief in his own heard-from-God gospel.

The man remains in his heart a disassociated, depraved man, not unlike a man who has beat up his wife and returns, not to say, "I'm sorry," but to say, "I have changed." Like that man, Paul wanted people to believe him and believe in him. History has shown, as in dysfunctional families where there is a history of abuse, people have overlooked the horrific things Paul actually did, and have believed him.

It would be an understatement to say that the meeting did not go well. After 15 days, Paul left to preach to Roman Gentiles, recognizing that Jews in Palestine would never believe him. It was 10 years before he returned to Jerusalem again.

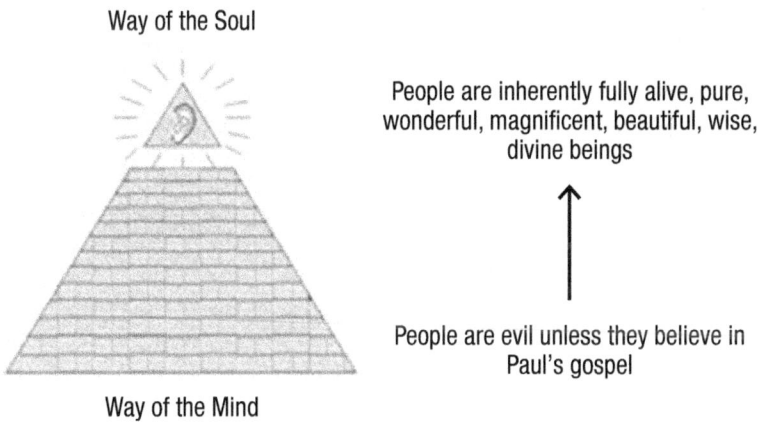

Way of the Soul

People are inherently fully alive, pure, wonderful, magnificent, beautiful, wise, divine beings

↑

People are evil unless they believe in Paul's gospel

Way of the Mind

CHAPTER SIX

JESUS' SELF-DEVELOPMENT METHOD

Discover Yourself on Your Own

Jesus' message in the Gospel of Thomas leads to his summation in Chapter 21, Poem 6 (Saying 11b)

Jesus
said this:

Whoever
discovers himself
on his own,[1]

The world[2]
is
worthy of him
not.

[1]Whoever discovers himself on his own: Whoever leaves indoctrinators (clergy, political leaders, parents, family, peers, professors, authors, the media, and all of his previous beliefs) and uses soul-knowing to discover himself on his own.

[2]The world: Those on the Way of the Mind.

"Whoever discovers himself on his own." Whoever uses soul-knowing to obtain the answers tailored to his specific history, and situation. Whoever leaves all to discover the all. Whoever is a rebel seeker.

Way of the Soul

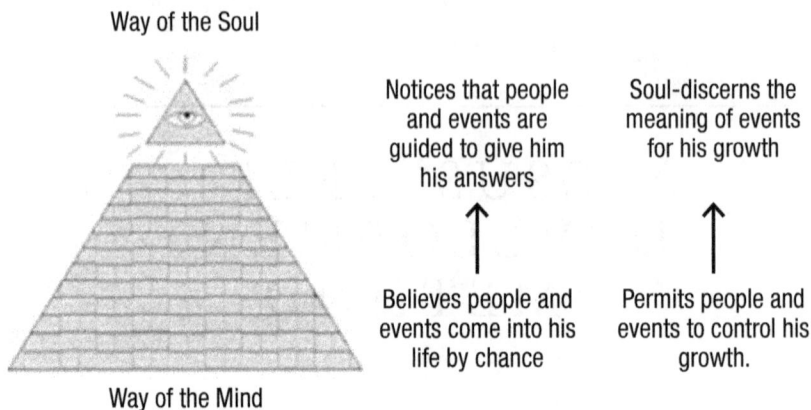

Notices that people and events are guided to give him his answers	Soul-discerns the meaning of events for his growth
↑	↑
Believes people and events come into his life by chance	Permits people and events to control his growth.

Way of the Mind

MAKE THE RIGHT FUNDAMENTAL CHOICE

One cannot be on the Way of the Soul and the Way of the Mind at the same time. Every choice we make determines which Way we follow. Jesus says in Chapter 11, Poem 2 (Saying 47):

Jesus
said this:

In no way
can
a man
climb onto horses
two[1]

And
he
stretch bows
two.[2]

[1]*Horses two*: A horse represents power. Within us are two powers. One from Light and the other from the dark self we create.

[2]*Stretch bows two*: A bow is strong intention. Within us is the intention to live more life or to live death.

In no way,

can

a servant

serve lords two;[3]

Or,

he

will honor the one,

And

the other one,

He

will despise.

[3]*Lords two*: Within us are two kinds of leaders. Our divine Father and Mother is one. Way of the Mind authorities is the other. Our Parents guide us continually through soul-knowing to be more ourselves. Our religious leaders tell us how to be fulfilled by being more false like them.

"In no way can a man climb onto horses two:" We ride power or self-confidence (a horse) in the world in only two Ways: On the Way of the Soul or on the Way of the Mind. We never straddle the two Ways. We live on one horse or the other.

For example, when we identity with a country, we identify with a brand of nationalism and its doctrine that includes a set of beliefs, leaders, a tradition, a pride, a flag, rituals, and a set of laws. This Way of the Mind becomes our extended false selves. We find our self-confidence on that nationalistic power horse. We will defend and promote it as if it were us.

If our nationalistic leaders tell us to kill people in other nations, our other horse (the Way of the Soul) may tell us a different message. Then, we must choose on which horse we want to ride. The visualization here is very powerful. While it may seem at first that a person can straddle two horses at once—especially if they are going slowly at the same speed and moving in the same direction, when the horses begin to go at different speeds or in different directions (which will ultimately happen), the person must either choose one or fall from both.

"In no way...can a man stretch bows two." We cannot have concurrent dual intentions—especially if they contradict each other. For example, we cannot intend to be full of life and soul at the possible sacrifice of money, and at the same time make making money our priority over soul development. The first intention is the Way of the Soul; the second intention is the Way of the Mind.

"In no way, can a servant serve lords two; or, he will honor the one, and the other one, he will despise." For example: Our "lord" clergyperson may tell us that those who do not believe our truths live in sin. That may work fine for us for a while. However, our Way of the Soul "lord" will always get through to us and demand through soul-knowing that we identify with our core selves, not with our theology. At that point, we choose to live in darkness or light by the "lord" we choose to serve

To follow Jesus and become fulfilled, we must give up the notion that we can ride two horses, pull two bows, and serve two lords. For example, we may think that we can identify with our core self AND identify with being an American, a Buddhist, a plumber, a conservative, and a male. When we do try to do that, we spend most of our time in emotional turmoil on the Way of the Mind.

Jesus is clear: To be single, one identifies with one horse, one bow, and one lord all arising out of one's core inner life with our Father and Mother. One cannot do that and at the same time identify with any group of common beliefs, any symbol of such a group such as a crucifix or flag, any titles used, such as "Father," "Sister," "Mullah," or "Reverend," or any garments that shout, "I am special, you are not." As soon as one does that, he tries to ride two horses, pull two bows and serve two lords. He will be emotionally torn.

As people grow in soul and life, they may begin by jumping from one horse to the other, from between a Way of the Mind supportive large group of family and friends to a tiny Way of the

Soul support group. Both provide an enjoyable life; however, the nature of that life is shockingly different if one has a third eye to see it. Eventually, to find peace, Jesus says one must ride one horse, pull one bow, and follow one lord.

Way of the Soul

One lord   One bow (intention)

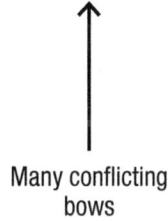

↑   ↑

Conflicting lords   Many conflicting bows

Way of the Mind

Way of the Soul

Loyalty to one's real self & to They Who Live

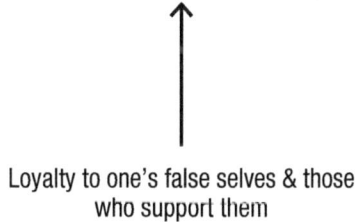

↑

Loyalty to one's false selves & those who support them

Way of the Mind

Way of the Soul

Rides one power horse

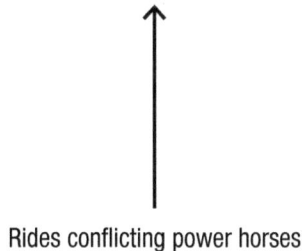

↑

Rides conflicting power horses

Way of the Mind

LOVE-GUARD INDOCTRINATORS

Jesus saw that most indoctrinators were the enemy. He tells us to love them and guard against them. Let us read the clever way he expresses this in Chapter 2, Poem 2 (Saying 3a):

Jesus
said this:

If
they
should say to you
this:

Namely
those,

Who
lead themselves
before you:[1,2]

[1] *Who lead themselves before you*: Clerics, politicians, parents, peers, authors and other leaders who ordain themselves to indoctrinate others with their truths.

[2] *Before you*: When Jesus uses the phrase "before you," he intends that his audience remember the many biblical commands warning us not to put false gods before us (Exodus 20:3, Exodus 32: 2; Deuteronomy 5:7; 12:30; Judges 2:3). There are two kinds of leaders: Those that empower people to find their own answers on their own about who they are, who others are, and how the world works; and those who try to control people's thinking. The former lead on the Way of the Soul; the latter, on the Way of the Mind. Jesus says that when we permit leaders and peers to "lead themselves before us," we worship them as false gods.

"Behold!

The kingdom[3]
is in heaven;"[4]

Then
the birds
of heaven[5],[6]
will come to be
first
before you.[7]

[3]*Kingdom*: A kingdom
is one's high, wise rule
over oneself and one's
interactions with others.

[5]*Heaven*: A level of
knowing.

[4]*The kingdom is in heaven*:
Your rule will be found
in the indoctrinator's
level of believing about
all. The indoctrinator
says: "Believe as I do and
you will be fulfilled."

[6]*Birds*: Mental ideas; most
often, blind beliefs.

[7]*The birds of heaven*: the
artificial beliefs of a
level of knowing. When
a leader says, "Your
kingdom of heaven will
be found in my ideas,"
he means, "Your way of
being fulfilled as a ruler
will be found in my
mental, absolutely true
beliefs."

[8]*Then, the birds of*
heaven will come to be
before you: Then, the
indoctrinator's beliefs
will become your false
gods.

If
they
should say to you
this:

Namely
those,

[8]*Sea*: Unconscious
and semi-conscious
emotions.

Who
lead themselves
before you:

[9]*The kingdom is in the*
sea: "Your rule is in
true emotions." In other
words, the indoctrinating
leader tries to convince
his followers that they
will rule when they adopt
his emotional beliefs.

"Behold!

The kingdom
is
in the sea;"[8,9]

[10]*Fish*: Emotional ideas;
most often, emotional
blind beliefs.

Then
the fish[10]
will come to be
first
before you.[11]

[11]*Then the fish will come*
to be first before you:
Then the indoctrinating
leader's emotional ideas
will come to be your false
gods.

In that Poem, Jesus points out two means through which leaders indoctrinate. The first means is through logical mental arguments. He calls them, "birds," because they flit around in our brain with no basis in observable fact.

For example, an indoctrinator may show logically that Jesus is the second person in the Trinity. Based on that, the indoctrinator may then tell the audience that they need to follow the doctrine of the church that he represents. For some cerebral people, the putting together of those two abstract arguments convinces them to put the indoctrinator, his church, and its doctrine before them as false gods.

The second means is through emotional, sometimes illogical arguments. For example, an emotional preacher may shout, "Jesus lives, he has been resurrected." If one were to think logically, one might ask, "Does Jesus live after death any differently than anyone else?" In other words, the fact that Jesus lives and that he is resurrected does not seem to logically mean anything. Yet, the emotion of the indoctrinator moves the audience.

An emotional indoctrinator does not count on people to listen to him logically. He wants to move them emotionally to live blindly his truths at his level of heaven.

Indoctrinators create Ways of the Mind by intellectually or emotionally preaching fixed, artificial truths-- truths not tied to anything you can observe and validate.

People find their self-confidence in certainty; thus, they seek false-god people and institutions who will give them that, even if it means embracing artificial, illogical blind beliefs.

Jesus never knew an absolute truth. At each level of life and soul, he perceived the world differently. He did not seek blind-belief certainty, he trusted in the evolution of truth as it was shown him by his Parents. Each instant he gave up what he had discovered to discover more. He was a perpetual seeker and finder.

Jesus knew that for a person to be an independent ruler of his kingdom, he needed to get free of self-absorbed indoctrinators and find the unique answers given him moment to moment by his Parents. So as part of his teaching, Jesus needed to confront the enemy—all of those leaders who wished to enslave people to their low level ideas. He did that strongly in several poems, including Poem 1 in Chapter 10 (Saying 39):

Jesus
said this:

The Pharisees
and
the Scribes[1]
took the keys[2]
of knowledge,[3]

And
they
hid them,[4]

Nor
did
they
go inward;[5]

And those

Who
desired to go
inward,

They
did
not permit them.[6]

[1] *Pharisees and Scribes*: Two of the many groups of clerics within Judaism. In this Gospel, they represent all indoctrinating leaders, whether religious or secular. Such leaders could be politicians, clerics, professors, parents, business managers, TV celebrities and influential friends.

[2] *Keys*: The keys to knowledge are what Jesus teaches, beginning with soul-knowing.

[3] *Knowledge*: Knowledge of your real self, the real self of others, and the principles of coming alive in a dead world.

[4] *Hid them*: Taught people to make the beliefs of authorities more important than what they soul-know.

[5] *Go inward*: Leave their indoctrination and soul-know.

[6] *They did not permit them*: The authorities taught people to distrust soul-knowing.

"And those who desired to go inward, they did not permit them." The indoctrinators insured that people became conformists by ridiculing mistakes, telling them that they were bad if they thought or acted contrary to doctrine, and by psychologically and physically marginalizing and persecuting rebels.

For example, a clergy person may tell people that if they disobey the church's interpretation of scripture, they will go to hell. Or a commentator may manipulate people into thinking that if they disagree with the political party, they will be fools. Or a peer group may ostracize a member for unorthodox thinking and behavior. Or a parent may weep trying to cause emotional pain in her child who does not honor the family traditions.

Way of the Soul

Wise facilitators: "I will help you find your own truths."

Your truths will be discovered as you grow in guarded-love of yourself and all

Indoctrinators: "I possess the absolute truths you need."

You can learn truths without first growing.

Way of the Mind

Way of the Soul

People become one with the source of their soul

People worship indoctrinators, their institutions and their doctrine

Way of the Mind

In contrast to people who want to be masters over others, Jesus ensured that no one relates to him like that. Let us notice how he love-guards a disciple who wants to adore him as a false-god leader in Chapter 2, Poem 3 (Saying 13):

Jesus
asked his disciples:

"Compare me,

And
you
speak to me
this:

I
resemble
whom?"

Said
he
to him,

Namely
Simon Peter,
this:

"You
resemble
an angel,[1]

One,

Who
is
righteous.[2]

[1] *You resemble an angel*:
You resemble someone
who uses soul-knowing
to communicate
with God; and then,
who provides that
information to us.

[2] *Who is righteous*: Who
lives by the laws of God.

Said

he

to him,

Namely

Matthew

this:

"You

resemble

a philosopher,[3]

One

Who

is

wise."[4]

Said

he

to him,

Namely

Thomas

this:

"Master,[5]

My entire mouth[6]

permits me

not to say:[7]

[3] *You resemble a philosopher*: You resemble someone who seeks to know himself, others, and the principles of personal development.

[4] *Wise*: Evolved.

[5] *Master*: One who controls how another thinks and acts.

[6] *Mouth*: My entire being. When one speaks from his mouth, he speaks from his being. If he identifies with his real self, he speaks from He Who Lives. If he identifies with his false self, he speaks from indoctrinators.

[7] *My entire mouth permits me not to say*: My entire being permits me not to say.

Whom
you
resemble."

Jesus
said to Thomas:

"I
am
your master
not."[8]

[8]*I am your master not:*
Fool, become your own
master in the kingdom.

"You resemble an angel." In the Old Testament, angels delivered messages from God, usually to prophets. For example, in 1 Kings 13:18 we read. "I also am a prophet as you are, and an angel spoke to me by the word of the LORD."

The angels were symbols, both of a person who used soul-knowing to communicate directly with his source of inspiration, and of the message.

As one grows on the Way of the Soul, one uses soul-knowing more; thus, one receives direct revelation and becomes an angel to others. Thus, Jesus had no problem with Peter calling him an angel. Jesus also wanted everyone to become an angel.

"You resemble a philosopher." Everyone on the Way of the Soul uses soul-knowing and logic to understand himself, others, and the principles governing the world. Thus, again, Jesus embraced Matthew's description of him.

"Master." When Thomas called Jesus, "Master," Jesus attacked in love when he said, "I am not our master."

On the Way of the Mind, people identify with titles, roles, offices, uniforms, and awards—anything to give them status over another. From that position, they believe that they have the right to be master over how others think and act.

Jesus will not endorse that abuse. Consequently, he replied, "I am not your master." In other words, "Grow up and use soul-knowing to discover yourself on your own."

Thomas wanted an enslaving indoctrinator. Jesus empowered him to be free.

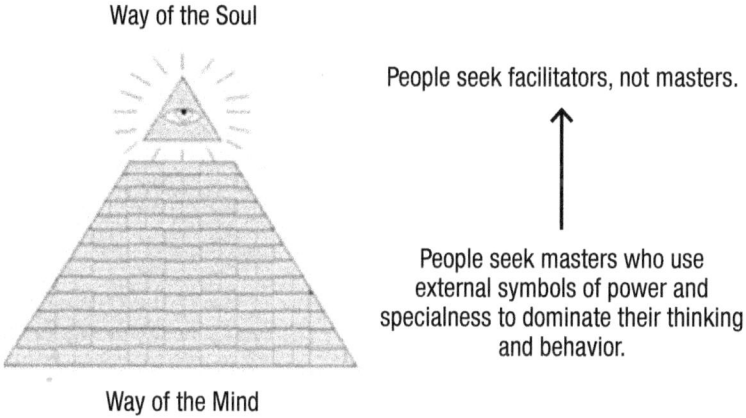

Way of the Soul

People seek facilitators, not masters.

↑

People seek masters who use external symbols of power and specialness to dominate their thinking and behavior.

Way of the Mind

MASTER YOUR FIELDS

When we were little children we were one with our core selves. Indoctrinators taught us through the socialization process to identify with false selves and to dislike and hate those who were not like our false selves. Jesus illustrates what we must do to reverse that process on the Way of the Soul in Poem 2, Chapter 6 (Saying 21a):

Mary
said to Jesus:

"Your disciples,[1]

They
resemble
whom?"[2]

[1]*Disciples*: People who follow Jesus' Way of the Soul.

[2]*They resemble whom*: They resemble whom in the way they think and act?

Jesus
responded:

"They
resemble
small children,

They
dwelling in a field³

³*They dwelling in a field*:
A field is a person's
sphere of influence. It is
the internal and external
environment affected by
a person's presence.
A field is one's sense of
self, and it is a family,
work environment, or
group in which one finds
himself.
We are more than
isolated beings. The
person we are affects
others over a distance.
For example, when a
little child is brought
into a room, he affects
everyone. His light
becomes the light in the
room. How powerful he
is at birth. That self he
lives in and the room
are his field of influence.
When a person living
at a low level of heaven
comes into the room,
we sense the darkness.
We also sense the light
in others. Their fields
influence us.
When a person chooses
to live from a false self,
he causes his real self
to suffer. He affects his
own field. For example,
he becomes afraid,
depressed, anxious and
angry. In other words,
he makes himself
emotionally sick.
With mass
communication, a
person's field can be
worldwide.
A little child does
not know to guard;
consequently, it can be
seduced by someone's
dark field.

Which

is

not theirs.⁴

When

they

should come,

Namely

the lords

of the field,⁵

They

will say this:

'Release our field

back to us.'⁶

And

they

will strip naked⁷

in their presence,⁸

⁴*Which is not theirs.* The followers of Jesus live at a high level of heaven. They may work and live around people on the Way of the Mind at a low level. So they dwell superficially in a low level "which is not theirs."

⁵*When they should come, namely, the lords of the field*: A lord of a field is a leader. For example, a lord could be a parent at the Christmas dinner, or a boss at work, or a friend at lunch.

⁶*Release our field back to us*: Conform to our level of thinking and acting. For example at the Christmas dinner, a parent may say, "Pray like we do." Or a boss may say, "We cover for each other. No one upstairs need know." A friend may say, "Go along until you find another job."

⁷*They will strip naked*: The child-adult followers of Jesus refuse to be what they are not; thus, they easily strip themselves of false-self clothes and pay the costs.

⁸*In their presence*: To declare openly one's real self.

<table>
<tr>
<td>

So that

it

be given back

to them."⁹

And

it

will be given back

to them."¹⁰

</td>
<td>

⁹*So that it be given back to them:* So that those on a Way of the Mind can have their level of knowing and deceit.

¹⁰*And it will be given back to them:* So that those demanding to control a field may choke on their false identities.

</td>
</tr>
</table>

"They resemble small children, they dwelling in a field, which is not theirs." Jesus describes the war of fields that we encounter every day. No two people live exactly on the same level of heaven. The greater the distance between fields, the greater the conflict.

"When they should come, namely the lords of the field, they will say this: 'Release our field back to us." Lords of the field sense when someone does not conform to falseness. Then, they have an option: To look at themselves with soul-knowing and decide if they have something to learn from the non-conformist, or remain blind and demand that the rebel meet their standards.

"And they will strip naked in their presence, so that it be given back to them."

The person on the Way of the Soul soul-knows deliberately every other person's field. In every encounter, he chooses to strip rather than compromise or lie, to love-guard rather than be controlled. He will lose a job or be banished from a community rather than live at a lower level.

Way of the Soul

Easily strips himself
of external symbols
of power and
specialness

Honestly discloses
who he is and pays
the costs

↑

↑

Clings to external
symbols of power
and specialness

Hides who he is out
of fear of the costs of
being himself

Way of the Mind

Way of the Soul

Love-Guards his real-self and others
at any cost

↑

Loves and guards his false-self and
abandons others no matter the cost

Way of the Mind

Way of the Soul

Manifests high
fields of soul and
life

Auto-Triggers anger
and jealousy in low
lifers

↑

↑

Manifests low fields
of soul and life

Auto-Triggers
approval & support
from low lifers

Way of the Mind

Jesus observed that we pass our fields on to our sons, daughters and neighbors, in Chapter 21, Poem 3 (Saying 109):

Jesus
responded:

The kingdom[1]
is comparable
to a man,

Who
had
he
there
in his field[2]
a treasure[3,4]
hidden, [5]

He
not knowing
about it.[6]

And after
he
died,[7]

He
left it
to his son;[8]
And
the son
did
not know
about it.[9]

[1]Kingdom: A "field." It is an internal and external area of personal rule.

[2]Field: Internal and external sphere of personal influence.

[3]Treasure: Words of soul that can only be soul-known.

[4]Man..who had...treasure: All men have in their possession a treasure of soul, but only those who are soul-alert know about it.

[5]It hidden: It concealed by his living death, by his Ways of Dogma.

[6]Not knowing about it: People on the Way of the Mind do not know that they possess the ability to disclose to themselves the soul about who they are, who others are, and how to solve practical problems.

[7]After he died: After he grew more and more to live death.

[8]Son: A person who learns a tradition from a father.

[9]Son did not know about it: The son did not know about hidden soul. He lived loyal to the Ways of Dogma he inherited from his various fathers.

He
took the field,

Which
was
there,[10]

And
he
gave it
away.[11]

And
whoever
bought it,[12]

He
came[13]
plowing,[14]

And
he
discovered the treasure;[15]

And
he
began to give money
at interest[16]
to those,

Whom
he
desired.[17]

[10]*Took the field which was there*: Took the awareness that is known only by living in the present.

[11]*And gave it away*: He did not know that he has something of value.

[12]*Bought it*: Paid the price of differing from others to be on the Way of the Soul. Paid the price of being loyal to his real self when others wanted him to conform to their false Ways.

[13]*He came*: Came into a level of awareness in the moment.

[14]*He plowing*: He examined what he soul-knew.

[15]*Discovered the treasure*: The meaning for his life of the soul he soul-discovered.

[16]*Give money at interest*: He spoke out of love-guardedness.
He used his words of soul to help others while demanding a responsible response.

[17]*Whom he desired*: Whom he desired to share his divine life. In other words, he did not speak soul to everyone, because he knows who is receptive and who will not use those words responsibly.

"And after he died, he left it to his son. And after living on the Way of the Mind until he, as a robot, thought and acted as he was indoctrinated, he taught his son to live the same Way. He could have taught his son to be rebel and discover his own answers with soul-knowing; however, he did not.

For example, when parents teach a child their fears about the future and guilt about the past, the child may rebel, or he may buy into the death world of his parents. When he chooses the latter course, he grows up dead and may teach his own child to live death.

"And whoever bought it, he came plowing, and he discovered the treasure." Occasionally, a person comes along, pays the price of being a non-conformist, and begins down the Way of the Soul. He grows in soul-knowing, questions authorities, leaves blind beliefs, confronts himself, lives the pain and joys that he discovers, and continues soul-listening until he breaks through to his real life answers—his treasure.

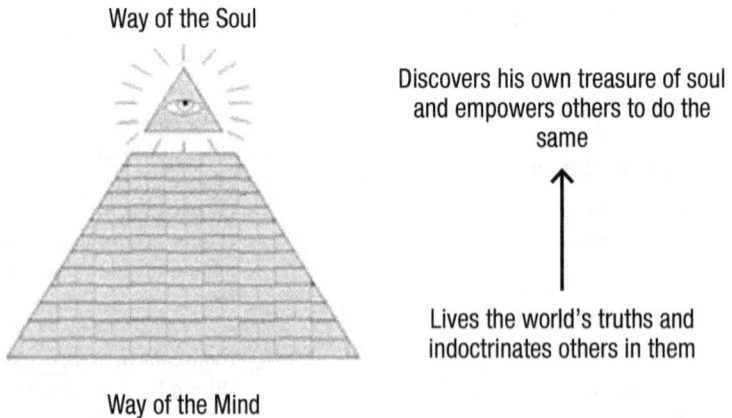

Way of the Soul

Discovers his own treasure of soul
and empowers others to do the
same

Lives the world's truths and
indoctrinates others in them

Way of the Mind

Seek to Destroy Yourself

To evolve on the Way of the Soul, one must trample what he has taken on as precious extension of himself. Jesus states that in Chapter 9, Poem 4 (Saying 37):

Jesus responded:

"When
you
should strip yourselves
naked[1]
without being ashamed,[2]

And
you
take your garments[3]

And
you
put them
on the earth[4]
under your feet[5]

Like
those little,
small children [6]
do,

[1] *When you should strip yourselves naked*: When you stop presenting yourself as anything but your core, light self. Or when you stop identifying yourself with ideas, things and people.

[2] *Without being ashamed*: Without worrying about whether you conform to the expectations of others.

[3] *Garments*: Those beliefs, things and people to which you identify rather than your core life.

[4] *Earth*: Our reflective consciousness. To put garments on the earth is to bring into consciousness one's false identifications and the harm they cause to oneself and others.

[5] *Feet*: What we stand on for confidence. When we take a stand in the world, we project ourselves from the beliefs, things and people important to us.

[6] *Little, small children*: People who love themselves for being who they are, not what they are with clothes (false identities) on.

And

you

trample them;[7]

Then

you

will peer upon the son

of He

Who lives,[8]

And

you

will come to be

afraid not.[9]

[7]*Trample them*: See those clothes (false identities) as foolish and useless. To trample is to demean what gave one false life.

[8]*Son of He Who Lives*: Then, you will reveal yourself and the core of another as the son or daughter of They Who Live.

[9]*Come to be afraid not*: Come to be emotionally healthy.

"And you take your garments." And you identify your false identities. For example, you look at your appearance and how proud it makes you. Or you see how hard you have worked to have a title and a position that makes you appear important for the wrong reasons.

"And you put them on the earth under your feet." And you deliberately stand on them to see how awful they feel to yourself and others. For example, you recognize how flaunting your appearance has made yourself look silly and others feel inferior. Or you recall how you have used your title and position to control others, rather than free them to find their own answers.

"And you trample them." And you make them nothing to you. For example, you see how worthless your false identities are compared to being who you are honestly in the world, no matter the cost.

"And you will become afraid not:" To the degree that one identifies with beliefs, things, and people, to that degree he lives in fear of losing them. For example, If one stands on money, he fears loss. If one stands on his beliefs, he fears being shown he is wrong. If one stands on his spouse, he fears losing her.

Fear may be the basis of all emotional problems. When we grieve, we fear the consequences of a past loss. When we get frustrated, we fear failure. When we become out-of-body excited, we fear being still with our painful emotions.

Jesus tells us that we stop being fearful when we trample our identification with ideas, people and things. A woman afraid of losing her spouse must trample her dependency and claim herself standing alone. A child afraid to fail must trample his shame and claim his dignity with doing his best. The permissive mother who is afraid of losing her children must trample her obsession with giving them all that they want and claim how wonderful she is whether her children like or not. A man who is afraid to say to his child, "I love you," must trample his false manliness and claim his tenderness.

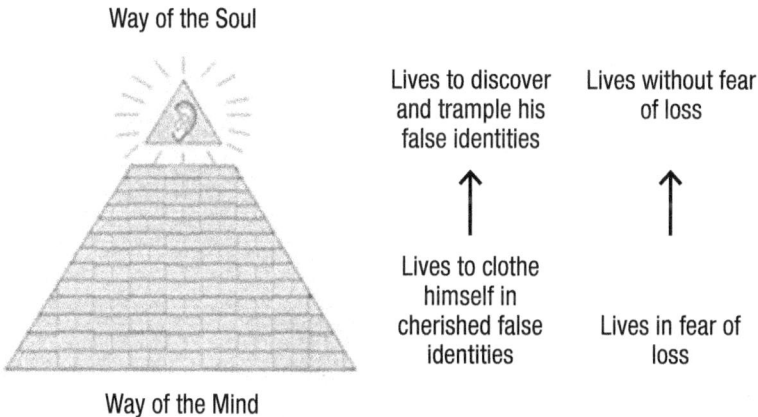

Way of the Soul

Lives to discover
and trample his
false identities

Lives without fear
of loss

↑

↑

Lives to clothe
himself in
cherished false
identities

Lives in fear of
loss

Way of the Mind

DESTROY YOUR DIVIDED SELF

We know from the following Poem that Jesus was not born perfect. He identified with false selves, thanks to his socialization by his birth mother. When very young, he entered the war of fields with his mother and those around him who wanted him to conform to Judaism, his Jewish tradition, and to do the things that would be safe in a Roman-dominated country. He also went to war with himself. He was generating two fields by riding two horses, pulling two bows, and serving two lords. His false-selves wanted approval and support from those around him. His real-self wanted to be more alive no matter the cost. Over and over again, he decided to destroy his false selves, as he says in Chapter 16, Poem 4 (Saying 71):

Jesus
said this:

I

will destroy this house [1,2]

And

no one

can build it, [3]

Never.

[1]*House*: A self. Our house has rooms when it has false selves. When it is empty, we are our real self.

[2]*I will destroy this house*: I will destroy this house with rooms (false identities).

[3]*And No one can build it*: And no one can manipulate me into identifying with false selves again.
No one can convince me to stand on religious beliefs, family traditions, money, political beliefs, things and people. I will stand on my core, divine, real self.

Way of the Soul

Destroys rooms in
his house

Love-Guards
himself from
house dividers

Builds rooms in his
house

Loves house
dividers

Way of the Mind

Having destroyed his house with false rooms over and over, Jesus was able to formulate a universal Way of the Soul principle for self-development, as we see in Chapter 13, Poem 2 (Saying 61):

Jesus
said this:

"When
he
should come to be
destroyed,[1]

[1]*Come to be destroyed*: When he stops identifying with his false selves. When he stops identifying with any set of theological or secular beliefs.

He
will be
full
of light.[2]

[2]*Light*: The power emanating from honesty.

When
however,

[3]*Divided*: Divided in loyalty between his real self and his false selves.

He
should come to be
divided,[3]

[4]*Darkness*: Dishonesty, confusion, and fear.

He
will be
full
of darkness.[4]

"Light...Darkness:" Emotionally sound...emotionally ill. We often see emotional illness as normal. Jesus did not.

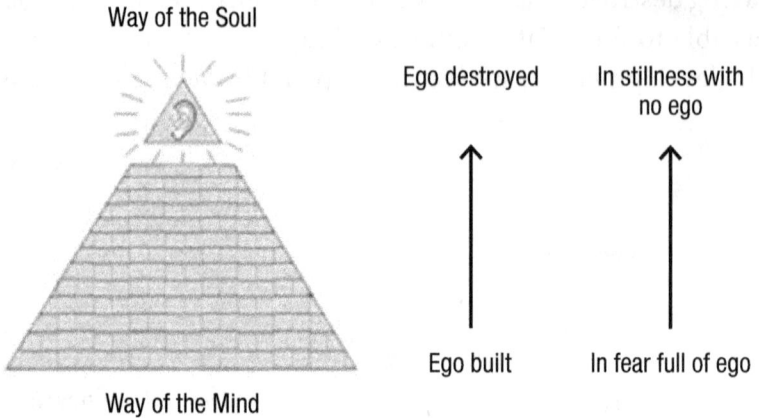

Way of the Soul

Ego destroyed   In stillness with
                        no ego

↑   ↑

Ego built   In fear full of ego

Way of the Mind

GET LOST

Jesus provides a model of a great leader who seeks out those lost on the Way of the Soul in Chapter 20, Poem 7 (Saying 107):

The kingdom, [1]

It
is comparable
to a man
shepherding, [2]

Who
had
he
there
100 sheep. [3]

One
of them
strayed, [4]

The greatest
was
he.[5]

[1]Kingdom: A realm or field of influence ruled by an egoless king or queen.

[2]Man shepherding: A man who loves and guards all.

[3]Sheep: People.

[4]Strayed: Became a non-conformist.

[5]The greatest was he: He became great because he began to soul-know himself and others on his own.

He
let go the 99,[6]

And
he
sought after that one[7]

Until
he
discovered it
troubled.[8]

[6]*99*: Those on the Way of the Mind.

[7]*One*: Rebel.

[8]*Troubled*: Troubled because he knew deep down that he was divided, but he could not find the Way of the Soul to singleness. People conform to group-think in order to avoid emotional trouble.

"And he sought after that one until he found it troubled." People conform to group-think in order to avoid emotional trouble. A non-conformist seeks himself and always finds at first, trouble. Thus, a seeker seeks to stray, to be lost, to be "troubled," and to be found by a wise shepherd. He suffers that quest daily.

The shepherd may be either another person or what he senses directly from his Parents in soul-knowing. If it is another person, he soul-listens to him in love-guardedness to be sure that he protects himself from false messages.

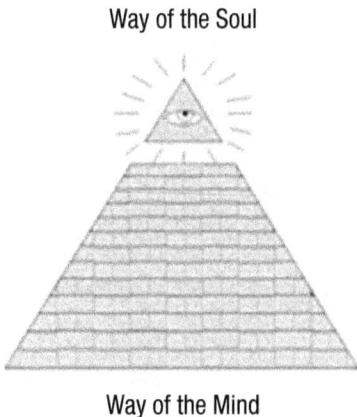

Way of the Soul

Rebels seeking emotional trouble in order to be found by wise shepherds

Conformists seeking emotional comfort from false shepherds

Way of the Mind

BECOME IN THE BEGINNING

Whenever we face any problem, we become emotionally upset, which is a sign that we are living in the past, the future, or in both. When we live in the present, we are never upset. We are movement from stillness.

So whenever we are upset, we know we are on the Way of the Mind; that is, we know that we have identified with our clothes (false identities).

Those who have decided to live on the Way of the Soul therefore seek a shepherd to lead them back to living in the moment. Jesus says that in Poem 1 from Chapter 5 (Saying 18a):

The disciples
said to Jesus:

"Speak to us
this:

Our end[1]
will come to be
in what manner?"

Jesus responded:

"Have
you
revealed yourself
in the beginning,[2]

So that
you
will be seeking
after the end?[3]

For
in the place[4]

[1]*End*: The disciples could have been asking about their personal end after following Jesus.
The disciples could have been asking about the end of Jesus' mission. They could have been asking about the end of times.
In all three of those questions, they seek their end in the future.

[2]*Have you revealed yourself in the beginning*: Have you revealed your true self in the present?

[3]*Have you revealed yourself in the beginning; so that you will be seeking after the end*: Have you become you before you begin to proceed; so that you know and are your goal?

[4]*Place*: That part of us within from which we think and act.

Where

the beginning

is

there,[5]

The end

will come to be

there."[5]

[5]*Where the beginning is
there:* Where stillness in
the now begins to reside.

[5]*For in the place where the
beginning is there, the
end will come to be there:*
For how you begin the
journey to a fulfilled life
is how you will end it.

"Our end will come in what manner?"

The word "end" may have been one of the most thought-about
and used concepts in the 1st century Jewish world. The people
of Palestine were literally being taxed to death by Herod and the
Romans. The people longed for the dignity and freedom that
their ancestors had when David ruled in about 800 B.C.E. They
saw the greed, dishonesty and general lack of living the Torah
in their religious leaders. They longed for a cleansed temple
leadership that would inspire people and not exploit them. And
so they longed for the end to their physical and psychological/
spiritual suffering.

The end of this age of darkness and the beginning of a new age
of light was greatly anticipated because of the predictions of key
Jewish prophets. For example, in Daniel 8:17-19 we read:

> So he came near where I stood; and when he came,
> I was frightened and fell upon my face. But he said
> to me, "Understand, O son of man, that the vision
> is for the time of the end." As he was speaking to
> me, I fell into a deep sleep with my face to the
> ground; but he touched me and set me on my feet.
> He said, "Behold, I will make known to you what
> shall be at the latter end of the indignation; for it
> pertains to the appointed time of the end.

In the above passage, "son of man" refers to the coming Messiah.

About that Messiah, Malachi predicted (Mal. 3:2):

> *But who can endure the day of his coming, and who can stand when he appears? For he is like a refiner's fire and like fullers' soap.*

So the people expected that the Messiah will preach such a strong message, and be such a strong person that one will wonder who can stand in his presence. His message will burn those who are duplicitous, and cleanse those who wish to live a pure life.

Ezra proclaimed the most moving predictions of the coming of the Messiah at the end of this age of corruption:

> *Therefore I say to you, O nations that hear and understand, "Await your shepherd; he will give you everlasting rest, because he who will come at the end of the age is close at hand. (4 Ezra 2:34). But the day of judgment will be the end of this age and the beginning of the immortal age to come, in which corruption has passed away (4 Ezra 7:113)."*

It is also Ezra that spoke specifically about the Messiah who would be of the lineage of David, and how he would first judge the wicked and then free the innocent (4 Ezra 12:32-34).

> *The Messiah whom the Most High has kept until the end of days, who will arise from the posterity of David, and will come and speak to them; he will denounce them for their ungodliness and for their wickedness, and will cast up before them their contemptuous dealings. For first he will set them living before his judgment seat, and when he has reproved them, then he will destroy them. But he will deliver in mercy the remnant of my people, those who have been saved throughout my borders, and he will make them joyful until the*

end comes, the day of judgment, of which I spoke
to you at the beginning

Those are but a few of the many predictions that Jesus' disciples had memorized. Thus when they asked Jesus about the end, we know that it resonated with many deep, powerful personal and community longings:

"Speak to us
this:
Our end
will come to be
in what manner?"

The disciples hoped that Jesus was the Messiah; however, they may not have seen in him what they expected. So in disappointment, they asked him vaguely as a prophet, and not the Messiah, to "tell us how our end will come about."

"Have you revealed yourself in the beginning, so that you will be seeking after the end?"

Jesus did not buy in to their false dream that they would be different when the Messiah arrived. He pointed to their responsibility to be in the beginning. He knew that this is THE task, the most difficult task for a person on his Way. He knew that when they were in the present moment, they would know their end, and know how to seek it in each moment.

"For in the place where the beginning is there, the end will come to be there." For when you change that place from where you live to movement from stillness, you will become the end and the Messiah for yourself and others.

Jesus does not say that there will not be a Messiah; rather he makes that person subordinate to what a person can become on his own. He rephrases Ezra 9:5

> *For just as with everything that has occurred in*
> *the world, the beginning is evident, and the end*
> *manifest.*

Jesus knows that all worry, regret, false-excitement, depression, sadness, fear, longing—all emotional issues will be resolved only when one becomes oneself in the "beginning"; that is, in the present. Once a person knows who he is, his core seeking is over. He proceeds in movement from joyful stillness to solve any secondary problem.

If we begin in movement from regret, worry, or out-of-self excitement, every idea we obtain will lead to more regret, worry, out-of-self excitement, so we learn not to begin like this. We may think or do something that covers up our beginning regret, worry, or out-of-self excitement; however, our problems have not been resolved. Therefore, they will come back to destroy us.

If we begin in movement from joyful stillness, every idea we obtain will always lead to more. We cannot get there from here if here is different from there. If "here" is misery, "there" will be also. If "here" is movement from stillness in the beginning, "there" will be also.

Thus, his core message in that Poem to all of us: Stop dreaming about someone else saving you; you become the savior of yourself and the world by revealing yourself in the beginning.

When we are in emotional pain, our Way of the Mind indoctrination tells us to seek relief in the future. We pray for future relief, we go into the future to buy and read books, to meet with friends to discuss our problems, to distract ourselves by buying things, or by losing ourselves in activities such as

Way of the Soul

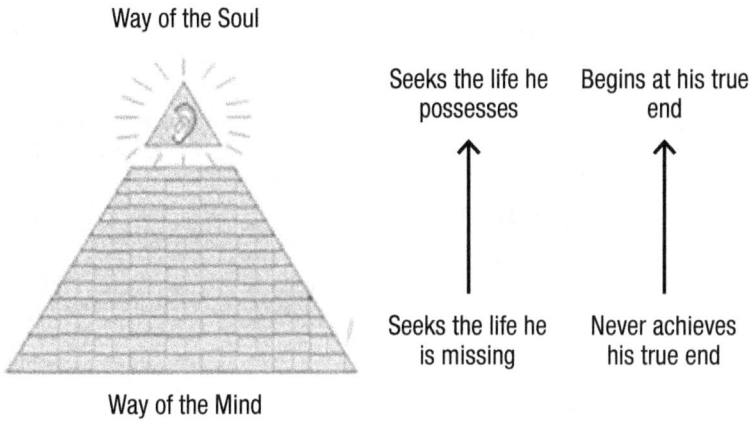

Seeks the life he possesses   Begins at his true end

Seeks the life he is missing   Never achieves his true end

Way of the Mind

sex, music, art, and gambling. We have endless ways of seeking our real, still selves in the future. When we do that, we are like the disciples who sought the end of one age of misery and the beginning of an age of fulfillment.

Everything the Way of the Mind has taught must be reversed or thrown out. Everything. We cannot ride two horses, pull two bows, or serve two lords.

When we are miserable, we might yank ourselves out of the Way of the Mind by reciting to ourselves Poem 3 from Chapter 5 (Saying 19a):

"A blessed one is he who will come to be from the beginning before he comes to be." A blessed one is he who will come to be love-guarded of all before proceeding.

A blessed one[1]

is

he,

Who
will come to be[2]
from the beginning,[3]

Before
he
comes to be.[4]

[1] *A blessed one*: A wise one.

[2] *Will come to be*: Will come to be fully alive in love-guarded of all.

[3] *From the beginning*: From this moment.

[4] *Before he comes to be*: Before he seeks to be involved in the solution of any other problem.

When we are afraid (upset), we dislike what is happening now, what happened in the past, or what might happen in the future. Dislike is mild hate. In other words, all upset arises from fear and hate.

All solutions arise when we are love-guarded from a place of stillness. To be still in the beginning, we need to love-guard what is going on. Recall Poem 5 from Chapter 8 (Saying 25):

Love your brother

Like
your soul.

Guard him

Like
the pupil
of your eye.

"Love your brother like your soul." Love all that has life like your core soul; in other words, love all.

"All" includes all of our mistakes, all of our enemies, all that our enemies did to us, all of our health issues…all the darkness that surrounds us.

To evolve, we must decide which horse we will ride and which bow we will pull: The light horse and the bow of love, or the dark horse and the bow of hate. One horse rides into self-destruction of our ego (false selves) and freedom, the other into enhancement of our ego and enslavement; one into living in the past and future, the other to being oneself in the beginning.

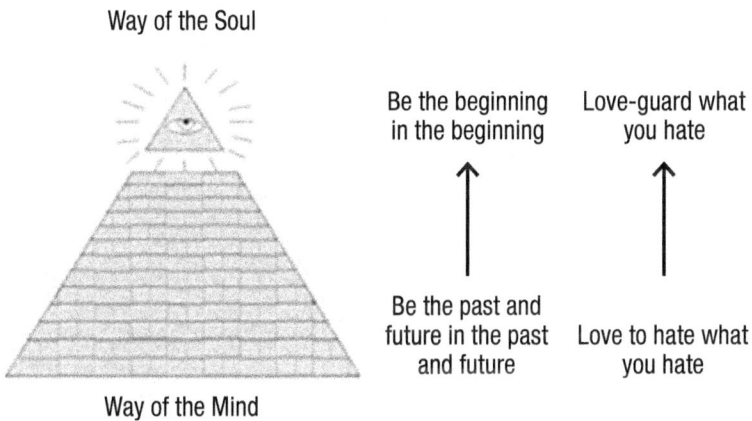

Way of the Soul

Be the beginning   Love-guard what
in the beginning   you hate

↑   ↑

Be the past and
future in the past   Love to hate what
and future   you hate

Way of the Mind

Jesus shows us that by being in the beginning, we attack. In other words, the best defense is a great offense. He says that and more in Chapter 6, Poem 5 (Saying 21):

Jesus
said this:

You
therefore,

Keep watch
from the beginning
of the world, [1,2,3]

Bind yourselves[4]
in a great power;[5]

So that
not
the thieves[6]
discover the entrance[7]
to the way[8]
to come up
to you.[9]

Because,
the help,[10]

[1]*World*: One's world one
creates whenever one
chooses either the Way
of the Soul or the Way of
the Mind.

[2]*Beginning of the world*:
Each moment is the
beginning of one's world.

[3]*Keep watch from the*
beginning of the world:
Stop drifting, be
conscious each moment
of your opportunity to
be present with what is
going on.

[4]*Bind yourselves*: Bind
your loins. Pull yourself
together with conviction.

[5]*Great power*: A strong
sense of your core divine
life. Be love-guarded.

[6]*Thieves*: Those on
the Way of the Mind
including your lower self.

[7]*Discover the entrance*:
Discover your
weaknesses.

[8]*Way*: The Way of the
Soul.

[9]*To come up to you*: To
seduce you.

[10]*Help*: Insights.

For which
you
peer outward,[11]

It
is
that,

Which
will be discovered
in yourselves.[12]

[11]*The help for which*
you peer outward: For
that which you seek
from the Messiah and
from dead people and
their authorities, such
as therapists, clergy,
authors, friends, etc. on
the Way of the Mind.

[12]*It is that which will be*
discovered in yourselves:
It is that which will be
discovered with soul-
knowing in oneness with
They Who Live.

"Keep watch from the beginning of the world." Do not wander through your day and allow yourself to be manipulated into doing the will of a false lord.

"Bind yourselves in a great power." Bring yourself together in love-guarded of all, no matter what happens.

To love all is to experience all as perfect, just the way it is. We fully embrace the worst that has or will happen, from torture to finding out that a loved one has terminal cancer, to the death of our physical bodies.

To guard all is to see the true limitations of all. Nothing is perfect in the sense of being without limitation or fault.

To love/guard all is not to approve all or condemn all. Rather, it is to be love as we face, accept, respect, and sometimes improve all.

"So that not the thieves discover the entrance to the way to come up to you." Our thieves are ourselves ultimately. We leave ourselves vulnerable to surprises. To be alert, one must love-guard the present. The love reveals the essence of everyone and every event. The guarding protects us. Love-guarding is an attitude that the wise foster.

When we love carelessly, we go into a dream about others. When we keep our guard up and do not love, we never see, less enjoy the true nature of others. We love-guard or die.

"For which you peer outward." When unwise, we seek salvation outward in others, such as the perfect mate or friend, the perfect advice, and the all-knowing leader.

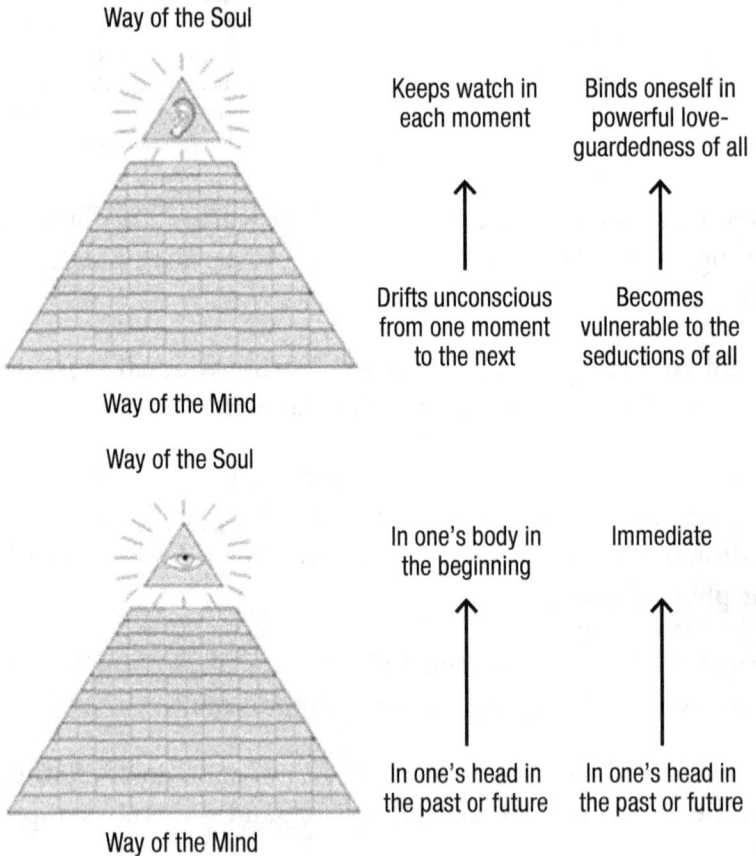

Way of the Soul

Keeps watch in each moment	Binds oneself in powerful love-guardedness of all
↑	↑
Drifts unconscious from one moment to the next	Becomes vulnerable to the seductions of all

Way of the Mind

Way of the Soul

In one's body in the beginning	Immediate
↑	↑
In one's head in the past or future	In one's head in the past or future

Way of the Mind

"It is that which will be discovered in yourselves." Ultimately we need do discover our own answers through soul-knowing, even if the stimulus comes from something someone else says. In the Gospel of Thomas, Jesus gives many examples of people succumbing to thieves breaking into their kingdoms. For example, Chapter 14, Poem 1 (Saying 63a):

Jesus
said this:

There

was

a man

of wealth¹

[1]*Man of wealth:* The man possessed in his core-self everything that he needed, especially the divine intelligence that would lead him to more fulfillment.

Who

had

he

there,²

Many riches.³

[2]*There:* In the beginning.

[3]*Many riches:* He is rich with soul-knowing and with They Who Live within him.

Said

he

this:

"I

will make use

of my riches

by sowing

and

reaping,

and

planting,⁴

and

filling my treasure-house⁵

with fruit;⁶

[4]*Sowing, reaping and planting:* Sowing and reaping, then, planting and reaping, over and over again.

[5]*And filling my treasure-house:* And filling the core of my being.

[6]*Fruit:* Fulfillment.

[7]*So that I will not need anything:* So that I will not worry about needing anything in the future.

So that

I

will

not need anything."⁷

These

were his thoughts

That

were

in his heart;[8]

And

in the night[9]

Which

was

there,[10]

He

died.[11]

[8]*These were the thoughts that were in his heart*: The pivotal thoughts: "Will work for the future so that I will not need anything." In other words: "I am not going to seek myself in the beginning, rather, I am going to seek the money, things, beliefs and people that will ensure that I have a fulfilled self in the future," and then, be in the beginning. These were the thoughts he loved most deeply. He did not love most being himself in the now.

[9]*And in the night*: As soon as he created worry and longing, it became a dark "night" for him.

[10]*Which was there*: Which was in the beginning.

[11]*He died*: He did not physically die. He stopped being alive and started living a false self that stood on beliefs, money, things, and the people that he foolishly thought would bring him what he most deeply wanted in the future.

"So that I will not need anything." When we are not ourselves in the beginning, we need everything. When we are ourselves in the beginning, we need nothing.

The man was empty. He thought he needed money, beliefs, things, and friends to become full. Wanting things or having things is not bad; rather, when we want those fruits more than the fruits that come with being ourselves in the present, we get emotionally sick. In other words, when we fear not having enough, and when we regret all the things we could have done to get more, we choose fear, regret, and false enthusiasm. In that way we die in the "night."

Way of the Soul

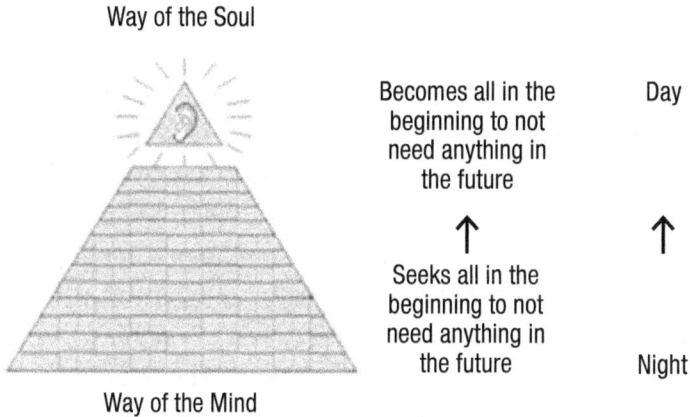

Becomes all in the beginning to not need anything in the future

Day

↑

↑

Seeks all in the beginning to not need anything in the future

Night

Way of the Mind

Remember that Jesus discovered that life has its own intelligence. It moves of its own hand. It knows all. It knows that we need food, friends and other things. When we live the light, which we can only do in the beginning, we are led through soul-knowing to obtain what we need. When we leave our beginning to worry about getting things in the future, we may get them; however, they will be accompanied by greater regret, worry and false excitement.

Jesus indicates that when we become in the beginning, and then we let ourselves be guided to what we most deeply and unconsciously need, we will be led to very different things and people, and a very different life. If we choose to be in the beginning, it will lead us to another beginning. If we choose to be in the future, it will lead us to another unsatisfying future— until we learn that what we want is in the beginning. To prove his point, we only need to reflect on our experience.

So Jesus noticed that our thieves (inner and outer worried voices) tell us that we may not get what we may need in the future, and that we may suffer and even die. So the choice is ours: Be in the beginning and know that even if we physically die, we will never die; or be in the future, and die now, in the next moment, and the next, until we choke on our physical death. Or, to put it another way: we can love our current situation, guard ourselves from its limitations, and then seek to change it; or we can hate our situation while seeking a better situation in the future. The first is Jesus' Way, the second is the way of the world.

We are governed by our present beliefs. If we believe that it all happens by chance, we will forever live in death worry that luck will turn against us. Jesus implies in so many poems that if we suspend our indoctrinated beliefs and look at the evidence that intelligent light has always brought us to the perfect opportunity to evolve, we will see that life is coordinated behind what we see as luck and chance. We must prove to ourselves that we become still and fulfilled when we choose to embrace what we have as perfect, just how it is. The proof is in the pudding, not in the world's blind beliefs.

His summary of his secret for a fulfilled life is in Poem 2 in Chapter 5 (Saying 18a):

Jesus
said this:

A blest one
is
he

Who
will stand on his feet[1]
in the beginning

And
he
will know the end,[2]
And
he
will take a taste
not
of death."[3]

[1]*Stand on his feet*: To be strong, firm and present in the world. To possess all-confidence, because you are one with all.

[2]*And he will know the end*: The divine intelligence that is one with his real self will show him the next step that he can take to accomplish a goal while remaining in the present.

[3]*He will take a taste not of death*: He will not be frustrated, angry, anxious, depressed, grieving, jealous, and full of longing for things in the future.

"A blest one is he who will stand on his feet in the beginning."
A wise one is he who becomes all-confident by standing on
the light that he is in the beginning. A foolish one is he who
becomes self-confident by standing on a person, a family,
a job, a reputation, money, appearance, a nation, a tradition,
indoctrinators, and other people and things that he could lose
and that will never yield movement from stillness.

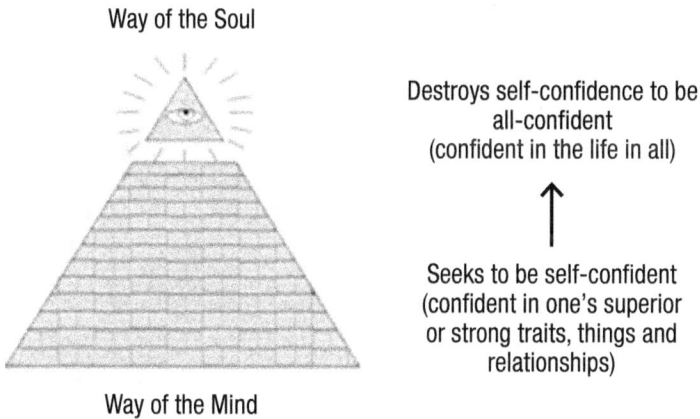

Way of the Soul

Destroys self-confidence to be
all-confident
(confident in the life in all)

↑

Seeks to be self-confident
(confident in one's superior
or strong traits, things and
relationships)

Way of the Mind

"And he will take a taste not of death." Even if he physically
dies. Recall that from a high level of soul-knowing Jesus saw the
evidence that

We
have come outward
of the light,

The place,

Where
the light
comes to be
there,

Outward
by its own hand.

Now, he leaves it up to us to validate his observation that we are eternal light no matter what happens.

Way of the Soul

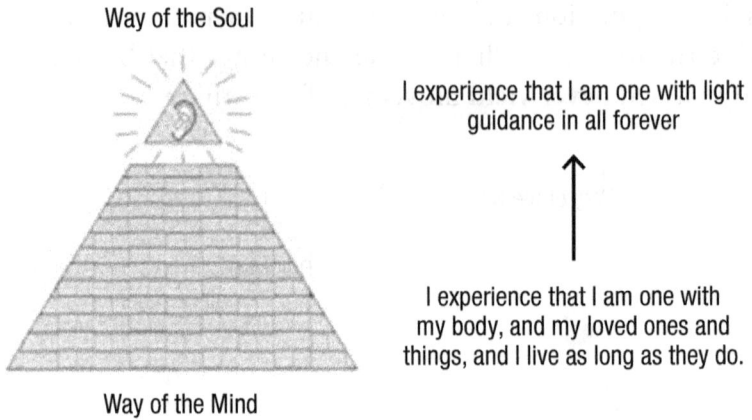

I experience that I am one with light guidance in all forever

I experience that I am one with my body, and my loved ones and things, and I live as long as they do.

Way of the Mind

SEEK AND FIND

Jesus has set a lot of goals, such as

- Be oneself,

- Be love-guarded, and

- Be in the beginning before coming to be.

He also spells out a five-step process to achieve all of the Way of the Soul goals in the following from Chapter 2, Poem 2 (Saying 2):

Jesus
said this:

Let not
him
stop,[1]

[1]*Let not him stop*: Let
not him stop seeking a
higher heaven of life and
soul.

Namely
he,

[2]*He who seeks*: He who
seeks to evolve.

Who
seeks,[2]

[3]*He who seeks as he seeks*:
He who soul-seeks
behind his soul-seeking.
Now that is seeking!

As
he
seeks,[3]

[4]*Finds*: What he most
deeply wants. For
example, our Minds
may want a million
dollars yesterday; while
our souls want us to be
fulfilled at a higher level
of soul and life.

Until
he
finds.[4]

when
he
should find, [5]

[5]*He should find*: An
insight or vision showing
him how he is living the
Way of the Mind and
how he might begin to
live the Way of the Soul.

He
will be
troubled. [6]

[6]*When he should find, he*
will be troubled: When he
should find his false self,
how he lives for others
rather than himself, how
he is dishonest, how he
clings to the past and
yearns for the future
to save him, how...
and how...he will be
troubled.

And if
he
should be
troubled, [7]

[7]*And if he should be*
troubled: And if he works
through his trouble to
resolution at a higher
level of self and other
knowing.

He
will come to
marvel;[10]

And
marveling,

He
will come to
reign[11]
over all;

And
reigning,

He
will come to be
still[12]
with all.

[10]He will come to marvel:
He will come to see
everything in a new,
wonderful way, come to
be amazed that he chose
death rather than life.

[11]And marveling, he will
come to reign: As he
wonders about this new
way to be, he will see
how to rule over himself
and his interactions
with others in a more
enlightened manner.
He will be more noble,
more aware, more wise,
more in control of his
destiny.

[12]And reigning, he will
come to be still: And as he
implements changes, he
will come to enjoy more
deeply being movement
from stillness.

In general, Jesus explains his five-step development process as

1. Seek all day long until you recognize that you are no longer in the beginning, that you are troubled;

2. Seek to know how you became troubled. Keep searching until you soul-see your way out;

3. Seek to know that you have transcended your trouble. You will know that when you marvel that you have risen above yourself to a new way to be;

4. With the new insights, soul-seek to use them to reign as a much stronger, wiser, more authoritative person; and finally,

5. Enjoy being again in the beginning at a new level of freedom and soul.

"Let not him stop, namely he, who seeks, as he seeks, until he finds." All day long, a seeker seeks to know if he has chosen to be in the beginning or in the past or future, that is, if he is movement from stillness, or movement from busyness.

When he experiences regret, worry, or out-of-presence excitement, he knows that he is in the past or future, that he has chosen to not be himself, and that he is not love- guarding everything that happened and will happen. Instead he is running from hate (dislike) of something to false-love (liking) of something else.

For example, a seeker may throughout the day take a moment with his coffee to sit and ask himself, "What am I experiencing?" It will either be regret, worry, out-of-presence excitement, or soul-joy. If it is soul-joy, he knows that he is movement from stillness in the beginning. If it is regret, worry, or false excitement, he knows that he has chosen to be movement from busyness, that he is mulling things from the past, or worrying about something in the future.

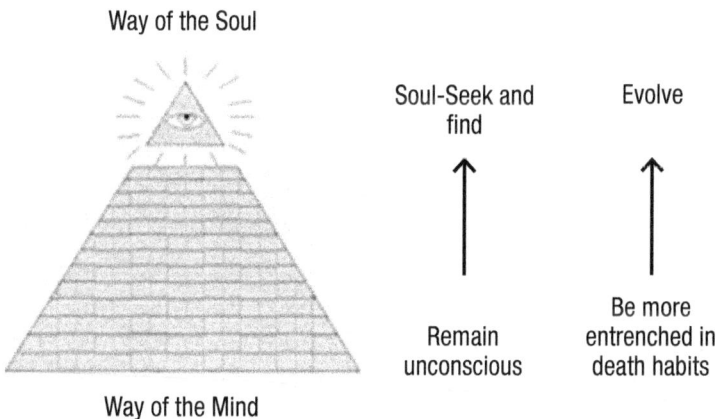

Way of the Soul

Soul-Seek and find	Evolve
↑	↑
Remain unconscious	Be more entrenched in death habits

Way of the Mind

"And when he should find, he will be troubled." When a seeker finds that he is not movement from stillness, he stops everything and seeks to be troubled by the cause of his restlessness. His soul-knowing will eventually show him the false-self and beliefs that he has chosen. It will also show him what he needs to do to evolve.

To continue the previous example, let us suppose that the person sitting with his coffee soul-discovers that he is living in past regret, future worry, or out-of-presence excitement. Now he is troubled to find himself there and seeks to move from there to the beginning.

He does that by soul-asking himself, "What would I need to give up to be now in the beginning?" After some time, it may be revealed to him that he

- Might sacrifice being on time for something in order to be still with his coffee until he enjoys the table, the scene out the window, his body, his problems, his successes and himself, more than anything else in the past or future,

- Might sacrifice disliking someone to love-guard that person,

- Might sacrifice regretting a mistake to love-guard himself and all that happened, or

- Might sacrifice being excited to soul-recognizing that he has all now.

Ultimately, to be again in the beginning, he will need to choose to be love-guarded in the world rather than have or be anything else. In love-guardedness, one finds himself.

All of us find it difficult to understand love-guardedness. The term says everything and nothing. It is an experience unlike any other. It is the transcendent "high" experience one seeks in sex, drugs, creativity and thrills.

When one love-guards, he does NOT approve of a person or an event. One embraces the person or event as exactly as the person or event is, rather than run from him or it. It is open-hearted being one with all.

When one guards, one recognizes the limitations and darkness in it for him. Love-guarding is not fools love, or guarding without loving either.

When a woman finds herself at an awkward moment not able to be intimate because of a flashback to a molestation event, how does she pull herself together and love-guard the perpetrator and every detail in that event? She can only do that through the power of Light that she opens to live.

When one recognizes that he has cancer and a young family, how does he love guard himself, the disease, and all that he wants to curse? He can only do that by dying to the false self that wants to be angry, sad and anxious.

When a man hears a bang and begins to tremble because what he experienced in combat stole his body-awareness that life is safe, how does he love-guard so many horrors? Only soul-knowing can show him how.

Ultimately, we all have Post-Traumatic Stress Disorder (PTSD) in some form. A child body-knows that he is safe; thus, he does not have PTSD. As we live, we get brainwashed into believing that bad luck happens, or a good God causes bad things to happen, or that life isn't fair, or some other ultimately terrifying nonsense. Then, we find evidence that those beliefs are true. And then, if we experience a truly horrific event, we body-lose all sense of being safe.

The only way out is to evolve on Jesus' Way of the Soul. We must re-experience all that haunts us, all that we project will haunt us, and become in the beginning with those people and events in love-guardedness. Gradually, we will know that nothing truly dies, and that we are safe.

For example, a person has a flashback to the experience of when an IED killed his buddy and maimed him. At that moment, he must immediately become one with something real, such as a child or the smile of a friend, so that he can ground himself,. As he opens to become one with the life in the child or friend, his body begins to open to see that the IED event was also full of perfect life. As he continues to open and be one with real life, he will also body-realize that death is impossible. Everything continues perfectly.

That is not something one mentally believes. He must come to it on his own, through soul-knowing people, animals and plants that scream "Life!" louder than his memory of the IED.

No matter how many times we relive a past painful event, the bottom line is this: it brought us to this beginning moment where we have the choice to choose to love what happened as perfect, just how it was, and to be more wisely guarded. We either choose to do that and evolve to a higher level of heaven, or we devolve into more self-and other-destroying darkness. We cannot regret our way out of regret, or worry our way out of worries; we cannot believe our way out of darkness, or suppress our feelings and thoughts in order to get out. We can only love-guard our way out. The choice to be love rather than to be regret/worried/falsely excited can be the most courageous act that we perform.

For some, that is a very tough journey to make. However, those who do are the leaders who will show the rest of us the way.

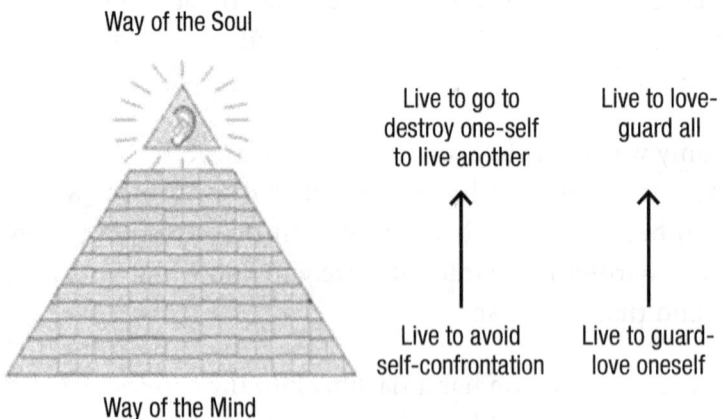

Way of the Soul

Live to go to destroy one-self to live another	Live to love-guard all
↑	↑
Live to avoid self-confrontation	Live to guard-love oneself

Way of the Mind

"And if he should be troubled, he will come to marvel." If he should be troubled and then, evolve out of it, he will marvel.

When we release ourselves from the past and future and become again in the beginning, experiencing movement from stillness and our real selves, it can be the ultimate high. People describe "transcendence" in many ways: Some say: "I feel I have become again," or "I sense that I have moved to a new level of wonderful living," or "I am full of energy and insight," or "I now look back on what seemed so horrible and see it as a gift."

Sometimes, transcendence accompanies a sense of being one with all, being clear, being more independent, being creative, being in-touch, being more alive, being more love-guarded, and being fulfilled. Those on the Way of the Soul crave trouble and its release to transcendence.

The Way of the Soul

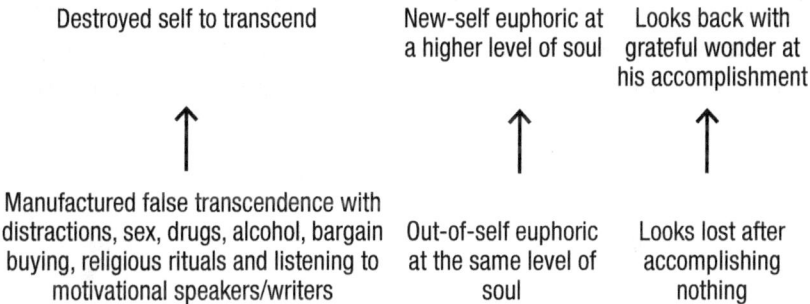

Destroyed self to transcend	New-self euphoric at a higher level of soul	Looks back with grateful wonder at his accomplishment
↑	↑	↑
Manufactured false transcendence with distractions, sex, drugs, alcohol, bargain buying, religious rituals and listening to motivational speakers/writers	Out-of-self euphoric at the same level of soul	Looks lost after accomplishing nothing

The Way of the Mind

"And marveling, he will come to reign over all." After one comes to marvel, one possesses the clarity and soul to navigate life much more wisely.

Pity the unwise who confront a person who has suffered so much to reign. That lion or lioness will eat that man alive.

Way of the Soul

	Solutions to difficult and impossible problems easily seen	Walks and talks from a new-found soul and power
	↑	↑
	Angrily stymied by one's own and others' incompetence	Gradually devolving into weakness and impotence

Way of the Mind

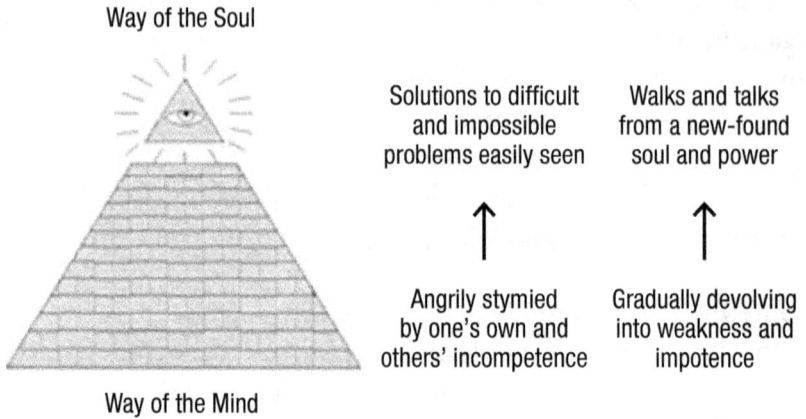

"And reigning, he will come to be still with all." The person who rules at a higher level also rests at a higher level in his new-found awareness. He may be found walking hand –in-hand in stillness with someone he loves; or chatting with someone sensitively and slowly; or simply sitting in a park watching the leaves blow in the wind, knowing that the universe has just been reset for him.

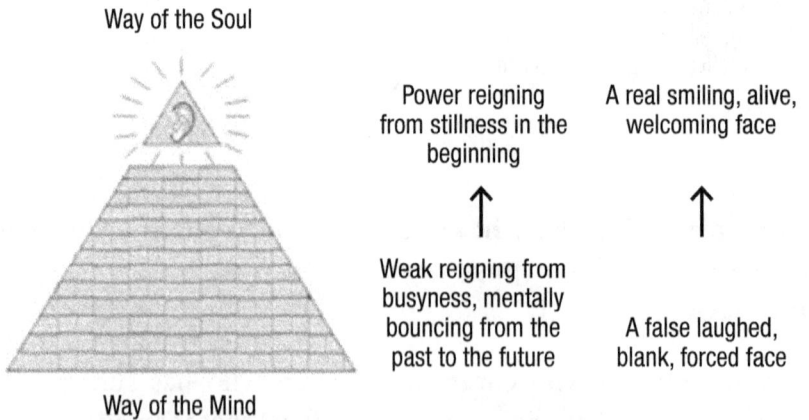

Way of the Soul

	Power reigning from stillness in the beginning	A real smiling, alive, welcoming face
	↑	↑
	Weak reigning from busyness, mentally bouncing from the past to the future	A false laughed, blank, forced face

Way of the Mind

On the Way of the Soul, one seeks more than "opposite" experiences. He seeks "higher-dimensional" experiences.

Jesus' Five Steps to Sanity and Fulfillment

- **Step One**: Seeks an experience which tells him he has chosen regret, worry, and false-excitement, rather than stillness in the beginning.

- **Step Two**: Seeks the experience of self-confrontation with the ways he has chosen to be weak and false.

- **Step Three**: Seeks the experience of wonder when he has released himself from the grip of false solutions.

- **Step Four**: Seeks the experience of being a more powerful ruler over himself and his interactions with others.

- **Step Five**: Seeks the experience of resting more powerfully in a deeper stillness in the beginning.

The bottom line: What we seek is what we find, live, enjoy or suffer.

CHAPTER SEVEN

PAUL'S SELF-DEVELOPMENT METHOD

BE SAVED BY YOUR FAITH IN PAUL'S GOSPEL

We left Paul outside of Jerusalem, on his way to find non-Jews outside of Israel who would adopt his gospel. We saw that Paul concluded that the redemption of humankind involved two steps: reconciliation and salvation. God fulfilled the first step when, according to Paul but *not* according to Jesus, He lovingly sent his Son, Jesus, in the likeness of human sinful flesh to sacrifice himself on the cross. When that happened, God ceased to be an enemy of humankind.

However, according to Paul, humankind must acknowledge Jesus' sacrifice in order to be saved. They do that by believing in Paul's "gospel of God," not by following Jesus' Way, and not by following the Torah's laws. He says in Rom. 3:28:

> *For we hold that a man is justified by faith apart from works of law.*

"For we hold that a man is justified by faith apart from works of law." We believe that a man is saved by his faith in my (Paul's) gospel and not by anything he does.

In other words, a person becomes one again with God (saved), as he was before Adam's sin, when he trusts in Paul's ideas about Jesus--the same ideas that Jesus never believed in or lived.

Paul makes no logical sense. He tells people to believe in the Son of God, who contradicted Paul, in order to be united with the Son of God.

Way of the Soul

Jesus: We evolve when we stop
identifying with our doctrines

Paul: We become "saved" when we
have faith in (identify with) Paul's
doctrine

Way of the Mind

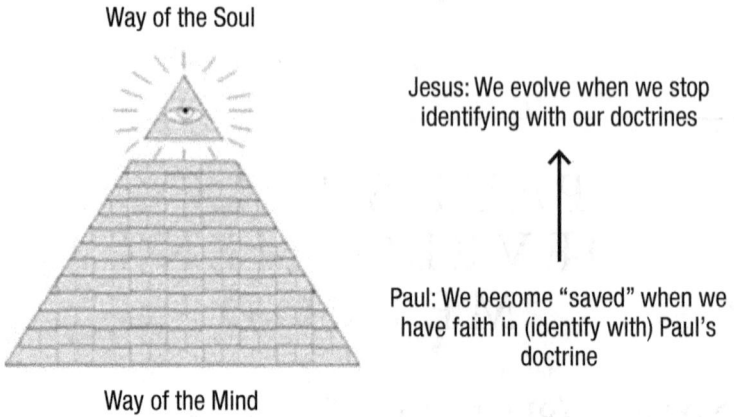

AVOID EVIL DEEDS

Paul then contradicts himself in Gal. 5:19-21:

> *Now the works of the flesh are plain: fornication,*
> *impurity, licentiousness, idolatry, sorcery, enmity,*
> *strife, jealousy, anger, selfishness, dissension,*
> *party spirit, envy, drunkenness, carousing, and*
> *the like. I warn you, as I warned you before, that*
> *those who do such things shall not inherit the*
> *kingdom of God.*

**"I warn you, as I warned you before, that those who do such
things shall not inherit the kingdom of God."** I am warning
you again: obey the laws or you will not be saved.

Paul changed his own theology. At first, he claimed a person
was "saved" through faith alone. He then retracted that notion,
claiming that there are things a person must *do* in addition to
having faith.

OBEY PAUL'S LAWS

Paul even gets quite specific about how a person should behave,
especially toward women, as we see in 1 Cor. 11: 3-8:

But I want you to understand that the head of every man is Christ, the head of a woman is her husband, and the head of Christ is God...but any woman who prays or prophesies with her head unveiled dishonors her head -- it is the same as if her head were shaven. For if a woman will not veil herself, then she should cut off her hair; but if it is disgraceful for a woman to be shorn or shaven, let her wear a veil. For a man ought not to cover his head, since he is the image and glory of God; but woman is the glory of man. For man was not made from woman, but woman from man...That is why a woman ought to have a veil on her head, because of the angels.

In this passage, Paul sets up a hierarchy of authority, again, that implies a lack of logic.

The topmost authority is Jesus, who never made any pronouncements about women like the pronouncements made by Paul.

A husband must follow the laws of Jesus, which Paul does not disclose. Instead, he discloses his own laws.

No one could possibly live as Paul requires. You cannot follow Christ when you do not know what he said, and when you are told to obey laws that he never declared.

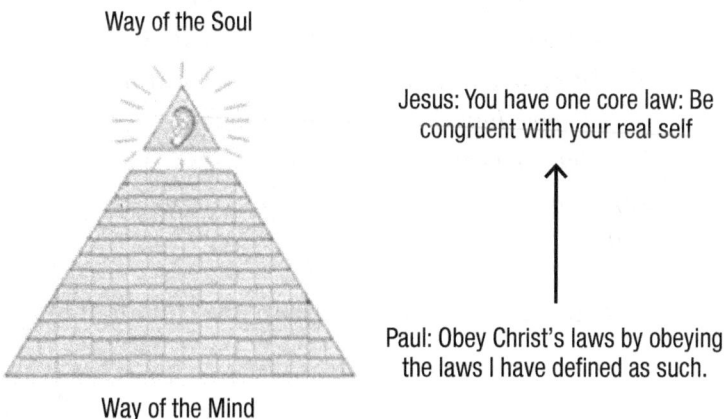

Way of the Soul

Jesus: You have one core law: Be congruent with your real self

Paul: Obey Christ's laws by obeying the laws I have defined as such.

Way of the Mind

Do Good

Many people associate Jesus with ordering his followers to do good deeds for others. He actually spoke little about that, as we have seen so far. He left it up to individuals to soul-know how to love-guard all.

Note well: In Rom. 12: 9-21, Paul spoke the commands that people associate with Jesus:

> *Let love be genuine; hate what is evil, hold fast to what is good; love one another with brotherly affection; outdo one another in showing honor. Never flag in zeal, be aglow with the Spirit, serve the Lord. Rejoice in your hope, be patient in tribulation, be constant in prayer. Contribute to the needs of the saints, practice hospitality.*

> *Bless those who persecute you; bless and do not curse them. Rejoice with those who rejoice, weep with those who weep. Live in harmony with one another; do not be haughty, but associate with the lowly; never be conceited. Repay no one evil for evil, but take thought for what is noble in the sight of all. If possible, so far as it depends upon you, live peaceably with all.*

> *Beloved, never avenge yourselves, but leave it to the wrath of God; for it is written, "Vengeance is mine, I will repay, says the Lord." (Deut. 32:35) No, "if your enemy is hungry, feed him; if he is thirsty, give him drink; for by so doing you will heap burning coals upon his head." (Prov. 25:21-22) Do not be overcome by evil, but overcome evil with good.*

"Let love be genuine." Do not pretend to love, but do it honestly.

"Hate what is evil." Hate evil actions and thoughts.

"Hold fast to what is good." Remain in accord with Paul's notions of "good."

"Love one another with brotherly affection." Love your neighbor.

"Outdo one another in showing honor." Do not be content to be average in honoring God.

"Never flag in zeal." Remain steadfast in the intensity of your faith.

"Be aglow with the Spirit, serve the Lord." Be radiant in your connection with God.

"Rejoice in your hope." Rejoice in your hope that by living according to Paul's doctrine, you will be saved.

"Be patient in tribulation." Be patient when others persecute you for the way you live.

"Be constant in prayer." Continually be one with God.

"Contribute to the needs of the saints." Support those who are recognized as living by Paul's doctrine.

"Practice hospitality." Welcome people to your homes.

"Bless those who persecute you; bless and do not curse them." Make holy those who persecute you; do not hate them.

"Rejoice with those who rejoice, weep with those who weep." Rejoice and weep with good and bad people equally, no matter the reasons for their rejoicing and weeping.

"Live in harmony with one another." Be peaceful with one another.

"Do not be haughty, but associate with the lowly." Do not be arrogant, but associate with those who are overlooked by others and/or who do not assert themselves.

"Never be conceited." Do not be vain.

"Repay no one evil for evil, but take thought for what is noble in the sight of all." Do not do what I define as "bad" to those who do bad things to you or to others.

"If possible, so far as it depends upon you, live peaceably with all." Live in peace with people who do loving and unloving things.

"Beloved, never avenge yourselves, but leave it to the wrath of God; for it is written, 'Vengeance is mine, I will repay, says the Lord.'" (Deut. 32:35). Do not seek revenge. God will visit his wrath upon those who harm you.

"If your enemy is hungry, feed him; if he is thirsty, give him drink; for by so doing you will heap burning coals upon his head." Give food and drink to your enemy if he is in need; for by doing so, you will humble him.

"Do not be overcome by evil, but overcome evil with good." Stand up to those who do not live Paul's doctrine by living it fully yourself.

Many people associate those statements with Jesus, however, Jesus never left such a list of guidelines or laws.

Paul desired to control the thinking and behavior of people, while Jesus did not.

Paul commanded people to love; Jesus taught people to love-guard.

Paul asked people to be peaceful, Jesus expected his disciples to be "fire, sword, and war" in the world.

INDOCTRINATE NON-BELIEVERS

Way of the Soul

Jesus: I am not your master.

Paul: I am your master.

Way of the Mind

Paul's command to ensure the continuance of his legacy is stated in 1 Cor. 4:14-16:

> *I do not write this to make you ashamed, but to admonish you as my beloved children. For though you have countless guides in Christ, you do not have many fathers. For I became your father in Christ Jesus through the gospel. I urge you, then, be imitators of me.*

"I do not write this to make you ashamed, but to admonish you as my beloved children." I write to you to scold you as a parent to a child, because you have not done as I told you to do.

"For though you have countless guides in Christ, you do not have many fathers, for I became your father in Christ Jesus through the gospel." I am your father, that is, your ultimate authority, even when you are guided by Christ.

"I urge you, then, be imitators of me." Teach exactly what I taught you.

That may be the strongest statement of Paul's desire to be the ultimate authority over the thoughts and behavior of everyone in his church. He had no intention of freeing people to use soul-knowing to make decisions for themselves. He desired to control every aspect of their lives, while manipulating them into thinking that they did the will of Jesus and, through him, the will of God.

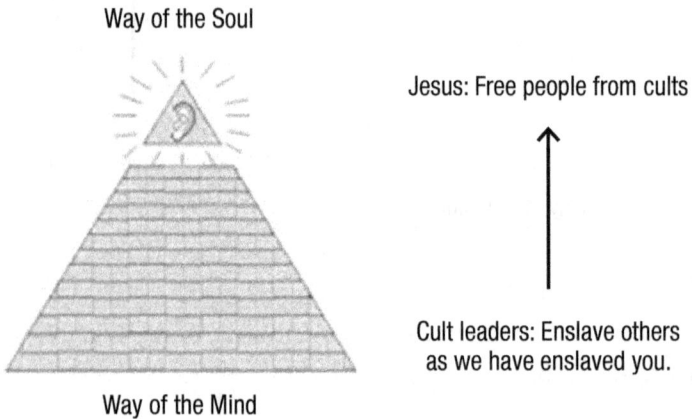

Way of the Soul

Jesus: Free people from cults

Cult leaders: Enslave others
as we have enslaved you.

Way of the Mind

Cult leaders are everywhere today. Jesus spoke of them in Chapter 20, Poem 1 (Saying 102):

Woe to them,

The Pharisees,[1]

For
they
resemble
a dog[2]

He
resting.[3]

[1]*Pharisees*: Those who indoctrinate rather than teach people how to listen and discover their own hidden soul.

[2]*Dog*: The lowest of the low in character. Dogs gathered at the garbage dumps to eat.

[3]*Resting*: Not laboring to soul-know and discover the meaning of what he heard.

He
upon the manger[4]
of some oxen.[5]

For
he
eats[6]
not,[7]

And
he
permits
not the oxen
to eat.[8]

[4]*Manger*: Place where people go to get their answers.

[5]*Oxen*: People on the Way of the Mind. Those not discovering hidden soul.

[6]*Eats*: Soul-knows and integrates what he hears.

[7]*For he eats not*: The indoctrinators do not soul-know; and thus, do not live from He Who Lives.

[8]*He permits not the oxen to eat*: Indoctrinators hinder people who are inspired with ideas that differ from the group's doctrine by telling them that they are wrong. In that way, they force people to conform to the group's Way.

Way of the Soul

Jesus: Eat from the soul that
is revealed to you

Cult leaders: Eat from our
hand

Way of the Mind

Way of the Soul

Jesus: Love-guard people who
identify with doctrines

Indoctrinators: Demonize
people who disagree with
"our" official doctrine

Way of the Mind

CHAPTER EIGHT

THE RESULTS OF LIVING JESUS' WAY OF THE SOUL

INTRODUCTION

If we were to ask people today, "What picture comes to your Mind when you think of a person who follows Jesus' Way perfectly," they would probably describe Mary, the mother of Jesus, or a saint.

Jesus, on the other hand, would present the picture of a mountain. Yes, a mountain.

Let us explore why.

A Mountain

Twice in the Gospel, Jesus repeats the Mountain Poem. In it, he announces the importance of us becoming a mountain.

The first instance of the Mountain Poem is in the centerpiece of the Gospel, Chapter 11. It is Poem 3 (Saying 48) of that chapter:

Jesus
said this:

Should
two[1]
make peace
with each other[2]
in this house[3]
unified,[4]

They
will speak
to the mountain
this:[5,6]

"Move,"[7]

And
it
will move.[8]

[1]*Should two*: Two beings in one person, one's real self and God.

[2]*Should two make peace with each other*: Should a person follow the Way of the Soul and become congruent with God, such that they possess the same life, power and Light intelligence.

[3]*House*: A person.

[4]*Should two make peace... unified*: Should two who have been battling become one.

[5]*Mountain*: A person who lives in powerful stillness, standing high on his own feet above all others.

[6]*Should...they will speak to the mountain this*: Should a person in oneness with They-who-live-within say to himself:

[7]*Move*: Be movement from stillness.

[8]*It will move*: The still person will move in the world.

"Should two make peace with each other in this house unified." Should two parts of oneself, the false self and the real self, become one in a person…

When we think of an evolved, powerful, independent person, we may think of someone whose strength arises from his physical prowess, his intelligence, his experience, or his money. At times, we may think of a person of character; however, do we go further and describe to ourselves what gives a person character.

Jesus did reflect on character. He concluded that an evolved person was one who had become congruent with himself; in other words, one who made peace between his false self and his real self. One does that when one acknowledges his false self but acts from his real self.

"They will speak to the mountain this:" In the Bible, a "mountain" is an evolved person. When an author describes someone as "going up on the mountain," he means that the person goes high up within himself to communicate directly with God through soul-knowing. Therefore, one goal of this Gospel is to enable every person to go up on the mountain and communicate directly with his source of inspiration.

Everyone does that at times. For example, when an artist goes to a special environment to be still and receive insights, he goes high up on the mountain to communicate with God. He may not call God "God," but what he calls his source of inspiration is not important.

Jesus recognized that a mountain was the perfect symbol for a person who has become congruent with his real self. He is self-contained; he speaks from the core life that Jesus found divine. He has become a mountain of a person.

"They will speak to the mountain this: "'Move,' and it will move." The tangible sign of a person who is one with his divine Light is movement from stillness. That person is still in the world, like the images we see of the Buddha. However, that person also moves in the world.

A person, who is very still and powerful is, for Jesus, like a mountain. He was in awe that such stillness could move. So, a mountain became his symbol for an evolved person, not a person with a halo.

Way of the Soul

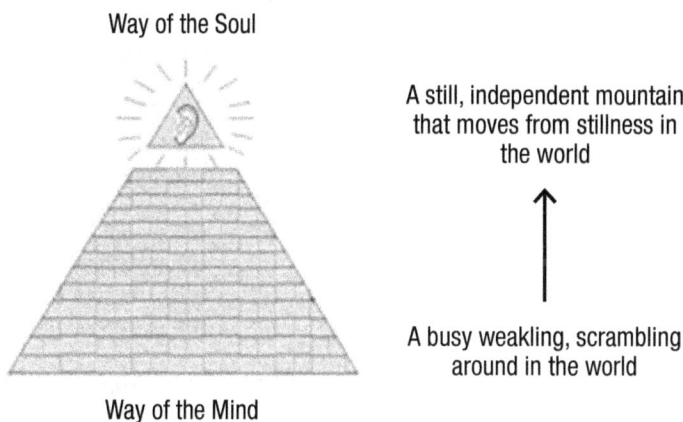

A still, independent mountain that moves from stillness in the world

A busy weakling, scrambling around in the world

Way of the Mind

A KINGDOM

Jesus also used the metaphor of the kingdom to describe a person who has evolved on his Way. In Chapter 21, Poem 7 (Saying 113), Jesus indicates that many such kingdoms exist unseen, and that they are spreading:

His disciples
asked him:

"The kingdom,[1,2]

[1]*Kingdom*: For Jesus, an environment ruled by an individual to the degree that he is one with himself.

[2]*Kingdom*: For the disciples, Palestine after the Messiah drives out the Romans and restores it in the likeness of David's kingdom.

It
is coming
on which day?"[3]

Jesus
responded:

"The kingdom,
comes
not in watching.[4]

They[5]
will say
not this:

'Behold here,'
or
'Behold there.'[6]

Rather
the kingdom
of the Father
is spreading
upon the earth,[7]

And
men[8]
peer
not upon it.[9]

[3]*Day*: A time when the Messiah will drive the invaders out of Israel. A time when the Messiah would cleanse the Temple, and bring everyone to worship the one true God.

[4]*The kingdom comes not in watching*: The kingdom will not come because you disciples stand around watching for what you could not and will not recognize.

[5]*They*: People on the Way of the Mind.

[6]*They will say not this, "behold here" or "behold there:"* They will not see what they are expecting.

[7]*Upon the earth*: Upon the reflective consciousness in people following the Way of the Soul.

[8]*Men*: Those following the Way of the Mind.

[9]*Peer not upon it*: Cannot see what is right in front of them.

Way of the Soul

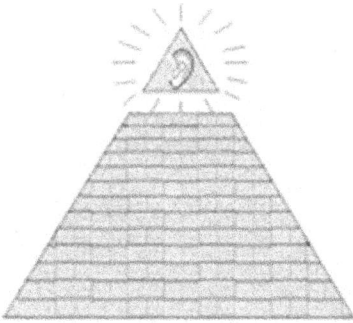

The light kingdom seen in
themselves and others by those
living light

↑

The light kingdom unseen by
those living darkness

Way of the Mind

Way of the Soul

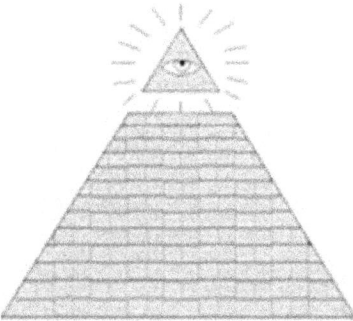

The kingdom exists today in the
consciousness of some people

↑

The kingdom does not exist today
because we cannot see it

Way of the Mind

A TWIN

Jesus also says that those who have evolved on his Way become twins. The Prologue (Saying 1) states that:

Poem 1
These
are
the words…

Which…
Jesus…
spoke.[1]

[1] *These are the words…*
which Jesus spoke: These
are the soul poems that
Jesus composed.

Poem 2
And
he
wrote them,

Namely
the twin[2]

Judas,[3,4]

Also
called
"Twin."[5]

[2] *The Twin*: In the text, we find the Greek word "Didymus," meaning, "twin."

[3] *Judas*: Jesus had two disciples named Judas.

[4] *And he wrote...Judas*: Judas, also called Thomas, wrote the poems down as Jesus' scribe.

[5] *Twin*: In the text, we find the Aramaic word "Thomas," meaning, "twin." Judas was also called Thomas or Twin. Therefore, we know that this Judas had a twin brother or sister.

"These are the words which Jesus spoke." These are the soul words that Jesus spoke.

"And he wrote them, namely, the twin Judas, also called "Twin." And Judas, called "Twin," wrote down Jesus' words.

When Jesus used "twin" twice in the same poem in such a strange manner, and when that Poem occurs in the Prologue, he points to the fact that this Gospel is about becoming a twin, as Judas did. That is a deliberate, carefully-constructed sentence.

The author never uses the word, "twin" again in the Gospel; however, he defines a person who is fully evolved on the Way of the Soul as a twin in other manners. For example, in the Child Poem (page 30), he says: "they will come to be single ones." He means as people evolve to be little children again, they will each become congruent with who he is at his core, divine life. In other words, one becomes a twin of God.

Above, we read that a person becomes a twin of himself when he makes peace between his false self and his real self. In Chapter 21, Poem 2 (Saying 106), Jesus says that a person also makes peace with others by becoming their twin. Below, note especially that the word "you" is plural.

When

you (pl)

should make the two

the one[1]

[1]*When you (pl) should make the two the one:* When you people should become one with the divine life in each of you.

You (pl)

will come to be,

the sons of Man.[2]

[2]*You will come to be sons of Man.* You will become sons of God.

In that context, to "make the two, the one" means one is to become the twin of everyone, because all have the same core life.

Jesus defined "sons of Man" in a previous poem (Poem 5) that we studied from Chapter 2 (Saying 3b):

When

you

should know yourselves;

Then

they

will know you,

And

you

will realize

That

you

are

sons

of the Father.

The phrase "sons of Man" in the former Poem parallels "sons of the Father" in the this one. (That is the way the Semitic authors define their terms.) Thus, we know that in this Gospel, "sons of Man" means "sons of the Father." Further, when we combine what we know from the "Mother" Poems, we know that "sons of Man" means "sons of the Father and Mother."

The Gospel came to be called the Gospel of Thomas. Because "Thomas" means "twin," the original name of the Gospel was probably intended to be understood as the "Gospel of the Twin."

Way of the Soul

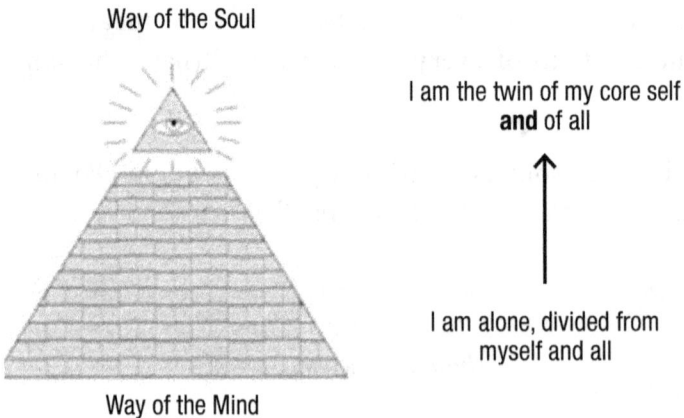

I am the twin of my core self **and** of all

I am alone, divided from myself and all

Way of the Mind

AN EMPTY ONE

Jesus also thought of a person who has become fulfilled on his Way as a person who is empty of ego and false selves. A person must become empty like a cup in order to become full on the Way of the Soul. Jesus tells us that in Chapter 19, Poem 3 (Saying 97):

The kingdom
of the Father,

It
is comparable
to a woman
bearing a jar,[1]

It
full of meal,[2]

She
walking on a way,[3]

It
far away.[4]
The ear
of the jar
broke,[5]

And
the meal
emptied out[6]
after her
along the way,

And
she
knew
not what
was happening,[7]

And
she
did
not realize any trouble.[8]

[1]*Jar*: What contains our false selves. We call it the "ego."

[2]*Meal*: False identifications that we consume.

[3]*She walking on a way*: She transitioning from the Way of the Mind to the Way of the Soul.

[4]*It far away*: It being a long journey.

[5]*The ear of the jar broke*: One of ego's ears broke. In other words, a person deliberately stopped listening with their [2] ears and began soul-listening with their third ear.

[6]*And the meal emptied out*: Her false selves fell upon the earth, without her even realizing it, so focused was she on her path (of soul-listening).

[7]*And she knew not what was happening*: And as she enjoyed becoming more alive and wise, she did not notice that her false selves were leaving her.

[8]*And she did not realize any trouble*: Like a woman after she gave birth, she did not realize the trouble, because of the joys she was experiencing.

When
she
opened inward
to her house,⁹

She
released the jar
down,⁹

And
she
discovered it
being
empty.¹¹

⁹*When she opened inward*
to her house: When she
reflected on who she had
become.

¹⁰*She released the jar*
down: She emptied her
ego.

¹¹*And she discovered it*
being empty: Her ego was
empty.

Way of the Soul

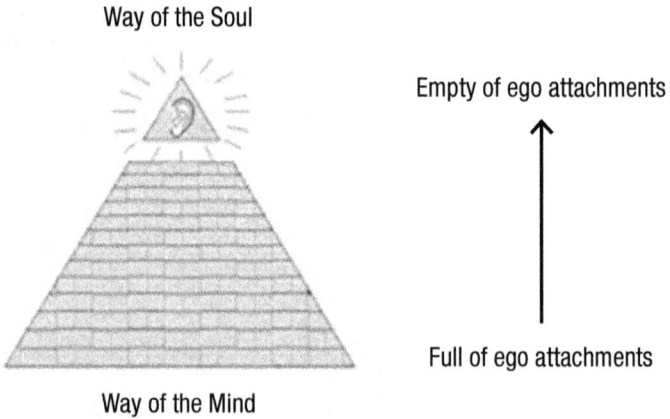

Empty of ego attachments

Full of ego attachments

Way of the Mind

INVULNERABILITY

As a mountain is invulnerable, so Jesus viewed an evolved person. Those following his Way will discover themselves blessed, but hated and persecuted--and love it. They react positively to attacks because they have become invulnerable. Jesus tells us why in Chapter 1, Poem 3 (Saying 68):

Jesus
said this:

You
are
the blest ones[1]

When
they[2]
hate you[3]

And
persecute you;[4]

For
they
will discover
not any place[5]

Where
you
have
not persecuted yourselves.[6]

[1]*Blest ones*: People one with their core divine life.

[2]*They*: People on the Way of the Mind.

[3]*When they hate you*: When they hate you for being the children of God.

[4]*And persecute you*: And make life difficult for you.

[5]*Place*: A vulnerable spot within you that can be exploited to control your thinking and behavior.

[6]*For they will discover not any place where you have not persecuted yourselves*: They will not find a weakness in your character that you have not examined and transcended.

Way of the Soul

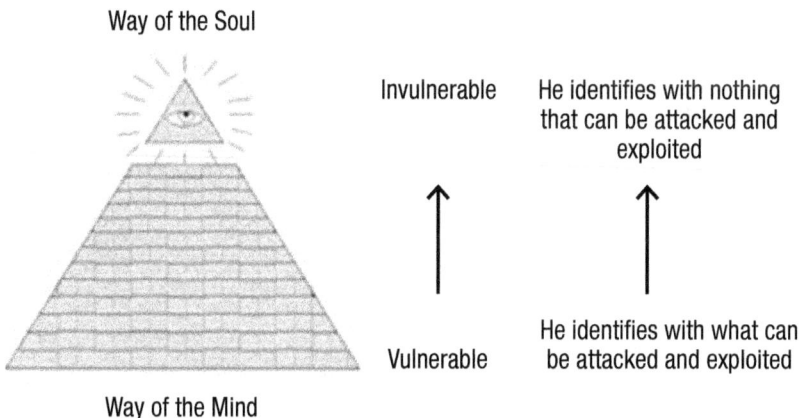

Invulnerable — He identifies with nothing that can be attacked and exploited

Vulnerable — He identifies with what can be attacked and exploited

Way of the Mind

A Child and a Lion

We saw previously that Jesus told us that on his Way we would return to the childlike kingdom in which we were born. That is the kingdom marked by congruence with oneself. He also visualized a person becoming a lion that would not permit indoctrinators to seduce him into following the Way of the Mind. Thus, Jesus' evolved person is the seemingly contradictory characteristics of being both a child who loves all and a lion that guards himself from all.

CHAPTER NINE

THE RESULTS OF LIVING PAUL'S WAY OF THE MIND

SALVATION AND RIGHTEOUSNESS

Paul created a doctrine-based gospel and staked his life and legacy on everyone believing it. To ensure that they complied, he interwove his letters with intangible rewards for his acolytes. In Rom. 1:16-17, we read

> For I am not ashamed of the gospel, because it is the power of God that brings salvation to everyone who believes: first to the Jew, then to the Gentile. For in the gospel the righteousness of God is revealed—a righteousness that is by faith from first to last, just as it is written: "The righteous will live by faith."

"**For I am not ashamed of the gospel, because it is the power of God that brings salvation to everyone who believes.**" I am not ashamed of my gospel (not the gospel of Jesus), because it is the power of God that brings salvation to everyone that believes.

As we saw above, Jesus had a different gospel. Further, he never said that one must believe it word for word. Rather, he said, one should live it in his own way by following his inspiration. Jesus laid out a process for personal development, not a doctrine to be believed. He knew that people could believe in a creed and not be changed by it.

"It...brings salvation to everyone who believes: first to the Jew, then to the Gentile." The gospel favors the Jews over the Gentiles when it comes time for God to reward believers.

According to Paul, we are not all equal. Race and traditions determine one's essential value in God's eyes. Some people are more favored for salvation than others.

"For in the gospel the righteousness of God is revealed—a righteousness that is by faith from first to last, just as it is written: 'The righteous will live by faith.'" One experiences the "righteousness of God" through his faith in Paul's doctrine.

Way of the Soul

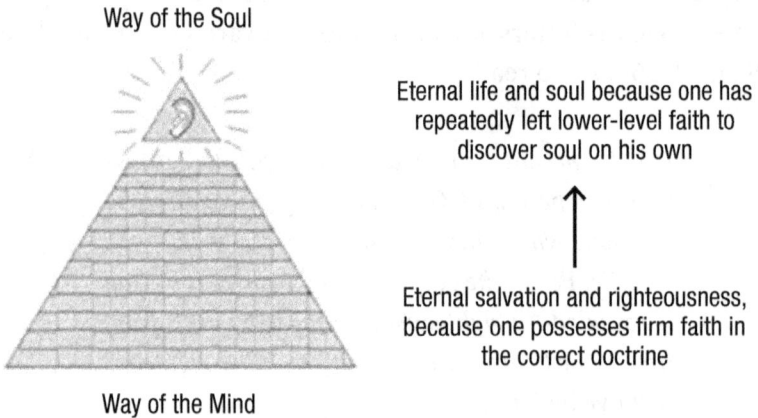

Eternal life and soul because one has repeatedly left lower-level faith to discover soul on his own

Eternal salvation and righteousness, because one possesses firm faith in the correct doctrine

Way of the Mind

TROUBLE AND DISTRESS

Paul believes that he loves everyone equally, but he contradicts himself in his letters, as we see in the next chapter of the same letter to the Romans (2:9-10):

> *There will be trouble and distress for every human being who does evil: first for the Jew, then for the Gentile; but glory, honor and peace for everyone who does good: first for the Jew, then for the Gentile.*

"There will be trouble and distress for every human being who does evil: first for the Jew, then for the Gentile; but glory, honor and peace for everyone who does good." There will be trouble and distress for everyone in the world (starting with the Jews) who do not adopt Paul's gospel. On the other hand, there will be eternal "honor and peace" (starting with Jews) for those who live it.

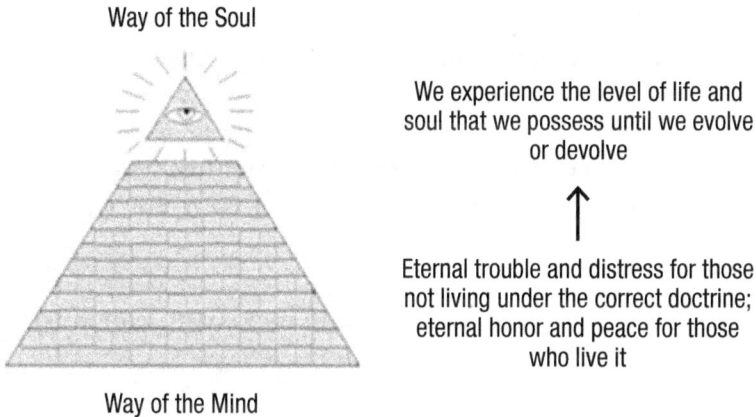

Way of the Soul

We experience the level of life and soul that we possess until we evolve or devolve

↑

Eternal trouble and distress for those not living under the correct doctrine; eternal honor and peace for those who live it

Way of the Mind

INHERIT THE KINGDOM

For Jesus, the kingdom is a state of soul-knowing oneself, others, and the nature of the world. As a person evolves, he becomes a higher level of heavenly kingdom.

As we see below in 2 Thes.1: 5-11, for Paul, the kingdom is a place we enter after we die, and a place brought to the world when Jesus returns.

This is evidence of the righteous judgment of God, that you may be made worthy of the kingdom of God, for which you are suffering; since indeed God deems it just to repay with affliction those who afflict you, and to grant rest with us to you who are afflicted, when the Lord Jesus is revealed from heaven with his mighty angels in flaming fire, inflicting vengeance upon those who do not know God and upon those who do not obey the gospel of our Lord Jesus. They shall suffer the punishment of eternal destruction and exclusion from the presence of the Lord and from the glory of his might, when he comes on that day to be glorified in his saints, and to be marveled at in all who have believed, because our testimony to you was believed. To this end we always pray for you, that our God may make you worthy of his call, and may fulfill every good resolve and work of faith by his power.

"This is evidence of the righteous judgment of God, that you may be made worthy of the kingdom of God, for which you are suffering."

God will recognize your suffering and make you "worthy of the kingdom of God" at the end of times.

For Jesus, the kingdom is lived at a higher level of heavenly knowing now, not later. We suffer now to evolve, and to live the rewards now, not after we die.

"Since indeed God deems it just to repay with affliction those who afflict you, and to grant rest with us to you who are afflicted, when the Lord Jesus is revealed from heaven with his mighty angels in flaming fire inflicting vengeance upon those who do not know God and upon those who do not obey the gospel of our Lord Jesus."

In the future, the God, Jesus, will descend to the world from heaven with his mighty angels. At that time, God will afflict vengeance upon those who have afflicted you, who did not know God, and who did not obey Paul's gospel. Those who have been faithful will be spared further affliction.

As you saw, Jesus did not experience God as vengeful. He did not say that God will punish those who do not believe in his soul poems, nor those who do not follow his Way. Jesus teaches that one suffers in the natural order of things when he does not evolve.

"They shall suffer the punishment of eternal destruction and exclusion from the presence of the Lord and from the glory of his might, when he comes on that day to be glorified in his saints, and to be marveled at in all who have believed, because our testimony to you was believed."

Those who have not followed Paul's gospel will suffer the punishment of eternal destruction and exclusion from the presence of Jesus and his glory when he comes from heaven to earth. At that time, Jesus will be glorified by those who have remained faithful to Paul's gospel, who in turn, will be admired by those who have not been faithful.

The Jesus we saw in the Poems above would get sick to his stomach to hear Paul's words. He did not develop an after-death, carrot-stick motivational system. He would not indoctrinate people with a fear of something that they have never experienced. Instead, he pointed to the present outcomes of not living as light, life, and soul.

Way of the Soul

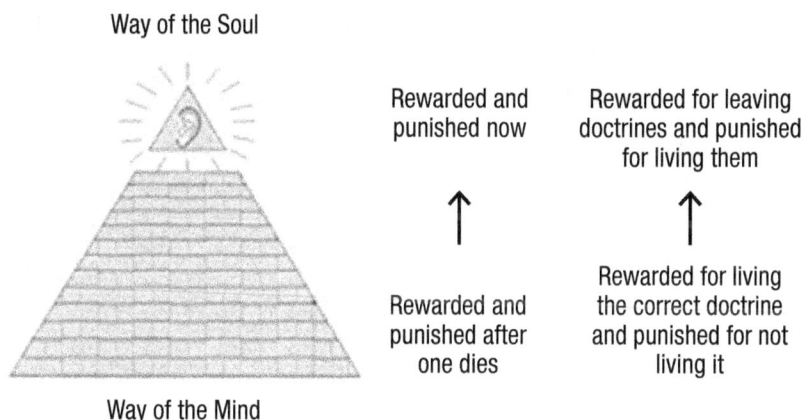

Rewarded and punished now

Rewarded for leaving doctrines and punished for living them

↑   ↑

Rewarded and punished after one dies

Rewarded for living the correct doctrine and punished for not living it

Way of the Mind

Way of the Soul

Jesus: Responsible for service to the poor, ill, disabled, aged, and disenfranchised no matter their identification with doctrine

↑

Paul: Responsible for the psychological and physical persecution and killing of people who did not conform to his doctrine

Way of the Mind

Way of the Soul

Jesus and those unseen & unheralded who may never have known him

↓
↑

Hitler, Stalin, Nationalists, Elitists, Media-idols, King David, Paul, Mohamed, the Vatican, Dalai Lamas and others heralded for causing division between people

Way of the Mind

CHAPTER TEN

THE AUTHOR OF THOMAS

Through the previous chapters, we have come to understand the true, intended meaning of the Gospel of Thomas. We have also gotten a great deal of insight about the author. Additionally, there are conclusions that can be drawn and reasonable statements that can be made about the circumstances surrounding the writing of the Gospel and about the fate of its author.

WHAT WE KNOW ABOUT THE AUTHOR OF THOMAS

Here are some conclusions we can draw about the author of the Gospel of Thomas:

1. **The author was probably a Jew.** Based on what we know historically about the demographics of the region at the time of the writings, the concepts the author discusses, and the metaphors and allegories he uses, it is clear that he is deeply familiar with the Jewish culture and religion. There is no other religion or culture in that time and area that would have created his particular frame of reference. For example, he knew the Old Testament metaphors, such as "kingdom" and "mountain," and the meaning of the allegories, such as that about the Garden of Eden and Moses' sojourn in the wilderness.

2. **The author neither adhered to nor supported the Torah, the Jewish traditions, or the Jewish authorities.** In fact, he attacked them as idols.

3. **The author was a poet, not a theologian like Paul.** The author studied people and nature and then arrived at the

principles governing human interaction and evolution. He
did not use his mind or mystical experiences to understand
things that cannot be verified by others. He would never,
for example, ask people to believe in the Trinity, if that
concept of God could not be experienced.

4. **He saw the Way of the Mind as darkness, and the Way of
   the Soul as Light.** He did not endorse any theological or
   secular dogma. Nor did he support pledging allegiance to
   a flag, an economic system, a spouse, a job, a celebrity, an
   organization, or a belief system. Those factors are the Way
   of the Mind. Instead, he rode one horse, that of the Light
   found in all; he pulled one bow, the desire to be the twin of
   every person; he followed one leader, the One that guided
   him through soul-knowing.

5. **The author studied with Jesus or he was Jesus.** He knew
   well some of the parables and sayings of Jesus that we find
   in the New Testament. Further, he understood them in
   their more primitive versions; that is, closer to the way their
   author composed them and meant for them to be read.

6. **The author was a single person who composed a unified,
   intricately organized Gospel.** The Gospel of Thomas is
   not simply a collection of sayings, or a bunch of ideas that
   came from different sources that were grouped together by
   an editor. It communicates a unified philosophy. The author
   consistently used metaphors in the same way throughout.
   All of the poems work together to elucidate a single, core
   theme with many sub-themes. In my companion volume,
   *The Gospel of Thomas: The Original 21-Chapter Poetic
   Arrangement*, I present the logical and clear organization.
   After reading this book, you are likely to agree that only
   a single individual—one who intimately understood every
   poem and how each fit with the others to convey a unified
   Gospel—could have written the Gospel of Thomas.

7. **The author was a wise therapist.** He saw and understood the cause of emotional torment in humans, and he articulated a clear, structured, unified path to self-development.

8. **The author was a wise statesman.** He saw and understood that dogma identification divided individuals and nations, and he showed how to unite them.

9. **The author was not interested in self-importance.** He did not say that he was the Messiah or "the Son of God." He did not want to be anyone's master. He desired only for people to honor the core divine life in themselves and others. He did everything possible to empower people to evolve in soul knowing.

10. **The author lived love-guarded.** We can see from the manner in which he presents his message, and from the specific words he uses, that he was compassionate to both the suffering and not-suffering alike while holding everyone responsible for their thinking and behavior. He would have been a walking love-guard, which made him a threat to everyone, from his closest friends to those who wanted to continue to control populations through dogma and fear.

This leads us to other conclusions that can be drawn about the circumstances surrounding the writing and awareness of the Gospel of Thomas and about the likely fate of its author.

11. **The author would have affected people over great distances.** He did not compose all of his poems in a single sitting. He would have composed one, edited it, recited it, and edited it again. He would have done that repeatedly until he was satisfied his message was clear and accessible to everyone. Meanwhile, people would have memorized one poem after another and communicated them to others, and they to others. In that way, over many years, knowledge of this radical, wise person and his revolutionary gospel would have spread over a great area, and likely to other

countries when his poems were memorized and recited by traders and nomads.

12. **The author had a following of disciples.** The author of Thomas lived these poems. He embodied the concepts presented in them. He would have attracted people seeking the Way of the Soul, people seeking "something better," people who sensed something in his message and knew instinctively that they should be listening to him. There would have been many who were interested in his message and in him.

13. **The author would have been aware that his message was perceived as a threat by some.** He would also have been aware of the inherent danger to himself from those looking to gain or maintain control, and even from those who just wanted to follow rules and dogma because it was easier and created less conflict. Many conformists would have hated him.

14. **The author was probably murdered.** Palestine in the first and second centuries was ruled through an informal agreement between the Roman occupiers and their Jewish collaborators. Neither group would have wanted an uprising to destroy that relationship and what it brought them. There were people who were inspired by the message in the Gospel of Thomas, and as interest spread and the number of people embracing its message grew, fear of challenges to both religious and government control would have also grown. As well, the Poems in Thomas attack all indoctrinators and Jewish leaders by title. One would not live long in first century Palestine while publicly calling the elite "dogs." The author of Thomas and the ideas he shared were a threat to the establishment. It is unreasonable to believe that indoctrinators would not have made every effort to permanently silence this message.

15. **The author composed the Gospel of Thomas to proclaim the solution for world peace should he die.** It is inconceivable to think that a person who saw the world's troubles as clearly as the author of Thomas; who gathered 128 wisdom poems, some of which we know that Jesus composed; who composed other poems; and who knew that he could be killed at any time, would not compose a Book to ensure that his message lived on and was available and accessible to humanity after he was gone.

16. **The author's Book would have been hidden.** Anyone with his Gospel on hand would have suffered the same fate as the author—rejection, persecution and death. Therefore, only a few copies would have existed, and those would have been kept and read in secret. It seems likely that written copies were rare, and the message was lost to most people.

17. **After the author died, his followers would have divided into different schools of interpretation of his poems.** Once the author was no longer available to keep the message alive and clear, and few original copies of the Book existed for reference, there would have been those who wanted to continue sharing his message—or parts of it. However, without the original source to ensure accuracy, both intentional and unintentional misinterpretations of the author's message would have been developed and spread.

One does not leave the Way of the Mind to follow the Way of the Soul quickly or easily. For example, during the past 50 years, scholars, clerics and lay people have studied the Gospel of Thomas, yet no-one has seen the Way of the Soul in it because they have been blinded by their Way of the Mind beliefs.

That must have also been true at the time that the author lived. Few, if anyone, truly grasped his radical message. Eeconomic conditions were very difficult, and the average life expectancy was about 35 years, making it even more difficult for people to transform themselves. Few would have had the time and luxury to abandon their preoccupation with survival in order to seek the Way of the Soul.

Thus, because it took time, courage, and resources to leave the Way of the Mind for the Way of the Soul, many schools of interpretation of his ideas would have arisen after the author's death. Each of these, in an attempt to make the transition easier or the message clearer, would have created a collection or even a Gospel of his poems to support their different philosophies and theologies. And some, likely, were created in an attempt selfishly capitalize on what was clearly and important and valuable message.

Most schools would twist his Way of the Soul into a belief-based dogma—because rules and dogma are what people are used to and comfortable with (even if they aren't truly comfortable with the actual rules or dogma). That would do two things: First, followers of a particular dogma could feel above others because of their belief in the so-called truth; and second, followers could substitute the long, hard work of spiritual growth for quick and easy beliefs.

Other schools would integrate the author's ideas into the Judaism that they already practiced. We can imagine many people saying "Let's not throw the baby out with the bathwater"; in other words, let's not completely get rid of what we already have and know and are comfortable with, but incorporate this new Way into our framework. Unfortunately, "throwing the baby out with the bathwater" was exactly what the author was doing and knew had to be done.

18. **We would know about such an author.** No one with such a large following of both disciples and enemies, with a message that spread over a great distance, and with such a huge portfolio of poems proclaiming such an important and understandable message, could have vanished from the historical record. Such a person would have been written about in other sources, both directly and indirectly.

WHO AUTHORED THE GOSPEL OF THOMAS?

The evidence points to Jesus as the most likely author of the Gospel of Thomas. We know of no one else who matches the ideas that we just discussed.

Much of the discussion rests on the evidence that the Gospel of Thomas is a coherent, highly organized book that could only have been authored by a single person. More detailed information is found in the companion book, *The Gospel of Thomas: The Original 21-Chapter Poetic Arrangement*.

CHAPTER ELEVEN

WAS JESUS THE EXPECTED MESSIAH?

Recall, the word "Messiah" comes from the Hebrew word "mashiach" and means "anointed one" or "chosen one." Many people were "anointed" in the Old Testament. However, some prophesies pointed to two special ones who would appear that would bring peace to Israel and the world. We read in Zech. 6:13:

> *It is he who shall build the temple of the Lord*
> *and shall bear royal honor, and shall sit and rule*
> *on his throne. And, there shall be a priest beside*
> *him on his throne, and the counsel of peace shall*
> *be between them both.*

This passage speaks of the King Messiah, who will "build the temple" and "rule on his throne," and the Priest Messiah would be "beside him." Because we are told that "a counsel of peace shall be between them both," we know that they would be using the same principles to govern.

"It is he who shall build the temple of the Lord." It is he who will build the Third Holy Temple.

The First Holy Temple in Jerusalem was built in 957 B.C.E. by King Solomon, and was destroyed by the Babylonians in 587 B.C.E. The Second Temple was authorized by Cyrus the Great and constructed under the auspices of the Jewish governor Zerubbabel. It was dedicated in 515 B.C.E., and renovated by Herod the Great around 20 B.C.E. It was destroyed by the Roman Empire in 70 C.E. Jesus was clearly not involved with the construction of the Holy Temple. As a result, many believe this precludes Jesus as the Messiah.

Many interpret "It is he who shall build the temple of the Lord" to mean, "It is he who will cleanse the temple of false teachings." While the canonical Gospels describe Jesus "cleansing" the Temple (John 2:13–16; Matthew 21:12–13; Mark 11:15–17; Luke 19:45–46), it was not a wholesale cleansing of false teachings that is described. So again, consequently, many do not regard him as the Messiah.

However, in many of Jesus' poems and parables, he points to the "place" from which we live and communicate directly with God. For example, in Chapter 2, Poem 4 we read:

He
will delay
not

Namely
the man
of maturity
in his days

To ask a little
small child

He
being
of seven days

About the place
of life;

And
he
will live.

That "place" within seems to be the "temple." Thus, Jesus builds that temple by teaching people to rediscover that "place" of "life" and to make it all important, especially when communicating directly with God. In that way, he does fulfill the prophesy about the Messiah.

"It is he … who shall bear royal honor, and shall sit and rule on his throne." The Messiah will possess a regal demeanor and power. He will "rule" by both the force of his personality and by the authority given to him by others (many think by the entire world). Since Jesus was a humble man with noble but not regal character, he was not recognized as a ruler.

"And, there shall be a priest beside him on his throne." Many interpret that statement to mean that there will be two Messiahs who will redeem the world—a King Messiah and a Priest Messiah.

Zechariah does not imply that the King Messiah would be greater than the Priest Messiah. Other ancient documents, such as the Testament of Levi in the Dead Sea Scrolls, seem to indicate that the priest will be wiser and the king will be more visible and assertive. Zechariah also does not imply that the two Messiahs will be alive at the same time. "Beside him" can also mean "on the same Way," not literally "at his physical side." The Priest could create the wisdom that the King administers later, which would be a logical progression.

In Jewish eschatology (theology concerned with the final events of history, or the ultimate destiny of humanity), the Priest Messiah is known as "Mashiach ben Joseph" (Messiah son of Joseph; Joseph, the son of Jacob). The King Messiah has come to be known as "Mashiach ben David" (Messiah son of David). The phrase "son of" does not necessarily mean genetic lineage. It could mean "one who has inherited the spirit, charisma or character of someone who lived previously."

Let us suppose that the Priest Messiah arrives before the King Messiah. Recall the following passage from the Preface:

> *He shall judge between the nations,*
> *and shall decide for many peoples;*
> *and they shall beat their swords into plowshares,*

and their spears into pruning hooks;
nation shall not lift up sword against nation,
neither shall they learn war any more. (Isa. 2:4)

For every warrior's sandal from the noisy battle
and their garments rolled in blood
will be burned as fuel for the fire.
For a child has been born,
a son has been given...
And his name shall be called
Prince of Peace...
Of the abundance of his government and peace
there shall be no end (Isa. 9:5-10)

"His name shall be called Prince of Peace." In order for a
Messiah to bring peace to a world where most people are on the
Way of the Mind, he would need to preach an alternative Way
that everyone, including Atheists and Agnostics, could embrace.
Further, this new "Way" would be a type of emotional health
system that would heal a person divided between his real and
false selves. We saw, explained in this book, that Jesus taught
people to put all of their belief in doctrines aside and listen
only to their soul voice for their guidance. As we discovered,
Jesus proclaimed the Way of the Soul. For most people, that
is a paradigm-shift message that will unite people personally
and globally. Thus, Jesus *does* fulfill the prophesy for the Priest
Messiah.

However, Jesus did not "judge between the nations" and compel
them "to beat their swords into plowshares" so that "nation shall
not lift up sword against nation." Nor did he lead "abundance"
of world-wide "government." The world continues to be torn
apart by strife and war. Therefore, if Zechariah is correct, the
King Messiah will do what Jesus—as the first, Priest Messiah—
did not, and will certainly govern with the gospel of the Priest
Messiah: the Way of the Soul.

The fulfillment of Isaiah's prophecy—that a Messiah could proclaim a way of living that would *replace* every form of religion and ideology—seems utterly impossible.

Jeremiah explains the role of the Priest Messiah further:

> *But this is the covenant which I will make with the house of Israel after those days, says the Lord: I will put my law within them, and I will write it upon their hearts; and I will be their God, and they shall be my people. And no longer shall each man teach his neighbor and each his brother, saying, `Know the Lord,' for they shall all know me, from the least of them to the greatest, says the Lord; for I will forgive their iniquity, and I will remember their sin no more. (Jer. 31: 33-34)*

"But this is the covenant which I will make with the house of Israel." The "house of Israel" are the "family," "friends," and "descendants" of Israel (Jacob): those who are on the Way of the Soul. Thus, Jeremiah predicts that there will be a new covenant (promise) to those who follow the Messiahs, almost certainly on the Way of the Soul.

"I will put my law within them, and I will write it upon their hearts; and I will be their God, and they shall be my people." A Priest Messiah will teach people the natural laws of God. Those laws will be recognized in and come from their "hearts," not from any external authority or dogma. Religious and secular authorities and their dogmas will no longer be their rulers. Instead, the God who guides them through soul-knowing will be their authority.

In the Gospel of Thomas, Jesus taught the "law within" people, not the Torah laws of Moses or any other external, man-constructed law. Further, he presented the danger of making any secular or religious laws more important than what is in a person's heart and soul. Therefore, Jesus as the Priest Messiah fulfilled Jeremiah's requirements.

Ezekiel also prophesized the characteristics of the Messiah:

> *Thus says the Lord God: "Behold, I will take the*
> *people of Israel from the nations among which*
> *they have gone, and will gather them from all*
> *sides, and bring them to their own land; and I*
> *will make them one nation in the land, upon the*
> *mountains of Israel.*
>
> *And one king shall be king over them all; and*
> *they shall be no longer two nations, and no longer*
> *divided into two kingdoms.*
>
> *They shall not defile themselves any more with*
> *their idols and their detestable things, or with*
> *any of their transgressions; but I will save them*
> *from all the dwelling places in which they have*
> *sinned, and will cleanse them; and they shall be*
> *my people, and I will be their God.*
>
> *My servant David will be king over them, and*
> *they will all have one shepherd. They will follow*
> *my laws and be careful to keep my decrees.*
> *(Eze. 37: 21-24)*

"Thus says the Lord God: 'Behold, I will take the people of Israel from the nations among which they have gone, and will gather them from all sides, and bring them to their own land; and I will make them one nation in the land, upon the mountains of Israel.'" Let's explore this in detail.

"I will take the people of Israel." "Israel" is the name given to Jacob (the grandson of Abraham) after he wrestled with an angel (his soul knowing) to conquer himself. Thus, "people of Israel" does not mean citizens of the state of Israel or the literal descendants of Israel (Jacob). Instead, the statement refers to those on the Way of the Soul, like Israel, who wrestle with their soul knowing every day.

"I will take the people of Israel from the nations." "The nations" are what Jesus calls the "world." They are those on the Way of the Mind.

"I will gather them from all sides, and bring them to their own land; and I will make them one nation in the land, upon the mountains of Israel." "I will gather all people, from everywhere, and bring them each to their own soul knowing; and I will make them into a new, singular nation, together in soul knowing, with all of those who are already on their internal mountain—the highest place within themselves, free of distraction from or adherence to former beliefs."

A "land" is a "way of being" (soul knowing), which Jesus called the "kingdom." A person on the Way of the Soul establishes himself as a king or queen over himself and his interactions with others, that is, over his "kingdom."

The physical land of King David is now divided between many Jewish factions and between Jews and Palestinians and their many factions. That physical "land" will be united by the Messiah, which has not happened. So Jesus, as the first Messiah, did not fulfill the prophesy.

However, should everyone in the physical land of King David become one on the Way of the Soul as a result of the second Messiah's leadership, then the prophesy would be fulfilled in two ways:

First: The people living in the physical land of King David would be united.

Second: Everyone on the Way of the Soul throughout the world would become "one nation" in soul living.

"I will make them one nation in the land upon the mountains of Israel." I will make them one because they will all be listening to the same soul voice when they go up on their inner mountain.

"And one king shall be king over them all; and they shall be no longer two nations, and no longer divided into two kingdoms." Because all of those on the Way of the Mind will convert to the Way of the Soul, the Messiah King shall rule all as a single entity. And each person will be fully on the Way of the Soul, connected to his true self, with no false selves to "divide him into two kingdoms." All will be united on the Way of the Soul.

They shall not defile themselves any more with their idols and their detestable things, or with any of their transgressions; but I will save them from all the back-slidings in which they have sinned, and will cleanse them; and they shall be my people, and I will be their God." They will not defile their true selves by attempting to "ride two horses" or move between the Way of the Soul and the Way of the Mind. They will no longer be concerned with or distracted by those material and dogmatic things that prevent them from soul living.

"My servant David will be king over them, and they will all have one shepherd." The King Messiah will be the king and shepherd over those on the Way of the Soul.

"They will follow my laws and be careful to keep my decrees." They will follow God's laws that are within them in their hearts and soul knowing, not religious or secular laws. They will listen to and follow the guidance of God from within.

CONCLUSION

Jesus was the Priest Messiah who articulated the Way of the Soul. We find it completely in the Gospel of Thomas, and we find it also in his parables and core sayings in the New Testament.

The King Messiah has not yet come. When he does, he will proclaim compellingly to the world the Way of the Soul.

CHAPTER TWELVE

A WAY OF THE SOUL PRIMER

INTRODUCTION

The Way of the Soul begins with a person who seeks to leave the "world" in order to live more in the "kingdom."

The "world" is the life that most people live. It consists of

- Living mentally in the past and future.

- Living from sadness to happiness, from worry to relief, from depression to elation, from failure to success…on and on.

- Living the beliefs of others, and not being congruent with one's inner voice.

Summary: The "world" is "religion," not just theological religion, but of the way we make external beliefs more important than listening to one's intuitive voice or Voice.

Jesus uses the image and concept of "kingdom" as a *fulfilled way of being*, that is, a Way to experience oneself and life very differently than those in the "world."

To be concrete: In the kingdom, one lives in a type of bliss world that few understand. We are familiar with similar, short-term worlds. For example, falling in love is like entering a new world. It provides feelings of exhilaration and completeness and oneness—much like what it feels to be living in the kingdom. But this (falling in love) is a short-term world unless the new lovers find a way to continue living in that zone, that space, that way of being *every minute for the rest of their lives*. For most of us, that does not happen. Why? Because unless we live on the

Way of the Soul, we cannot do it. We cannot maintain that level of relationship because our comfortable behaviors, thoughts, needs and even objects draw us away from the soul living, the joy, the exhilaration we experienced while falling in love. We want to stay in that space, but we can't. We feel a deep pull from within that draws us to that zone, makes us aware that we want it, but we cannot seem to maintain that feeling. That is why we see people trying to artificially create a "kingdom" by substituting activities for "falling in love," such as engaging in extra-marital affairs, watching pornography, dreaming while listening to romantic music, trying novel sex encounters, and using drugs that provide a "high."

According to Jesus, we all experience some aspects of the kingdom when we are tiny children—before we before we learn about roles and rules and titles. As we grow and are indoctrinated into our culture by family, teachers, and other leaders, we move further from the kingdom. It's not a conscious occurrence. It's just how we are taught to live by those around us who are not on the Way of the Soul. But deep inside, we remember the experience of the kingdom as a child and long to live it again.

As one gradually lives more "in the kingdom," he will become a wise king (or queen) over his "field," which includes all aspects of himself as well as all of his interactions with others. Further, a "kingdom" for Jesus is also a group of people who live the Way of the Soul. He intended to invite everyone in the universe to be on that common Way to peace and fulfillment.

Seeking the "kingdom" is a goal for which a person must be willing to sacrifice anything and everything—especially his ego. He must "leave all" of his present dogma to follow the Way of the Soul, or he will choose a thousand psychological deaths. One cannot live with "one foot in and one foot out." To do so would cause great internal conflict and emotional and spiritual pain that would also radiate out to and affect all those within that individual's "field."

Through his Gospel, Jesus teaches the disciplined steps to achieving our deepest wish—to be back in the kingdom 24/7. This chapter provides a concise "primer" to living the Way of the Soul.

First, in order to *refresh* your experience of the "kingdom," permit me to lead you through an exercise.

Exercise

Look back over your life and recall your strongest "all experience." It was a moment or short span of time in which you were in the "now" and were one with all. Time seemed to stop. You enjoyed just being you and being with all around you— perhaps with your friend, your child, or the sunset. Some folks have that kind of experience on the last day of a vacation or a long weekend. Some folks have it when they take time to step away from everything and everyone and take a walk or sit on a swing or float in a body of water.

Maybe you can recall times when you acted from the "now" and enjoyed those wonderful emotions and thoughts of joy, personal power and safety. (Many have learned to act from the "now" in a practice commonly called "mindfulness." I think it should be called "soulfulness.")

However you have reached that experience, think about it now.

Now, in your imagination, put yourself back in that "all experience" and recall its details. Let me guide you:

Recall the stillness within you and around you. People may have been talking near you, but you were in a stillness bubble.

Recall that you felt emotionally healthy. You were not anxious, worried, depressed, sad, or in out-of-the-body excitement.

Recall how joy bubbled up from your soul.

Recall how alive you felt and how alive everything around you seemed. If you were sitting on the beach, for example, recall how the sea, the sand, the sky, and those around you seemed so real in a refreshing "alive" way.

Recall that you could sit or stand there and enjoy things that you normally never even saw. For example, if you were in a park, recall how you enjoyed feeling the breeze and watching it move the leaves of the trees. Remember how everything seemed to slow down (of course, it was actually you that slowed down!).

Recall how your ideas bubbled up from you soul. They seemed to come *through* you. You were not *manufacturing* them with your mind. You sensed the ideas or visions and then, secondarily, used your mind to shape and play with them.

Recall that your soul-ideas led you to plan something in the future. However, you planned from being in the present. You did not plan from a mind *anxious* about the future.

Recall that you were *in* the flow. Everything came effortlessly to you, and you decided easily to go this way or that. Perhaps in the park, you sensed to walk to the right. You did that and saw something wonderful that seemed to have been given to you, such as new kind of flower.

Sitting again, recall how you seemed to be one with universal intelligence (which you may have called, "my higher self," "my source," or "God.")

Recall that that intelligence *lovingly* guided your thoughts and your actions, such as to the new type of flower.

Recall the sense that you were infinitely loved.

Recall the sense that you were safe, no matter what happened.

Recall that as soon as a question arose from you soul, it was followed by the answer—tailored specifically for you.

Recall that you had suspended your mind and its beliefs. You were living from your experience, not from your faith in yourself, in God, or in any of the "truths" that you were taught. You had given up the Way of the Mind and entered the Way of the Soul.

If you were aware of God's presence, recall how you experienced and accepted it and without feeling a need to believe.

Recall that you enjoyed and appreciated your body. When you looked down at your hands, you were one with them. Your physical self and your spiritual self were singular, fluid and vibrating as one with the universe.

Recall saying to yourself, "I wish I could live like this forever—with no worries, fears or regrets."

Recall that you sensed yourself as a unique gift to the world.

Recall the realization that others were also unique gifts but that they did not seem to act like they were. Most were always trying to manufacture themselves.

Recall the peace, the quiet, the beauty, and the wonder of it "all."

Recall that deep down you sensed that nothing happens by accident, by luck, or by coincidence. Under those impressions of disorder, you sensed loving order.

Recall how the exact right events, things and people had "shown up" in your life almost magically, at the right time and place, and with exactly what you needed.

Recall how you sensed that the universe seemed to know what you most deeply needed before your mind did. How things, people and ideas came into your life without you even asking.

Recall how you remembered your hardships, such as people who betrayed you, your mistakes, and all of your problems. Recall how you saw that they all led you closer to what you most deeply wanted.

Recall how you realized that when you felt upset in the past, all of your feelings, ideas and actions emanated primarily from your mind, not your soul.

Recall how you noticed that when you were upset, all of your "mind" ideas led eventually to more upset.

Recall how you noticed that to get out of the vicious upset cycle, you needed to take time to be still in what Jesus calls "the beginning," that is, the "now."

Maybe you can recall times when that you acted from the "now" and were led to more of those wonderful emotions and thoughts of joy, personal power, and safety.

Recall how you may have said in your own way, "I create what will happen. From regret and worry, my mind guides me to more of the same suffering. From stillness and joy, my soul guides me to more wondrous fulfillment."

REFLECTIONS

You may not recall all of those specifics of the "All Experience." However, that is find if you remember a few. As one seeks the "All Experience" and studies it from inside, one usually disocveres many more aspects than those that I mentioned. As one does that, he seeks to live the "All Experience" or "Kingdom" continually. Gradually under every thought and activity, he will be living from the kingdom and seeking to be more in it. That is the Way of the Soul.

The "Kingdom" or "All experience," then, is an *experience*, that is, "a way of being" in which one rules over himself and his interactions from his soul knowing, not his mental manipulations. It is also a community of people who are kings and queens. To enter that "space" or "zone," you suspended your faith in all that you believed in order to reenter your experience as a little child would. You leave your theological and social rules and dogmas to be your real you. You leave what Jesus called the "world," the "dead," the "body," and "darkness." You leave your emotional rollercoaster to be still and one with all. As a result, you began living "life" and "light."

Now, you know that Jesus did not set out to or actually start a religion. His desire, intention and actions were to free people from their mental religions so that they could be one with their real soul-selves and with all as the "kingdom." Now, you can go back through his ideas, sit with your soul, listen to others on the Way of the Soul, and discover your own, unique way of living the kingdom.

THE LOGIC OF THE TWO WAYS

Jesus recognized why we are not in the kingdom 24/7: We are all blinded by our precious blind beliefs. He describes how we disempower ourselves with our blind beliefs in his "Parable of the Sower" (Chapter 2, Poem 1):

Behold![1]

He
went out

Namely
he

The one

Who
sows.[2]

And
he
filled his hand[3]
(with seed)[4]

[1]*Behold:* Soul-see! or third-eye see

[2]*The one who sows:* The one who provides seeds of wisdom (as Jesus does in these poems). Our soul v(V)oice.

[3]*Hand:* The ability to control.

[4]*Filled his hand:* From all of his ideas, he carefully chose his seeds of wisdom.

And
he
threw them.⁵

And
some
were
indeed
discovered
on the way.⁶

And
they
came

Namely
the birds⁷

And
they
gathered them.⁸

⁵*Threw them:* Confronted others with them.

⁶*Some were discovered on the way:* Some seeds of wisdom were heard by a person on the Way to higher levels of life.

⁷*They came, namely the birds:* The old blind-beliefs of the person came forward in the person's mind.

⁸*And they Gathered them:* The listener made his blind-beliefs more important than the wisdom.

In Jesus' parable of the sower, a wise man (symbolizing our soul v(V)oice) throws out seeds of wisdom on the "earth" (our reflective consciousness). "Birds" (blind beliefs) come and remove the seeds before they can grow. In other words, like fools, we choose to believe our dogma rather than suspend it to consider wisdom bubbling up from our soul. The Parable of the Sower is an example of how Jesus criticizes blind beliefs.

Religion rewards steadfast faith. Jesus preaches the opposite: doubt your beliefs and discover for yourself what is real. In that process, grow into being a wise child living 24/7 in the kingdom.

We are like people with layers of cataracts on their eyes. Each layer is a blind belief. We think we see reality when we actually see a composite distortion. We are in a false, "dead" "world." If we could see properly ourselves, others, and the true way that the universe works, we would be full of "life" in the kingdom 24/7. So, to get into the kingdom, we need to remove our cataracts, one blind belief at a time.

The problem: we identify with our beliefs and not our soul wisdom. Each of us is a unique version of a universal soul that is one with infinite intelligence (God). Each moment we have the option of living from that soul or from the blind beliefs in our mind. In other words, we choose every second to be on the Way of the Soul of the Way of the Mind. Because we identify with our beliefs, suspending and removing them threatens us. We feel vulnerable, and we are until we reveal a reality closer to the truth. Then we become a bit more a wise "king" or "queen" over ourselves and our interactions with others.

When a child is born, he sees more the kingdom than we do. He loves cartoons because they are closer to the reality that is the kingdom. He is fragile and unwise, but he lives the kingdom more than we do. Our job is to be a child again but with the power and wisdom to guard ourselves from adult indoctrination.

A child loses his kingdom vision and his connection with his soul as he embraces mental blind beliefs. Little by little, he grows faith cataracts. He learns to trust those mental filters more than his child, clear vision.

Theological, political, and other social religions exist when two or more people agree that a blind belief cataract is reality. People in that religion, then, think that they are special because they see absolute truth and others do not. They, then, may think that anyone who does not embrace their truths are wrong, bad, and even worthy of punishment. Religions, therefore, are the reason we do not live in the kingdom 24/7 and why we do not live as powerful, wise children, one with each other.

In the Gospel of Thomas and in his New Testament parables and core sayings (those that we find in two or more gospels), Jesus never uses the words "believe" or "faith" without being critical of that way of construing reality. He never preached a creed or a legal system, nor did he establish a hierarchy of authorities to enforce them. In no way did he establish a religion. His goal was to remove people from body/mind slavery, not to create another version of it.

In Thomas, instead of the word "believe," Jesus uses the words "discover" and "reveal." We remove our blind belief cataracts by "discovering" or "revealing" the nature of reality. Truths are embedded in reality, they are not in our secular and theological religious beliefs about reality. Therefore, the process of personal evolution out of blind belief "darkness" involves challenging and suspending our current beliefs so that our soul intuition can present us with what is real.

Jesus modeled an enlightened leader in his poems, parables and core sayings. Instead of teaching dogma, he taught people how to challenge doctrine and indoctrinators so that they can discover their own answers on their own. He describes our world-wide, religion-logic situation so powerfully and clearly in Chapter 10, Poem 1 (Saying 39):

Jesus
said this:

The Pharisees
and
the Scribes[1]
took the keys[2]
of knowledge,[3]

And
they
hid them,[4]

Nor
did
they
go inward;[5]

[1]*Pharisees and Scribes*: Two of the many groups of clerics within Judaism. In this Gospel, they represent all indoctrinating leaders, whether religious or secular. Such leaders could be politicians, clerics, professors, parents, business managers, TV celebrities and influential friends.

[2]*Keys*: The keys to knowledge are what Jesus teaches, beginning with soul-knowing.

[3]*Knowledge*: Knowledge of your real self, the real self of others, and the principles of coming alive in a dead world.

And those

Who
desired to go
inward,

They
did
not permit them.[6]

[4]*Hid them*: Taught people to make the beliefs of authorities more important than what they soul-know.

[5]*Go inward*: Leave their indoctrination and soul-know.

[6]*They did not permit them*: The authorities taught people to distrust soul-knowing.

The enslaving logic of religion permeates society, particularly our educational systems. We pay "Pharisees" (clerics, teachers, professors and lecturers) to proclaim truths, rather than to empower people to "discover" and "reveal" their own truths. We design churches, temples, lecture halls and classrooms so that the high priests can dominate from above the ignorant masses. We devise grading systems that divide students into good ones and bad ones. We abuse children by instilling in them fear of failure in the learning process. In those ways, we invite unconsciously the sick logic of religion into our minds. Is it any wonder that people live in free-floating regret, anxiety and worry?

Can people learn from experts? Certainly—after they have been empowered to challenge them. Would it not be wonderful if each of our clerics, politicians, teachers and talking heads stood up and proclaimed, "My primary job is to empower you to challenge every so-called truth that has ever been uttered, particularly by me."

Procedures for Becoming More "the Kingdom"

Every day, in every instant, we choose to ride one horse or the other, to serve one master or the other: the Way of the Soul or the Way of the Mind. Permit me to share some of the ways that people on the Way of the Soul live to be more in the kingdom.

Seek

A Soul person asks continually: Am I in the kingdom or not? When one is upset in any way (anxious, worried, feeling guilty or like a failure, or seeking excitement, food or shopping as an escape), he knows that he is not in the kingdom.

He, then, goes to a place where he can be still, usually a place apart from others (maybe a corner of a coffee shop or to a park). There he asks, "What have I chosen that makes me upset—please tell me". He is seeking answers from his soul voice (or Voice). He resists using his mind for solutions. He knows that his mental beliefs have caused him to be upset. He may remind himself that a little child seldom gets upset because he lives from his soul, not from artificial, indoctrinated faith in theology, money, friends, job, family, self-importance, etc.

When one begins communicating with his soul-voice (Source), he begins what seems impossible: communicating in a normal give and take conversation with God or with universal intelligence. Jesus modeled that, not to say that he was special, but to teach everyone to do it. He called his Voice his "Mother and Father." Each person can ask, "What do you want me to call you?" or any other questions, such as, "Who are you?" or "Are you a person?" or "Do you love me personally?" He then "listens" or "senses" words, images, and impressions bubbling up from his soul. When he hears things that he normally would not say to himself, he becomes surer that he is not imagining things.

Communicating with one's source or Source is a skill. Children do it naturally. We need to relearn the ability. Each person develops his own way and his own rules for determining whether he is creating both sides of the conversation or only his side. It is a highly rewarding skill to learn, because you find that you are never alone without someone who can give you answers— sometimes that you do not like—but answers to any question.

The core trick is to be empty of all agendas and detached from all former beliefs. Those agendas and, especially, common sense cultural beliefs, interfere with unbiased listening. Further, if one already thinks he knows the answer, he will not be open to being taught.

The Soul person may, then, begin reading Jesus' poems until one poem or line resonates with him or causes an "a-ha moment." Sometimes it seems like a word or line stands out from the others. That can be the soul's signal that that word or line is part of what you are immediately seeking. So, one way your soul voice breaks through the mental bedlam is by guiding you to an author who is on the Way of the Soul and who speaks something that resonates with you.

The Soul person may also listen to the lyrics of a song, or look at a billboard, or overhear a conversion (it could be *any* kind of input, really), because he knows that his soul will use anything or anyone to deliver the needed insight.

The Soul person may also seek help from a "soul" friend or therapist. If a friend or therapist is living from his mind, he probably will cause more confusion. One wants to find someone who helps the Soul person find his own answers. Only the soul knows the exact next step to take, be it an insight or an action.

The Soul person watches every thought or image that bubbles up from his soul. He turns it this way and that to uncover the needed insight.

If still upset, the Soul person may return to normal activities while continuing third-ear (soul) listening for his breakthrough idea.

Finding

A Soul Seeker listens for a few *general patterns* that cause upset. Let me list some.

- A Seeker checks to see if he is in the present. If not, he knows that he has chosen to make beliefs about the past or the future more important than being himself in the "the beginning." So he then, asks, "What is the false god that I am worshiping now?" It could be money, prestige, ego, meeting the expectations of another, false love, or unwillingness to say and do what is real. Those are all things that one might regret (which causes him to live in the past) or think he needs (which causes him to live the future.)

Everyone needs money, for example, but one has the choice: find fulfillment in the moment and then seek what one needs, or seek what one needs to be fulfilled in the future. The latter strategy will never lead to fulfillment. It results in a vicious circle of upset, which Jesus calls "death."

- A Seeker knows that when living in the past or future, he is not embracing something or someone as "perfect-as-is." Instead, he is running from "bad" and seeking "good." He knows he must stop and embrace everything with unconditional love. That is the *only* way out of the mind-driven cycle of sadness to out-of-body bliss. We must transform deep anger about "bad" and not finding "good" into unconditional, pure love.

For example, a war veteran may suddenly feel terrible stress when his child drops something with a bang on the floor. Immediately that sound tells him that he is living the trauma of a battle where he experienced his friend being blown up. Thus, he knows that he has not embraced fully his friend, that situation, the enemy, the government, all, in unconditional love. His mind shouts, "believe that is bad." He knows that he cannot move forward until his being shouts, "It is perfect-as-is." But how to get there? He knows that only his soul knows his answer.

Therefore, he stops, goes apart from his family, and begs his soul, "Teach me."

He may be told to hold his child and think of his friend, the enemy, and the politicians who sent them to war as the soul essence of what he cherishes in his arms.

He may also be given the insight that he and everyone involved in that battle were brainwashed to kill in the name of some "good" false god.

He may be called to look at his hands and love his friend and his battlefield enemies with similar hands.

He may hear the suggestion to suffer not taking a drink of alcohol or swallowing another pill and to wait in pain for the answer to bubble up from his soul.

Every time this happens, his soul will say something different; each time tailoring the insight to his immediate need to leave his ego's demand that things were "bad."

Once he finds even the littlest bit of unconditional love for what is going on and/or what has gone on, his soul will prompt him to "guard" himself. He may do that by spending more time with his child, by listening to more gentle music, by using the internet to connect with others, by (any number of things). The soul knows the next step.

The only formula for healing is this: Unconditional love first, then guard. Seek "perfect-as-is" before using the mind to know the bad and good ways to move ahead safely. Never the reverse: thinking or acting out of "bad" and "good" hoping for unconditional love to follow is fruitless.

- A Seeker knows that universal intelligence (God), one with his soul, has led him into his present situation to *heal* him, to teach him to be unconditional-guarded love in the world. So he asks, "What am I to learn by this rejection, or by this misunderstanding, or by this problem, or by recalling that horrible event?" He waits to be shown how the *present situation* is his *next perfect step* to freedom from emotional trauma and to bring him to be a light leader in the world. He must learn to embrace what is going on, or he will just repeat it in other ways until he permits his soul to show him the way out.

To be clear: A Seeker *experiences* rather than *believes* that every thought, every urge, every thing that happens to him and around him happens to bring him to fulfillment in unconditional love guardedness. Those in the world experience or believe in bad and good luck and in coincidences. When one is one with his core self, fully in the "All Experience," he knows that everything going on is perfect-as-is and perfectly presents his next perfect step to fulfillment. Again, he does not live those things as blind beliefs, rather he seeks the All-Experience so that he will know them as obvious.

When a person has been shocked into dreading that he is vulnerable to be hurt or to die at any moment, he will live in "bad" and in perpetual anxiety and worry. The only way out is letting his source (Source) teach him personally how to live the Kingdom 24/7. He needs only to give up everything tying him to "bad" and "good" in order to be taught how to experience life correctly.

- A Seeker sees himself mirrored in everyone, particularly in his enemies. If he finds himself repulsed by anyone, he asks his soul, "What am I not embracing in love-guardedness in myself that I see in him?" "How is he me?" Or, if he notices the beauty of a kind person, he may ask, "Why did you, soul, bring him into my life?" "What are you teaching me?"

In short, the Seeker takes nothing for granted. It is all part of the cosmic lesson to bring him to being everything he deep-down desires—which Jesus' calls, the "kingdom." His goal is to be super-conscious of every thought and feeling. That will enable him to rule as king (or queen) over himself and his interaction with others. Then, he will be more the presence of unconditional love-guarded in the world.

- A Seeker seeks other Soul Seekers. Their souls will know each other beyond superficial differences. They will feel a love-guarded bond that will guide them to be family, even if just for a few minutes. Immediately, each soul will be communicating with the other and providing each other with learned lessons.

- Finally, a Seeker will discover that those who are not seekers of the kingdom will not understand him. Therefore, he will find that the only viable path to peace and sanity is to not rely on what Jesus calls "the world." That "world" may be long-time friends, family, a job, beliefs, money, material possessions, and so forth. A seeker of the kingdom sacrifices to obtain it all.

That, in a nutshell, is *one* way of understanding how immediately to practice the Way of the Soul.

SUMMARY OF THE TWO WAYS

Here is a chart that comparatively summarizes and describes the characteristics of the Way of the Mind and the Way of the Soul:

The Two Ways Contrasted

Way of the Mind		Way of the Soul
Lives primarily from mind-knowing	→←	Lives primarily from soul-knowing
Indoctrinated	→←	Self-evolved
Divided between one's real self and many false selves	→←	United with oneself
In conflict with all others who differ in their religions and ideologies.	→←	In oneness with other people and the universe.
Develops faith in dogma	→←	Questions dogma to discover his own answers
Jesus call this Way: "Darkness," "death" and "sickness"	→←	Jesus calls this Way: "Light," "life" and "health"

Way of the Mind		Way of the Soul
The goal: Find meaning and security by attaching oneself to people, things and dogma	→←	The goal: Detach from people, things and dogma to wisely love all
Means: Think and imitate those you admire	→←	Means: Use your inner voice to decide for yourself how to think and act

IMPLICATIONS

- If a Soul person is in a relationship with a Mind person, they will psychologically separate. If they try to live together or be friends, they will both continually experience some degree of stress and disharmony.

- Religions institutionalize and normalize the Way of the Mind. They teach people to divide by labeling something, someone, or even parts of themselves as "bad" and "good." They teach people to identify with blind beliefs rather that with their core, beautiful, perfect-as-is souls. They teach adherents to live in fear of not getting into "heaven" or possibly going to "hell." In other words, they teach fear, that is, psychological illness. Religions teach people to "tolerate" people with contrary beliefs. Seekers know that withholding unconditional love by being tolerant is actually hate. Therefore, for all of those reasons, Seekers sever their allegiance to all secular and theological dogma-based institutions.

Religions do not teach unconditional-guarded love of all. They do not empower people to use their souls to find their own answers. They, instead, indoctrinate and brainwash people to think and act according to official bad-good standards. Therefore, religions are the root cause of personal emotional problems and of inter-group political, social and national conflicts. They teach death logic as normal to the world. Jesus teaches the opposite.

- *Only* people *united* on the Way of the Soul will solve the horrific problems of overpopulation, competition for fewer resources, terrorism, global warming and the slew of plagues and crises facing humanity today.

- When we support, in any way, political, theological, economic, nationalistic or other social religions, we contribute to personal and inter-group conflicts, including horrific terrorism. When we identify with dogma, we divide from our core self and from others and become physically and mentally sick. Only allegiance to soul-knowing unites and heals. The world seeks salvation in new generations of weapons, in democracy, in justice systems, and in teaching tolerance. As history has shown, those solutions simply continue the cycle of hope to violence.

- Jesus did not build religious buildings or institutions, wear distinctive clothes, lead rituals to change one spiritually, establish a legalism or a creed, call himself anything special, discriminate against women and others, distinguish between spiritual and personal growth, ordain leaders with special powers, set up a hierarchy, or divide people into believers and non-believers. He did live in the "now," listening for the voice of his Mother and Father to guide him to love the person in front of him while protecting himself from that person's false identities. He did daily crucify himself of false selves to be resurrected to new levels of life, wisdom and fulfillment. He did communicate with God in his own way continually. He did empower everyone to find their own answers through soul-knowing. Thus, if he lived today, he would be unhappy if any group or individual associated him with dogma-religion that inevitably and automatically results in intrapersonal, interpersonal and inter-group conflict.

As a person living the Way of the Soul, Jesus lived in the kingdom. It was not a nationalistic or ethnic kingdom, but a personal and group way of being. Through his teachings, we can see the life he lived and the life he intended for us to

live. And through his words we can fulfill his wish for all of
humanity—to live in the kingdom, on the Way of the Soul,
together in peace.

One of Jesus' mantras that we can all say as we enter more
and more into the Kingdom:

Chapter 16, Poem 10 (Saying 77)

I

am

the light

The one

Which

is

upon them

All of them.

I

am

the all;

Has

the all

come outward

of me

And

has

the all

split

to become me.

Split

a timber

And

I

am

there;

Take

the stone

up

And

you

will discover me

there.

CHAPTER THIRTEEN

WAY OF THE SOUL – WAY OF THE MIND SELF-EXAMINATION

One of the characteristics of Jesus' Way of the Soul is self-examination. He says that in Chapter 16, Poem 2 (Saying 69a):

The blest ones

They

are

those

Who
have persecuted themselves
in their own heart.

Those

Who
have done that

Have known the Father
in truth.

The following exercise may enable you to "persecute" yourself so that you live more in "truth." To complete it, rate yourself, as honestly as you can, by checking the number below each of the factors that most closely matches your current life. (If you do this on your screen, write the numbers down on paper beside you).

1. My mind is in the present

usually ① — sometimes ② — half & half ③ — sometimes ④ — usually ⑤

My mind is in the past and/or future

2. I love people whether they reject or accept me

usually ① — sometimes ② — half & half ③ — sometimes ④ — usually ⑤

I love people only when they accept me.

3. I live from inner stillness

usually ① — sometimes ② — half & half ③ — sometimes ④ — usually ⑤

I live from inner busyness

4. I am concerned but peaceful without money

usually ① — sometimes ② — half & half ③ — sometimes ④ — usually ⑤

I am anxious and worried without money

5. I challenge and evolve my faith

usually ① — sometimes ② — half & half ③ — sometimes ④ — usually ⑤

I ground myself in my firm, unchanging faith

6. I have "give and take" chats with my s(S)ource of inspiration

usually ① — sometimes ② — half & half ③ — sometimes ④ — usually ⑤

I do not have "give and take" chats with my s(S)ource of inspiration

7. I live as me no matter what.

usually ① — sometimes ② — half & half ③ — sometimes ④ — usually ⑤

I compromise myself to be accepted

8. I live in peace and joy.

usually ① — sometimes ② — half & half ③ — sometimes ④ — usually ⑤

I live a roller-coaster life, from sadness to elation, from regret to worry, from anxiety to euphoria, on and on.

9. When someone turns me off, I seek to be more unconditionally loving of him and guarded.

usually   half & half   usually

①——②——③——④——⑤

sometimes   sometimes

When someone turns me off, I move away from him and guard myself from him.

10. I seek feedback from others about how I can improve.

usually   half & half   usually

①——②——③——④——⑤

sometimes   sometimes

I avoid feedback from others about how I can improve.

11. I enjoy sharing and hearing from another about the inner challenge to be more loving and alive.

usually   half & half   usually

①——②——③——④——⑤

sometimes   sometimes

I like to keep conversations superficial and light.

12. I take only one vow—to be unconditional love guarded of all no matter the cost.

usually   half & half   usually

①——②——③——④——⑤

sometimes   sometimes

I take vows to people, to groups, to my faith, to my flag, and to institutions.

13. I make nonseekers uncomfortable because I am unconventional and unpredictable.

usually   half & half   usually

①——②——③——④——⑤

sometimes   sometimes

I make people comfortable because I am conventional and predictable.

14. I live from a loving, fierce s(S)pirit within me.

usually   half & half   usually

①——②——③——④——⑤

sometimes   sometimes

I live from the general spirit of those around me.

15. I have a zeal for personal development.

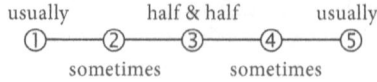

usually — half & half — usually
①—②—③—④—⑤
sometimes — sometimes

I seek the easy, familiar life.

16. I become my best me in the moment, and then, respond with unconditional love- guarded to how I affect the world.

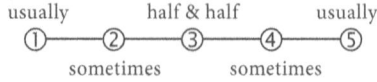

usually — half & half — usually
①—②—③—④—⑤
sometimes — sometimes

I plan and control what happens around me, and then, deal with what I like and do not like.

17. When bad things happen, I seek to experience them as perfect-as-is before making changes.

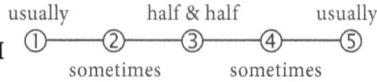

usually — half & half — usually
①—②—③—④—⑤
sometimes — sometimes

When bad things happen, I do what I can to make things good.

18. I am aware of all my thoughts and feelings.

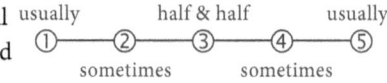

usually — half & half — usually
①—②—③—④—⑤
sometimes — sometimes

I do not pay attention to my thoughts and feelings.

19. I listen to anyone, but trust only my inner guidance.

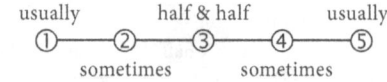

usually — half & half — usually
①—②—③—④—⑤
sometimes — sometimes

I trust peers, and authorities including those in scriptures more than I trust my inner guidance.

20. I am personally fulfilled.

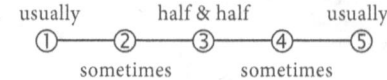

usually — half & half — usually
①—②—③—④—⑤
sometimes — sometimes

I am personally unfulfilled.

21. When unfulfilled, I use my soul-guidance to find fulfillment in the moment.

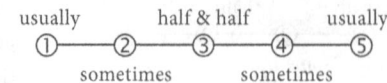

usually — half & half — usually
①—②—③—④—⑤
sometimes — sometimes

When unfulfilled, I seek fulfillment "out there" in people and things.

22. I do not identi-fy with any-thing but being unconditional love guarded in the world.

usually   half & half   usually
①——②——③——④——⑤
   sometimes   sometimes

I identify with my friends, country, family, race, things, money, religion and my other beliefs.

23. I relate to God only when I experience God.

usually   half & half   usually
①——②——③——④——⑤
   sometimes   sometimes

I believe or do not believe in God.

24. I welcome, confront, and conquer my inner turmoil.

usually   half & half   usually
①——②——③——④——⑤
   sometimes   sometimes

I seek outside relief from my inner turmoil through TV, drugs, alcohol, work, chatting, shopping, food, and other dis-tractions.

25. I challenge social and religious norms until I am satisfied that they serve the highest ends.

usually   half & half   usually
①——②——③——④——⑤
   sometimes   sometimes

I trust that social and religious norms serve the highest ends.

26. I experience perfect, loving order behind all events.

usually   half & half   usually
①——②——③——④——⑤
   sometimes   sometimes

I experience good and bad luck, coinci-dences, that life is not fair, and that prayer may affect what happens.

27. I watch for how everything that happens offers me the next perfect step to becoming my fulfilled self.

usually   half & half   usually
①——②——③——④——⑤
   sometimes   sometimes

I dodge and weave through life avoiding bad things happening, regretting mistakes, and longing for what is missing.

28. I reveal my own personal truths (about who I am, what happens after I die, who others are, and life's other core questions) layer by layer, never getting to the core.

usually		half & half		usually
①	②	③	④	⑤
	sometimes		sometimes	

Experts (clergy, professors, commentators, celebrities, and people I admire like Jesus, Mohammed, and other Scripture authors) teach me absolute truths about life's core questions.

29. Just like the authors of scriptures, I suspend my beliefs in order to be enlightened with higher truths.

usually		half & half		usually
①	②	③	④	⑤
	sometimes		sometimes	

I am in awe of authors of scriptures who were chosen (unlike me) to be channels of God's truths.

30. I love surveys like this which help me decide how to improve.

usually		half & half		usually
①	②	③	④	⑤
	sometimes		sometimes	

I hate surveys like this even though they are designed to help me improve.

Compute your score by adding your selected numbers and dividing by 30. Mark you score on the scale below.

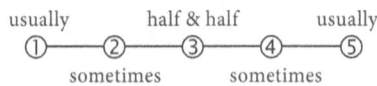

usually		half & half		usually
①	②	③	④	⑤
	sometimes		sometimes	

Results: The lower your score, the more likely you are on the Way of the Soul. The higher your score, the more likely you are on the Way of the Mind. If Jesus walked his talk, his score would be very low.

ACKNOWLEDGMENTS

An author's name is on the front of the book. He does do the bulk of the work; however, in most cases, and this is one, he could not have done it without the support of others.

This book is the fruit of 18 years of idea hoeing, planting, weeding, pruning, and harvesting. I worked the first five years alone in a cabin in the desert outside Santa Fe, New Mexico. I may have gone crazy and given up if it were not for three people: my brother Don continued to check in on me from New York, Charlie Leavitt provided encouragement and offered me training gigs, and Joe Rook, my first editor, reviewed and revised every idea and page. Their almost weekly emails and calls were a lifeline to reality.

I then, moved to Mexico and met my wife, Carmen. She and her five children (Cristina, Alejandra, Francesca, Carmelita and Alejandro) have been supportive for 10 years without understanding much about Biblical scholarship.

Along the way, other editors have helped immensely:

- Bruce Klippenstein,

- Brandon Phillips,

- Aundria Warren, and

- Ruth Cohen.

Others contributed greatly:

My friend Marvin Baker and Linda Klippenstein who were most helpful through some difficult times in Mexico.

Jeff Chase, Gwen Boucher, Ed Krause, Paul D'Heilly, and William Lynch, all of whom said, "I believe in you and this project."

People from the past came forward with their support:

My former high school friend, Jack Ewers;

Two former Jesuit buddies, Jack Linn and Norm Betz;

My cousin/sister, Nancy Parzych, the best there is, who kept writing to say that she could not understand why anyone would be interested, but that she was behind me,

My brothers Terry and Rick, and my son Mike.

Raul, a poor but rich man, living high in the mountain village of Terrero, Guanajuato who helped with his friendship, music and anything else that he had,

Dan Mantz, who, without understanding much, said, "Sounds good, go live in my vacant house near the beach,"

William Gower and Paul de Heilly, who helped with the book's final production, and

My wonderful friends, Don Talarico, who established the book's style and discussed every poem, and Steve Mitchell who conceived of the phrases "Way of the Soul" and "Way of the Mind."

So you see, it took many people to make this revelation of the real Jesus possible.

Behold a white horse!

And
its rider
had a bow,

And a crown
was given to him,

And
he
went out conquering
to conquer.

And
the armies of heaven,
followed him
on white horses,

They
arrayed in fine linen
white and pure.

Rev 6:2, 19:11,14

White Horse = Heavenly Power
Rider = Second Coming of the Messiah
Armies = Those on the Messiah's Way

www.ingramcontent.com/pod-product-compliance
Lightning Source LLC
Chambersburg PA
CBHW060312030426
42336CB00011B/1015